Tradition and Modernity in Arabic Literature

Professor Mounah A. Khouri, 1992

Tradition and Modernity in Arabic Literature

Edited by

Issa J. Boullata and Terri DeYoung

The University of Arkansas Press
Fayetteville
1997

Manufactured in the United States of America

01 00 99 98 97 5 4 3 2 1

Designed by Liz Lester

♾ The paper used in this publication meets the minimum requirements of the American National Standard for Permanence of Paper for Printed Library Materials Z39.48-1984.

Library of Congress Cataloguing-in-Publication Data

Tradition and modernity in Arabic literature / edited by Issa J. Boullata and Terri DeYoung.
p. cm.
"This volume is in memory of Professor Mounah A. Khouri, poet, educator, and scholar and is presented to him by his colleagues, friends, and former students"—CIP pref.
Includes bibliographical references (p.) and index.
ISBN 1-55728-447-4 (cloth : alk. paper)
1. Arabic literature—History and criticism. I. Boullata, Issa J., 1929– . II. DeYoung, Terri. III. Khouri, Mounah Abdallah.
PJ7510.T74 1997
892'.709—DC21 97-6667
CIP

This volume is in memory of Professor Mounah A. Khouri, poet, educator, and scholar, and is presented by his colleagues, friends, and former students.

Contents

Preface

As a teenager growing up in Jerusalem, Palestine, in the 1940s, I was deeply influenced by three persons as to my literary predilections: Mounah A. Khouri (1918–1996), Jabra Ibrahim Jabra (1920–1994), and Tawfiq Sayigh (1923–1971). The former two were my teachers of Arabic and English respectively at De La Salle College; the latter was their shy, sensitive friend and colleague whom I came to know better and better as time went by. Poets, creative scholars, and teachers, all three were at the threshold of literary careers that brought them together in Jerusalem until the 1948 war in Palestine separated them. Although they later met for short periods of time in Beirut, Harvard University, Oxford, London, and Berkeley, their life paths had diverged after leaving Jerusalem but their brilliant careers were continuously ascending.

Little did I know in the 1940s that I would be writing about them or that, after the Palestine catastrophe of 1948, I would even ever see them again. But as fortune would have it, I kept following developments in their lives from a distance and had the privilege of occasionally seeing them and corresponding with them and always remaining their friend. On Tawfiq Sayigh I wrote one of my earliest and best essays, "The Beleaguered Unicorn: A Study of Tawfīq Ṣāyigh,"[1] which was awarded the Arberry Memorial Prize by the Pembroke Arabic Group of Cambridge University in 1972. On him and Jabra, I wrote in 1978 another of my dearest and best essays, "The Concept of Modernity in the Poetry of Jabrā and Ṣāyigh,"[2] and I later wrote other essays on Jabra.[3] On Mounah Khouri, I have not yet had the opportunity to write anything, deserving though he was as poet, literary critic and scholar, professor of several generations of students of Arabic literature and language in the Middle East and the United States, and above all a dear friend

I knew for over half a century. It is therefore with a great sense of fulfilling a welcome obligation that I take this opportunity to pay a debt long due. In addition to writing an introduction on Mounah A. Khouri, a kind human being whose memory I will always cherish, I am pleased that a former student of his in the United States, Professor Terri DeYoung, agreed to edit this volume with me and that some of his colleagues, friends, and former students agreed to join us in paying tribute to him by contributing to this collection of literary essays. Originally planned to be a festschrift in honor of Professor Khouri, it is now published in his memory, for he regrettably passed away a few months before its publication.

Issa J. Boullata

1. Issa J. Boullata, "The Beleaguered Unicorn: A Study of Tawfīq Ṣāyigh," *Journal of Arabic Literature* 4 (1973): 69–93.

2. Issa J. Boullata, "The Concept of Modernity in the Poetry of Jabrā and Ṣāyigh," *Edebiyât* 3 (1978): 173–89.

3. See Issa J. Boullata: "Jabra Ibrahim Jabra," *Encyclopedia of World Literature in the 20th Century, vol. 5* (New York: Continuum, 1993), 5:329–30; "Jabra Ibrahim Jabra," *Encyclopedia of Arabic Literature* (London: Routledge, forth-coming); "Jabra Ibrahim Jabra," *Contemporary World Writers,* ed. Tracy Chevalier (London: St. James Press, 1993), 269–70; "Jabra (1920–1994)," *Jusoor,* ed. A. Munir Akash, 5–6 (1995): 145L–55L; "Jabrā wa-al-Khurūj min al-Madār al-Mughlaq," *Al-Qalaq wa-Tajdīd al-Ḥayāh,* ed. ʻAbd al-Raḥmān Munīf (Beirut: al-Mu'assasa al-ʻArabiyya li-al-Dirāsāt wa-al-Nashr, 1995), 49–57; "Translator's Preface," *The First Well: A Bethlehem Boyhood* by Jabra Ibrahim Jabra, translated by Issa J. Boullata (Fayetteville: The University of Arkansas Press, 1995), vii–xi; "Jabra Ibrahim Jabra," *World Authors 1990–1995* (New York: The H. W. Wilson Company, forthcoming); and a few other publications.

Publications of Mounah A. Khouri

COMPILED BY TERRI DEYOUNG

Editor's Note: The works listed below under each heading are arranged chronologically, beginning with 1955. Prior to 1955, all Professor Khouri's published works were poetry (for more information on these, see Issa J. Boullata's introduction in this volume). Dr. Kaissar Afif, founder and chief editor of the Arabic journal *Al-Ḥaraka al-Shi'riyya,* chronicled Professor Khouri's biography and detailed his life and achievements as teacher, scholar and poet in Lebanon, Palestine, and the United States, in a book entitled *Ḥiṣād al-Dhākira: Munaḥ Khūrī Yatadhakkar Mawāsim al-'Umr* (Harvest of memory: Mounah Khouri remembers the seasons of his life) (Sidon: Dār al-Jāmi'a, 1997). It includes all of Professor Khouri's early poems, published prior to 1955, as well as his most recent works in verse, which have been appearing regularly since his retirement in 1989, as well as three letters to him from Tawfīq Ṣāyigh, Antoine G. Karam, and As'ad Khairallah.

Books and Chapters in Books

Al-Tārīkh al-Ḥaḍārī 'Ind Tūyinbī [Toynbee]. Beirut: Dār al-'Ilm li-l-Milāyīn, 1960.

Toynbee's theories of history have had an enormous impact on the approaches adopted by modern Arab intellectuals (both secularist and Islamist) in writing about the development of Islamic civilization, and this was the book that first made those theories available to Arab readers in a comprehensive form.

The volume was reviewed at length by, among others, Mājid al-Sāmarrā'ī in *Āfāq 'Arabiyya* 3, no. 11 (Tishrīn al-Thānī [November] 1977): 98–101; and its contents were summarized and discussed by Professor Khouri himself in "Nushū' al-Ḥaḍārāt 'Ind Tūyinbī," *Al-'Ulūm* 3, no. 4 (Nīsān [April] 1958): 5–9, 65.

Advanced Arabic Readers I: The Novel and the Short Story. (William Brinner: co-editor.) Berkeley: University of California Press, 1961; reprinted as *Readings in Modern Arabic Literature, Volume 1: The Short Story and the Novel.* Leiden: E. J. Brill, 1971.

One of the most thorough, comprehensive and highly regarded collections of prose readings taken from modern Arab authors. Aside from its exhaustive attention paid to the development of students' vocabulary and grammatical skills, through the extensive glossary and notes, it is one of the few advanced readers to endeavor to place the readings in a larger framework of social and cultural concerns.

Advanced Arabic Readers II: The Essay and Expository Writing. (William Brinner: co-editor.) Berkeley: University of California Press, 1962.

A companion volume to Advanced Arabic Readers I: The Novel and the Short Story.

Al-Shiʿr Bayn Nuqqād Thalātha: Iliyūt [T. S. Eliot], Māklīsh [Archibald MacLeish], Ritshārdz [I. A. Richards]. Beirut: Dār al-Thaqāfa, 1966.

A landmark study that first made available to the Arab reader a comprehensive overview of the work of the most important Anglo-American modernist critics (Eliot, MacLeish, Richards, and Ezra Pound), as well as translations of their more important critical statements. In addition it emphasized the relevance of certain literary norms stressed in their writings to the development of a new sensibility in modern Arabic literature.

(with Peter Abboud, et al) *Elementary Modern Standard Arabic I and II* Ann Arbor: University of Michigan Press, 1968. Revised edition. Cambridge: Cambridge University Press, 1983.

For many years this was the most widely used textbook for the study of Arabic in the United States. It remains very popular. Among his other contributions, Professor Khouri supervised the composition of the volume's basic texts and ensured that they were integrated with the grammatical content of the lessons.

Poetry and the Making of Modern Egypt: (1882–1922). Leiden: E. J. Brill, 1971).

Based on a revision and expansion of Professor Khouri's Ph.D. thesis (prepared under the supervision of Professor Hamilton A. R. Gibb at Harvard), "The Role of Modern Arabic Poetry in Reflecting and Directing Social and Intellectual Currents in Modern Egypt, 1882–1922," this book was one of the earliest and remains one of the most substantive attempts to chart the interaction between literature and society in the modern Arab world. It can thus be seen as a precursor to Edward Said's classic *Orientalism,* a debt which has been acknowledged by that author in his notes.

Through its study in depth of the poetry of al-Bārūdī, Shawqī, Ḥāfiẓ, Muṭrān, Shukrī, ʿAlī al-Ghāyātī, and others, *Poetry and the Making of Modern Egypt* showed convincingly the decisive role these neoclassic and pre-romantic figures played not only in providing new directions for the renaissance of modern Arabic literature, but also in reflecting and directing social, political and intellectual movements and trends in modern Egypt during the British occupation. Thus, Khouri's study remains *the* pioneering effort in that important field of research. *Poetry and the Making of Modern Egypt* also documented extensively how the relative neglect of the poets Khalīl Muṭrān and 'Abd al-Raḥmān Shukrī had distorted prior critical assessments of early twentieth-century Egyptian poetry, and in this sense it continues to have an important impact on all attempts to write adequate accounts of the development of modern Arabic literary history.

The volume was reviewed at length by, among others, Salih J. Altoma in *JAOS* (1973): 107–8; in *Orientalistische Literaturzeitung* 71, n. 1 (1976): 62–63; and by Māhir Shafīq in *Fuṣūl* 3, no. 1 (Nov.–Dec. 1981): 279–86. A response to the last-mentioned review was made by Professor Khouri and published in *Fuṣūl* 3, no. 2 (Jan./Feb./Mar. 1983): 373–76.

An Anthology of Modern Arabic Poetry. (Hamid Algar: co-translator.) Berkeley: University of California Press, 1974.

The first bilingual anthology of contemporary Arabic poetry in English. It was designed not only to acquaint the reader with modern developments in one of the world's major poetic traditions, but to afford insight into the contemporary cultural situation of the Arab peoples.

It was reviewed by Edmund Ghareeb in *The Middle East Journal* 28, no. 3 (Summer 1974): 344–46; M. M. Badawi in *The International Journal of Middle East Studies* 8 (1977): 416–19; 'Abd al-Qaddūs al-Khātim in *Al-Yamāma* 29, no. 652 (22 May 1981): 64–65; and Roger Allen in *Journal of the American Oriental Society* 96, no. 2 (April–June 1976): 290–92, among others.

"Arabic Literature," In *The Genius of Arab Civilization,* edited by John R. Hayes, 17–45 New York: New York University Press, 1975. Paperback edition (Cambridge, Mass.: MIT Press, 1978), 17–45. Second rev. ed. (Cambridge, Mass.: MIT Press, 1983), 17–45. Third ed. (revised and expanded) (New York: New York University Press, 1992), 45–75. Arabic edition "Al-Adab," *'Abqariyyat al-Ḥaḍāra al-'Arabiyya.* Cambridge, Mass.: MIT Press, 1978, 27–57.

A wide-ranging and highly regarded scholarly introduction to the achievements of Arab civilization, whose popularity and lasting value is attested to by the several editions that have been published. It contains important articles on Arab accomplishments in science, philosophy, art and architecture, trade and commerce, as well as Professor Khouri's in-depth discussion of the developments in Arabic literature from pre-Islamic to modern times.

It was reviewed at length by Edward Said in *The New York Times Book Review* (October 31, 1976): 4–5 and 35–36, where he drew special attention to the literature section, calling it an "impressive piece of scholarly writing" and an "effective summary of [its] material." The work was also reviewed by Raymond A. Hare in *The Middle East Journal* 30, no. 1 (Winter 1976): 102–3; Michael Dols in the *International Journal of Middle East Studies* 11, no. 1 (February 1980): 138–39; and in *The Wilson*

Quarterly, 8, no. 3 (summer 1984): 149, among others. The Arabic edition was reviewed by Ḥusayn Fawzī al-Najjār in *Al-Ahram.*

Studies in Contemporary Arabic Poetry and Criticism. Piedmont, Calif.: Jahan Book, 1987).

A collection of previously published and newly written articles dealing with the literary and intellectual accomplishments of a number of leading modern Arab authors and evaluating their contributions to the development of Arabic literature. The articles focus on those groups—most notably from the Mahjar and Modernist poetic movements—who, like Professor Khouri himself, have sought to encourage and promote a cultural dialogue between the East and the West.

It was reviewed at length by, among others, Maḥmūd Shurayḥ in *Al-Nahār,* 26 (Tishrīn al-Thānī [November]) 1987.

Articles

"Fī Mawkib al-Shi'r." *Al-Adīb* 28, no. 10 (October 1955): 3–4, 72.

"Qara'tu al-'Adad al-Māḍī min al-Ādāb." *Al-Ādāb* 3, no. 4 (April 1955): 65–70.

"Ma'nā al-Ma'nā fī al-Shi'r al-Ḥadīth." *Al-Adīb* 28, no. 11 (November 1955): 3–5. Reprinted in Khouri, *Al-Shi'r Bayn Nuqqād Thalātha,* 159–65.

"Pound wa-Ahl al-Qalam." *Al-Adīb* 29, no. 2 (February 1956): 5–6. Reprinted in Khouri, *Al-Shi'r Bayn Nuqqād Thalātha,* 91–99.

"Amīn al-Riḥānī." In *Al-Riḥānī Memorial Volume,* edited by Albert Riḥānī, 52–53 Beirut: Dār al-Riḥānī, 1966.

"Mutran's Contribution to the Development of Modern Arabic Poetry." In *Linguistic Studies in Memory of R. S. Harrell,* edited by D. J. Stuart, 69–102 Washington, D.C.: Georgetown University Press, 1967.

"Lewis 'Awaḍ: A Forgotten Pioneer of the Free Verse Movement." *Journal of Arabic Literature* 1(1970): 137–44. Reprinted in *Critical Perspectives on Modern Arabic Literature,* edited by Issa J. Boullata, 206–13 Washington, D.C.: Three Continents Press, 1980.

"Revolution and Renaissance in al-Bārūdī's Poetry." In *Islam and Its Cultural Divergence: Studies in Honor of Gustave E. von Grunebaum,* edited by G. L. Tikku, 76–95 Urbana: University of Illinois Press, 1971.

"Tawfīq Ṣāyigh's Poetry: A Critical Evaluation" (in Arabic). *Al-Nashra: Bulletin of the American Association of Teachers of Arabic* 4, no. 2 (December 1972): 1–14.

"Prose Poetry: A Radical Transformation in Contemporary Arabic Poetry." *Edebiyât* 1 (1976): 127–49. Reprinted in *Critical Perspectives on Modern Arabic Literature,* edited by Issa J. Boullata, 280–303 Washington, D.C.: Three Continents Press, 1980.

"Al-Riḥānī as Critic." *Al-'Arabiyya* 9 (1976): 1–8.

(with Michael Zwettler) "Farḥāt's Poem: 'Wine, Love and Youth' Assessed and Rendered." *Mundus Arabicus: Arab Writers in America* 1(1981): 54–59.

"Al-Shābbī as a Romantic." *Mundus Arabicus: Arabic Literature in North Africa* 2 (1982): 3–17.

"Ḥawl Kitāb al-Shi'r wa-Ṣun' Miṣr al-Ḥadītha." *Fuṣūl* 3, no. 2 (1983): 373–76.

"Criticism of the Heritage: Adonis as an Advocate of a New Culture." In *Arab Civilization: Challenges and Responses,* edited by George Atiyeh and I. Oweiss, 183–207 Albany: State University of New York Press, 1988.

"Mikhā'īl Na'īmī: 'Imlāq al-Rūḥ wa-l-Qalam (Mikhail Naimy: A giant in spirit and pen)" *Al-Majāl Review* 212 (November 1989): 25–27.

"Jubrān fī 'Ālamihi al-Fikrī wa-al-Adabī (Gibran's literary and philosophical world)." *Al-Majāl Review* 225 (January 1992): 8–11.

"Shaykhunā al-Kātib Yanṭaliq min Kalimāt wa-Yastaṭrid ilā Abwāq wa-ilā Shu'arā'." (Introduced by Maḥmūd Shurayḥ.) *Al-Nahār,* 8 (Nīsān [April] 1994).

"Rumūziyyat Tawfīq Ṣāyigh: Shahwa Yan'atiq bi-hā khārij al-Daymūma." (Translated and edited with commentary by Henri Zughayb.) *Al-Nahār,* 30 (Nīsān [April] 1994).

"Taqī al-Dīn wa-Abū Shabaka: Kānā Wā'iyayn wa-fī 'Uṣbat al-'Ashara Ṭāfā bi-al-Kalimāt." (Introduced by Maḥmūd Shurayḥ.) *Al-Nahār,* 15 (Ailūl [September], 1994).

"La'āzar wa-Ḥabībatuh: Jadaliyyat al-Mawt wa-al-Inbi'āth fī Ru'yat Jubrān" (Gibran's *Lazarus and His Beloved (1929);* Rendered into Arabic Verse with a Critical Introduction). *Al-Ḥaraka al-Shi'riyya* 3, no. 2 (July 1995): 7–30.

Translations

"Aṣwāt al-Shi'r al-Thalātha li-T.S. Ilīyūt." *Al-Ādāb* 3, no. 1 (January 1955): 33–38. A translation of T. S. Eliot. *The Three Voices of Poetry.* Cambridge: Cambridge University Press, 1953. Reprinted in Mounah A. Khouri, *Al-Shi'r Bayn*

Nuqqād Thalātha: Iliyūt [T. S. Eliot], Māklīsh [Archibald MacLeish], Ritshārdz [I. A. Richards] (see below, 1966), 44–65.

"Mawhibat al-Shā'ir bayn al-Taqlīd wa-al-Tajdīd li-T.S. Ilīyūt." *Al-Adīb* 27, no. 1 (January 1955): 32–35. A translation of T. S. Eliot. "Tradition and the Individual Talent," In *Selected Prose,* edited by Frank Kermode, 37–44 New York: Harcourt, Brace, Jovanovich, 1975. Reprinted in Khouri, *Al-Shi'r Bayn Nuqqād Thalātha,* 74–87.

"Naẓra fī al-Naqd al-Adabī li-T.S. Ilīyūt." *Al-Adīb* 27, no. 3 (March 1955): 20–22. A partial translation of T. S. Eliot. "The Function of Criticism." In *Selected Prose*, 68–76. Reprinted in Khouri, *Al-Shi'r Bayn Nuqqād Thalātha,* 66–71.

"Al-Shi'r wa-al-Falsafa li-T.S. Ilīyūt." *Al-Adīb* 28, no. 7 (July 1955): 3–4. A translation of T. S. Eliot. "Poetry and Philosophy." In *Selected Essays,* 53–56 London: Faber and Faber, 1932. Reprinted in Khouri, *Al-Shi'r Bayn Nuqqād Thalātha,* 35–39.

"Al-Ma'arrī's Elegy for Abū Ḥamzah." (Hall Winslow: co-translator.) *Middle East Forum* 31, no. 2 (February 1956): 27.

"Mūsīqā al-Shi'r li-T.S. Ilīyūt." *Al-Adīb* 29, no. 3 (March 1956): 11–12. A translation of T. S. Eliot, "The Music of Poetry." In *Selected Prose,* 107–14. Reprinted in Khouri, *Al-Shi'r Bayn Nuqqād Thalātha,* 24–31.

"Al-Shi'r al-Ḥurr wa-al-Shi'r al-Ṣa'b, al-Ṣiḥāfa wa-al-Adab li-T.S. Ilīyūt." *Al-Adīb* 29, no. 4 (April 1956): 16–17. Translated from T. S. Eliot. "Reflections on Vers Libre." In *Selected Prose,* 86–91; "Difficult Poetry." In *Selected Prose,* 92–94; and "Journalism and Literature." In *Selected Prose,* 44–45. Reprinted in Khouri, *Al-Shi'r Bayn Nuqqād Thalātha,* 19–23 (as "Naẓarāt fī al-Shi'r al-Ḥurr"), 32–34 (as "Al-Shi'r al-Ṣa'b"), and 72–73 (as "Al-Ṣiḥāfa wa-al-Adab").

"Michel Ṭrād: Poems." (Hall Winslow: co-translator) in "Perspectives on the Arab World," a special supplement to *The Atlantic Monthly* 198, no. 4 (1956), 175.

Al-Shi'r Bayn al-Ra'y wa-al-Ru'yā: Ḥiwār Ḥawl Waẓīfat al-Shi'r. Beirut: Dār al-Thaqāfa, 1966. A translation of Archibald MacLeish's *Poetry and Opinion: A Dialogue on the Role of Poetry.* Urbana: University of Illinois Press, 1950.

"Modern Arabic Poetry II, III." (Hamid Algar: co-translator.) *Journal of Arabic Literature* 1(1970): 75–87, 117–28.

"Abū Māḍī's 'The Mysteries' (al-Ṭalásim)." in Mounah A. Khouri, *Studies in Contemporary Arabic Poetry and Criticism,* 53–71(Piedmont, Calif.: Jahan Book Company, 1987).

Poetry (Since 1989)

"Bāqat al-Ward: Ayn Yamḍī Shadhāhā?" *Al-Ḥaraka al-Shi'riyya* 1, no. 1 (Autumn 1992): 11–13.

"Nidā' min al-A'māq: Idhdhikāran li-Tawfīq Ṣāyigh—Shā'ir al-Karkadann." *Al-Nahār,* 28 (August 1993).

"Dam'at al-Fajr al-Nadī Tuwārī Ṭiflahā fī Rawḍa" (Other title: "Al-Ṭayr al-Mufāriq") and "Fī Mawkib al-Riyāḥ." *Al-Nahār,* 28 Tishrīn al-Awwal (October 1994).

"La'āzar wa-Jubrān, 'Ām 1929." *Al-Ḥaraka al-Shi'riyya* 3, no. 2 (summer 1995): 15–30.

"Ghurbat al-Ḍiyā'." *Al-Ḥaraka al-Shi'riyya* 4, no. 3 (summer 1996).

Introduction: Mounah A. Khouri

Issa J. Boullata

Mounah A. Khouri

Mounah Khouri was born in Rāshayyā al-Fukhkhār on the twenty-sixth of November 1918 into a Christian Orthodox family. His village, lying on the northern slope of Mount Hermon, would fall within the new boundaries of Lebanon drawn two years after his birth by the French authorities occupying the area at the conclusion of the First World War and the defeat of the Ottoman Turks. After finishing his elementary education at the Greek Orthodox school of his native village, he went to the Orthodox College of Jdaydat Marji'yūn, where he earned a *Brevet* on completing his high-school studies. He had hoped to be admitted to the Elementary Teachers' Training School in Beirut but his examiner in oral Arabic, the well-known Lebanese writer Khalīl Taqī al-Dīn, noticed his excellence and helped him obtain a full, three-year scholarship to study at the French Section of the International College of the American University of Beirut (A.U.B.), where he obtained a French *Baccalauréat (deuxième partie)* and graduated in 1938. Among his most influential teachers at this college were Khalīl Taqī al-Dīn and Kamāl al-Yāzijī.

Mounah Khouri then went to Palestine as an educator and taught Arabic language and literature at a number of the best private secondary schools in the country. Between 1938 and 1942, he taught at the Orthodox College in Jaffa and among his students were: George Ḥabash, later to be the founder and leader of the Popular Front for the Liberation of Palestine; and Muḥammad Bāmiya, later to be Chief of the Royal Chancellery at King Fahd's court. Mounah Khouri had begun writing poetry, love being his major theme as a young man in his early twenties involved in a passionate romance frustrated by restrictive social traditions and values. His love poems were published in the Palestinian periodicals of the day. In 1942 he moved from Jaffa to teach at the Gaza College, where he continued until 1943; his students there included Hārūn Hāshim Rashīd and Mu'īn Busaysū, both of whom were to become well-known Palestinian poets involved in the nationalist cause of their country. When Prince (later King) Sa'ūd visited Gaza that year, the Gaza College principal, Wadī' Tarazī, asked Mounah to write a poem in His Highness's honor, which he did and delivered, and it was published in *Filisṭīn* and *Al-Difā'*, the leading Arabic newspapers of Palestine.

Mounah Khouri then moved on and began teaching in Jerusalem, the capital of Palestine. From 1944 to 1946 he taught at De La Salle College, commonly called the Frères' or Brothers' College, where I was privileged to be his student along with others who have become well-known professionals in various fields. Then he taught at Bishop Gobat School from 1946 to 1948 where his students included Anīs Ṣāyigh, later to become a noted historian and the editor of *Shu'ūn Filisṭīniyya* (he is the younger brother of the poet Tawfīq Ṣāyigh). Mounah also taught part-time at Terra Sancta College.

During this period of over nine years in Palestine, Mounah Khouri participated in the intellectual and literary activities of the country, which, despite the political turmoil that eventually led to the termination of the British mandate in 1948, was enjoying a rising level of socioeconomic and cultural conditions. He gave public lectures on literary topics, published literary articles in the local press, and took part in poetry readings and festivals along with the leading Palestinian poets. I attended one such national festival held in the auditorium of the YMCA in Jerusalem on November 14, 1946. It was sponsored by the Dajānī Family Council and organized by its cultural committee, featuring poets like Ḥasan al-Buḥayrī from Haifa, Wahīb al-Bīṭār from Nablus, Muṣṭafā al-Dabbāgh from Jaffa, 'Abd al-Qādir al-Ṣāliḥ from Nablus, Muḥammad al-'Adnānī from Jaffa, Sayf al-Dīn Zayd al-Kīlānī from Nablus, Kamāl Nāṣir from Ramallah, Aḥmad Yūsuf from Haifa, 'Abd al-Raḥīm Maḥmūd from Nablus, and Mounah Khouri (the only non-Palestinian) from Jerusalem.

In 1947–48 Mounah entered the Law School of Jerusalem which offered evening classes under the supervision of the Palestine Law Council to prepare those wanting to qualify for the bar in a five-year program. Having joined it myself upon my graduation from De La Salle College, I found myself sitting next to my former teacher in courses on "The Principles of Jurisprudence," "Constitutional Law," "The Law of Contracts," "Majallat al-Aḥkām al-Shar'iyya," and "Waqf" given by British and Palestinian (Arab and Jewish) professors to a mixed student body of Arabs and Jews, men and women. The school was eventually closed down before the end of the academic year on account of the armed hostilities between Palestinian Arabs and Jews in the country and the eventual termination of the British mandate on May 15, 1948. Mounah abandoned the study of law, as did I, both of us wanting to concentrate on our first love—literature.

Teaching in Bishop Gobat School and all other schools in Palestine was also disrupted and then discontinued before the end of the academic year because of the hostilities. Mounah Khouri returned to Lebanon and between 1948 and 1956 held a teaching position (except for 1952–53) in the French section of the International College of the A.U.B. and headed the Department of Arabic there as well. Among his students at the college was As'ad Khayr-Allāh, later to become professor of Arabic literature at the University of Freiburg in Germany. Involved as Mounah was in teaching and administration at this college, he enrolled in the American University of Beirut to continue his studies. In the Arabic department of the A.U.B., where Anīs Frayḥa and Jibrā'īl Jabbūr were among his professors, he obtained his B.A. in Arabic literature in 1952; in the history department, where Nicola Ziadeh and Nabīh Fāris were among his professors, he obtained his M.A. in history in 1956. In the period between the two degrees and at the recommendation of Professor Nabīh Fāris, he was awarded a Rockefeller Foundation fellowship as a poet and critic for special study at Harvard University in the academic year 1952–53. Among his professors at Harvard, the ones who influenced him most were I. A. Richards and Archibald MacLeish, although he also took courses with W. J. Bates, R. Poggioli, and J. Conant; and among his student friends at the university, the ones who were most congenial were his Jerusalem friends Jabrā Ibrāhīm Jabrā and Tawfīq Ṣāyigh who, like him, were beneficiaries of Rockefeller Foundation fellowships. Mounah spent the summer of 1953 with Ṣāyigh in Oxford attending lectures with him at the university by Dylan Thomas, William Empson, and other English writers.

Upon his return to Beirut, Mounah Khouri was active in writing and publishing, in addition to his teaching and administrative duties at the French section of the International College. To *Al-Adīb* and *Al-Ādāb,* two of the leading Arabic periodicals in Lebanon at that time, he contributed literary articles and translations from English, introducing the theories of I. A. Richards and the ideas of Ezra Pound and studying in depth the literary achievements of T. S. Eliot who was destined to have an immense influence on modern Arabic poetry. Recoiling from the romanticism of the Arabic poetry of the 1930s and 1940s, the free-verse movement in the 1950s was now in full swing in the Arab world, particularly in Iraq, Lebanon, Syria, and Egypt, but Mounah chose to concentrate on publishing literary and cultural studies rather than writing poetry. Based on his M.A. research work, he prepared a critical evaluation of Arnold Toynbee's theories of history, with particular reference to his interpretation of Islamic civilization, and published it in 1960 as *Al-Tārīkh al-Ḥaḍārī 'ind Toynbee.*[1] The book still remains the most serious study of Toynbee in Arabic.

In September of 1956, Mounah Khouri married Julia Na'īm Bishāra who was born in Ismailiyya, Egypt, to parents originally from Nazareth, Palestine, and the Khouris were later to have two sons, Māzin and Mark.[2]

In the fall of 1956, the Khouris went to the United States, where Mounah entered Harvard University as a beneficiary of a second Rockefeller Foundation fellowship for studies leading to a Ph.D. degree. He took courses with Professor W. Langer on the rise of modern Europe, with Professor M. Gilmore on the world of humanism during the Renaissance and the Reformation, and with Professor H. S. Hughes on the intellectual history of Europe. But his major concentration was with Professor H. A. R. Gibb, with whom he took seminars on Islamic history, Islamic institutions, and Arabic literature. Under the supervision of Professor Gibb, he wrote a doctoral dissertation entitled "The Role of Modern Arabic Poetry in Reflecting and Directing Social and Intellectual Currents in Modern Egypt, 1882–1922." He obtained his Ph.D. degree in 1964 and published a revised version of his dissertation in 1971 under the title of *Poetry and the Making of Modern Egypt, 1882–1922.*

Having earlier completed all his other graduate requirements at Harvard University except for his Ph.D. dissertation, Mounah Khouri set out to establish an academic career for himself in the United States even before obtaining his doctorate. He taught Arabic language and literature at Georgetown University in Washington, D.C., in the academic year 1959–60; then he joined the University of California at Berkeley in the fall of 1960 as a lecturer in Arabic at the Department of Near Eastern Languages. During his first two years at Berkeley, he developed with William M. Brinner, his colleague at Berkeley, two volumes for the teaching of advanced Arabic through selected and annotated readings: *Advanced Arabic Readers I: The Novel and Short Story* and *Advanced Arabic Readers II: Expository Writing,* which were published by the University of California Press in 1961 and 1962 respectively; a revised edition of the former was published in Leiden by E. J. Brill in 1971 as *Readings in Modern Arabic Literature I: The Short Story and the Novel.*

With his doctorate in hand in 1964, Mounah Khouri was promoted to assistant professor and then, in 1966, to associate professor of Arabic language and literature with tenure. His courses at the Department of Near Eastern Languages at Berkeley covered the main aspects of classical and modern Arabic language and literature. He was invited in 1965–66 by the American University in Cairo as a visiting associate professor of Arabic literature. He represented this university, as well as the United States, at the international conference held in Beirut in November of 1965 in commemoration of the twenty-fifth anniversary of the death of Amīn al-Rīḥānī (1876–1940). While he was in the Middle East that year, Mounah published in Beirut *Al-Shiʿr bayn Nuqqād Thalātha,* collecting his translations of a number of literary and critical essays by T. S. Eliot, Archibald MacLeish, and I. A. Richards and his studies on them and relating their ideas to the development of a new sensibility in modern Arabic poetry.

Back in the United States, Mounah participated in the summer of 1968 with a group of Arabists from the newly established American Association of Teachers of Arabic, of which he was a founding member, in producing a two-volume textbook *Elementary Modern Standard Arabic,* which was to become a standard book for teaching Arabic in many American universities.

He was granted a sabbatical leave in 1968–69, and he spent the year in France and Lebanon doing research on the Lebanese poets of French expression: Charles Corm, Georges Schéhadé, Andrée Chédid, and others.

In 1970 he was promoted to full professorship, and in 1971 he was appointed chairman of the Department of Near Eastern Studies, a position he held until 1975. Meanwhile, he was elected as a member of the board of directors of the American Association of Teachers of Arabic for the years 1969, 1970, 1971 and again for the years 1973, 1974, 1975; following that, he was elected president of this association for the year 1976–1977.

A consortium of American universities appointed him as the United States director of their Center for Arabic Studies Abroad (CASA) between

1970 and 1974, a center located at the American University in Cairo. In the first semester of 1975–76, he was appointed distinguished visiting professor at this university, giving graduate seminars and public lectures on Arabic literature.

In 1974 he was appointed by the president of the Middle East Studies Association (MESA) as member of the quinquennial committee to review the performance of this association's journal, the *International Journal of Middle East Studies,* and he later served as member of its editorial board from 1978 to 1983.

Despite all his academic duties and professional activities, Mounah managed in cooperation with Hamid Algar, his colleague at Berkeley, to publish in 1974 a bilingual anthology of contemporary Arabic poetry entitled *Anthology of Modern Arabic Poetry,* which deliberately omitted the neoclassical poets to concentrate on contemporary ones, especially free-verse poets. Apart from A. J. Arberry's *Modern Arabic Poetry: An Anthology with English Verse Translations,* first published in 1950, reprinted in 1967, and now out of date, the Khouri and Algar *Anthology* remains the only bilingual collection of modern Arabic poetry, and offers excellent renderings of eighty poems by thirty-five poets representing three successive generations: the Arab-Americans, the Egyptian modernists, and the contemporary Arab poets of the free-verse movement.

Although Mounah Khouri continued to contribute to Arabic periodicals, he increasingly concentrated on publishing his scholarly essays as articles and chapters in English-language books and journals. His publications dealt with different aspects of Arabic literature, especially modern Arabic poetry, and the range of his scholarship covered a variety of topics. He easily moved from a historical and critical survey of the entire spectrum of Arabic literature, to studies on a neoclassical poet like al-Bārūdī, a pre-romantic poet like Muṭrān, and a romantic poet like al-Shābbī; he could treat in depth the Arab-American critic al-Rīḥānī as well as the Arab-American poet Farḥāt; he wrote perceptively on prose poetry and the free-verse movement and translated into English good, illustrative selections from them; he recalled the pioneering role of Lewis ʿAwaḍ and critically evaluated Tawfīq Ṣāyigh; and with remarkable acumen, he studied Adonis as an advocate of new Arab culture in one of the best essays written on current Arab cultural criticism.[3] He later collected some of these essays and, after revision, published them in 1987 in a book entitled *Studies in Contemporary Arabic Poetry and Criticism,* with additional essays on Nuʿayma as a critic, Abū Māḍī as a meditative poet, Abū Shabaka as a romantic, Ḥāwī as a mythmaker, and an admirable article on the paradise lost of Ṣāyigh's poetry.

At the same time, Mounah Khouri supervised dozens of Ph.D. dissertations and M.A. theses. Some of the doctoral dissertations under his supervision as chairperson or co-chairperson have later appeared in book form, such as Michael Zwettler's *The Oral Tradition of Classical Arabic Poetry* (Columbus: Ohio State University, 1978); Saad Sowayan's *Nabaṭi Poetry: The Oral Poetry of Arabia* (Berkeley: University of California Press, 1982); Kristina Nelson's *The Art of Reciting the Qur'ān* (Austin: University of Texas Press, 1985); and Joseph Zeidan's *Women Arab Novelists: The Formative Years and Beyond* (Albany: The State University of New York Press, 1995). Other doctoral dissertations included: Julie Scott Meisami's "New Forms in Modern Arabic Poetry" (1971); Muhammad Siddiq's "Patterns of Identity in the Hebrew and Arabic Novel" (1981); Samia Mehrez's "The Artist as Bricoleur: The Case of Jamāl al-Ghīṭānī" (1986); Terri DeYoung's "And Thereby Hangs a Tale: A Study of Myth in Modern Arabic Poetry" (1988).

In 1989 Mounah Khouri retired from his position at the University of California at Berkeley, but he has remained in touch with his former colleagues and students as well as with his friends everywhere. He has also continued to write and do research on topics he did not have sufficient time earlier to finish, such as the Lebanese poets of French expression. But he also resumed writing articles in Arabic such as "Jubrān fī 'Ālamih al- Fikrī wa-al-Adabī" in 1992 and "La'āzar wa-Ḥabībatuh: Jadaliyyat al-Mawt wa-al-Inbi'āth fī Ru'yat Jubrān" in 1995. Arabic periodicals published articles about him and his life's work, such as *Al-Ḥaraka al-Shi'riyya* in 1992 and *Al-Nahār* in 1994, recognizing his contributions and reporting his opinions on developments in Arabic literature.

Perhaps more important than all this is the fact that Mounah Khouri resumed writing Arabic poetry mostly in free verse and addressing metaphysical issues. Freed from the demands of daily academic life and unhampered by the rigor of scholarship taught him by the eminent H. A. R. Gibb, Mounah now felt he might again express in verse the innermost thoughts of his soul as meritorious creative literature in its own right, in continuation of his former poetic career that had experienced a temporary, but long, hiatus. Mellowed by time and the wisdom of experiencing life, his new poetry is a far cry from the vehement passion couched in the glowing language of his younger days, but it is no less representative of the man with a big heart that he has always been.

Mounah Khouri, the Poet

I wish I had more samples of Mounah's poetry than what is available to me at this time. Back in the 1940s, I collected newspaper and magazine clippings of his poems published in Palestine—I did that as an admiring, dutiful teenage student, unbeknownst to the master.[4] I preserved those clippings for many years but lost them during my traumatic move from Jerusalem to North America after the 1967 war in the Middle East had played havoc with my life and that of my wife and four little children in the Holy City. Despite his many moves, however, Mounah seems to have kept his own clippings of these poems in addition to those of earlier ones and of others he later wrote and published in Lebanon. When he was about to undergo a serious surgical operation in April of 1995, he feared for these poems written between 1938 and 1954, so he sent them to As'ad Khayr-Allāh and Maḥmūd Shurayḥ in Europe to be edited and prepared for publication in book form along with his more recent ones of the 1990s. Until this book of Mounah's poetry is published,[5] what I will say here will be preliminary, but it will also be the first treatment in English of his poetry.

When Mounah began writing poetry, he admired a number of contemporary Arab poets like Ilyās Abū Shabaka, Ṣalāḥ Labakī, Sa'īd 'Aql, and 'Umar Abū Rīsha who were very popular. Khalīl Muṭrān *(Shā'ir al-Quṭrayn,* and later *Shā'ir al-Aqṭār al-'Arabiyya)* and Bishāra al-Khūrī *(al-Akhṭal al-Ṣaghīr),* both of an earlier generation, were also popular and acclaimed as innovators. The neo-classicism of Aḥmad Shawqī and Ḥāfiẓ Ibrāhīm had come and gone, and the romantic movement was now at its height. Mounah Khouri rode the crest of its wave as the love of a young woman entered his life while he was teaching in Jaffa at the Orthodox College.[6] She was the daughter of a well-off physician from an established Palestinian family and he a school teacher with a meager salary. His love was reciprocated by the young woman he fictitiously calls Laylā in his poems, but her parents objected to him because of his limited income and their perception of his social status as a school teacher and of the unprestigious school he taught at. If it were Bishop Gobat School, they speciously argued, the situation might be different (that was the high school in Jerusalem from which the young woman's father had graduated). Her parents made her break off all relations with Mounah and marry a rich cousin of hers who was in the shipping and transportation business.

Mounah moved away from Jaffa to teach in Gaza and then in Jerusalem, but all the fountains of poetry burst open in his disappointed heart. He published his poems in Palestinian dailies like *Filisṭīn* and *Al-Difāʿ* and in Palestinian weeklies like *Al-Qāfila, Al-Ghad,* and *Al-Muntadā.* They were poems nostalgically remembering his happy relationship with Laylā, recalling its physical and spiritual pleasures in a language chiseled from the best Arabic diction of infatuation and bristling with subdued anger that sometimes exploded in a righteous expression of pride and self-worth. The imagery in these poems was presented in a vivid and highly metaphorical language that drew on novel ways of combining words for best effect. Their rhythm was that of the Arabic meters used for centuries to express deep emotions.

Perhaps one of his most representative poems of this period is the one he recited on graduation day of Bishop Gobat School, held in 1947 at the YMCA auditorium in Jerusalem under the auspices of the British High Commissioner. More than five years had passed since the relationship had ended, but Mounah was still smarting from its pain. What made the occasion more poignant was that Mounah had finally become a teacher at the very school that Laylā's parents respected. Moreover, they were present in the audience with Laylā herself because their son was one of the graduands. Mounah recited the poem he entitled "I Am Indeed the Teacher, Laylā":[7]

> Laylā, bride of my love and dawn of its world,
> Leave my heart alone, you're not its Laylā today.
> Say farewell to love, bereaved as you are at its death
> Within your bosom unable to bear its affliction.
> I gave you my heart, the most generous and the purest gift[8]
> That the abundance of life can offer to a thirsty person.
> And your mouth avidly lapped up quenching gulps from the cool,
> Fresh waters of its plenitude desired by Paradise's virgins.

The poem then goes on to enumerate his giving of himself, her enjoyment, and her ingratitude and rejection. Then comes his affirmation of self-worth:

> If fortune were fair, Laylā, it would have made shoes for me
> Of the foreheads of haughty people scorning their teacher.
> I am indeed the teacher, Laylā. My affiliation is to the Son
> Of Divinity,[9] or rather say, to God Himself.
> To Him I am attributed as well as all those bearing my title
> My riotous voice would not ring out if it were not for Him.

The poet then embarks on a long section extolling the virtues of being a teacher, the sacrifices a teacher makes to build up new generations, and the moral influence a teacher has on learners in his charge.

> Ask the young men whose generation I raised
> And the two crowns of my proud brow will inform you:
> I offered them the best aspect of my beautiful life
> And the most generous part of the spring of my youth.
> From my heart, I used to provide sustenance for them
> That they might eat the best oblation and the most vivifying.
> I squeezed my heart into a chalice and called out to them:
> Drink from the fountain of my heart the purest drink.
> Woe to my night, how often have I made its darkness flow
> In ink which my red blood nourished and gave to drink.
> I led them onto the path of Truth, boldly plunging
> Into the terror of calamities surrounding its world.

Addressing himself to Laylā, he then ends the poem asking her to rid herself of arrogance:

> I am indeed the teacher, my Laylā. So go easy
> And curb your tyrannical haughtiness and excessive arrogance.
> On the shore of the universe, I am a shining beacon
> Which I supply with the most radiant light of my eyes.
> And I am a boat plowing the fathomless waves, struggling
> To bring the passengers to happiness and dignity.

At times, Mounah may have rebuked himself for dwelling so long on a past love, nursing a wound that would not heal. In a poem entitled "Aṣnām" (Idols),[10] he says:

> How long shall I rise on my fancy's back
> And urge my wings to seek the impossible?
> Am I the light emitted in the skies
> To embrace in exaltation the throne of my God?
> O Spirit that makes me soar and go astray,
> Take me back to the world and leave my sky.
> You're in it a barren woman giving birth
> Today to the emptiness of my yesterday's life.

Despite all his attempts to the contrary, his old love kept haunting him, and he continued to write poems about it. His reason told him it was futile to dwell on an old flame, but his heart felt otherwise. Perhaps he was trying to cleanse his soul of all the old effects of love by remembering them in detail and highlighting the betrayal of his ungrateful beloved in order to emphasize the pride within him that makes him transcend all bitter feeling, as he did for example in the poem entitled "Ḍalāl"[11] (Going astray) published in 1947 in which he says:

Snub the eagerness of longings and take away
Your lips, Laylā, from my suckling lips.
Snub them and go astray, O ungrateful one, and tear open
The seals of your mouth in consenting embraces.
Snub them, O foster babe of my passion, and be unthankful
For my wine, my glasses, and my tender bed.
Snub them. For the vehemence of emotion has left nothing
For your love foundling but leftover drops of pride.
Swagger with intoxicated glee over shreds of him,
Your memory is dyed with the yearnings of my ribs.
O tawny woman, life's avid desire and thirst,
Whose blood veins call out for coveted pleasures:
Come with me, let us fold up time and seclude ourselves
In a world colored with wishes, do come with me.

The poet then remembers in detail love moments of the past in which he enjoyed the pleasures of youth with his beloved, but he occasionally stops to wonder whether that experience was real:

Was that encounter in imminent bliss real
Or was it a legend, O my Laylā?
Do say, for my thoughts are raging
Like a violent and stormy hurricane.
Why are you silent? Speak and don't conceal
My abundant love running in your veins.
On your lips, wretch, are bloody prints
Of my outpouring heart and shuddering death.
And in your soul, thirsty for my bosom's outflow,
Is a weaned baby's eagerness for its tender nurse.

And on and on the poet goes, enumerating past experiences of mutual love, but he returns, in the end, to the beloved who denied him the joys of togetherness. And in a final rhetorical flourish, he challenges her to forget him and all the pleasures he has given her.

In retrospect, however, Mounah Khouri's failed love experience turned out to be a great blessing. Not only did it motivate him to pursue in earnest his advanced studies at Harvard University, but also led to his auspicious marriage to a fine, attractive, loving, and cultured lady, Julia Na'īm Bishāra, mentioned earlier. Mrs. Khouri earned a B.A., with distinction, in French literature from the University of California at Berkeley in 1973 as well as teaching credentials for French and English in 1976. For many years she served in Berkeley and the San Francisco Bay area as an effective and caring teacher. At home, she was for Mounah the ideal wife and life partner. With unwavering love and devotion, she ushered him into a happy family life and a splendid academic and creative literary career. In 1971 he dedicated his book *Poetry and the Making of Modern Egypt, 1882–1922* to her in recognition of her support when, as a mother of two demanding little boys, she continued to encourage him and sustain his efforts to complete his doctoral research at Harvard and later to publish it as a book. To her (and to his sons Māzin and Mark), he likewise dedicated in 1987 his other book, *Studies in Contemporary Arabic Poetry and Criticism,* containing his most valuable scholarly essays written over a period of approximately two decades during which she never ceased to be the mainstay of his endurance and inspiration. To her also he dedicated in 1995 his long poem and interpretive study inspired by Gibran's *Lazarus and His Beloved* as a tribute to her love and to her strong faith and deep religious belief.

After many years given to scholarly research and writing, Mounah Khouri started writing poetry again in the 1990s, as mentioned above. Some of his recent poems include one entitled "Nidā' min al-A'māq"[12] (A call from the depths) written in 1993 in memory of his friend Tawfīq Ṣāyigh. It begins:

My misfortune
Is my existence
In a waste land
Far off, lonely
I call out
Anxiously:
My misfortune

Is my existence
In a waste land.

These recent poems also include one entitled "Bāqat al-Ward: Ayn Yamḍī Shadhāhā?"[13] (The bouquet of roses: Where does its fragrance go?). Blessed by a happy marriage, he returns in it to the theme of love, but this time in a pensive mood wondering about existence as he asks his beloved at the end of the poem:

Where does the fragrance go
When the roses come to naught?
Has it been an existence
Made of dreams and shadows?
Or an existence
Unaffected by extinction?
Save me [Sweetheart]
My wandering in loss
Has been too long.

Both the tone and the language of Mounah's recent poems are different from those of his earlier ones. His ideas are now meditative and expressed in a simple language that avoids the diction of classical and romantic Arabic poetry and uses the license of free verse to subject the rhythm to the patterns of his thought. He suggests but does not elaborate, he economizes on conjunctions and logical connectors, he uses vivid symbols and images, and leaves the reader to synthesize, assimilate, and absorb.

After reading Kahlil Gibran's one-act play, *Lazarus and his Beloved*,[14] Mounah decided to epitomize its quintessence in a single long poem in Arabic free verse entitled "La'āzar Jubrān 'Ām 1929" (Gibran's Lazarus in the year 1929).[15] In his introduction to it,[16] Mounah explains he does not intend to parallel Gibran's masterpiece or emulate Khalīl Ḥāwī's long poem, "La'āzar 'Ām 1962" (Lazarus in the year 1962), but rather to give his own reading of Gibran's unique work that has several possible readings.[17] In other words, Mounah wants to illumine what he believes to be the main thrust of Gibran's play, and he disagrees with its editors, Kahlil and Jean Gibran, who said in their introduction to the play that a real beloved was intended by the play's author. Mounah thinks that the beloved of Lazarus in the play, to whom Lazarus wanted so eagerly to return after being resurrected by Jesus, was his other self that he had known from eternity, with whom he was united after death, and from whom he was forcibly separated. Mounah puts the following words in Lazarus's mouth:

> My sublime dream
> Is to transcend limits
> Be free in space
> Be united with Existence:
> As roots are with branches
> As fragrance is with flowers
> As clouds returning
> To the vast sea
> In a running stream
> And in dew at dawn.

I believe that Mounah finds an echo of his own thoughts in these words of Lazarus and, indeed, in Gibran's portrayal of the character of Lazarus in the 1929 play he had been working on since 1914. Mounah rightly says in his introduction that Gibran completely identified his own private experience with that of Lazarus in *Lazarus and his Beloved* more than he ever could with any other character in his earlier masterpieces, *The Prophet* and *Jesus, the Son of Man.*[18] This was particularly so because in 1929 Gibran knew his own end was coming, for his doctor had told him that he could not recover from the disease that eventually caused his death in 1931. Furthermore, he knew he was losing his creative ability, as he himself explained to the two friends who followed him and found him sobbing after he had withdrawn from the studio of his Mexican friend José Orozco, where a party was held for him by friends on his birthday on January 6, 1929, at which he had read *Lazarus and his Beloved*.[19] Mounah also finds an echo of his own thoughts in the final words he makes Lazarus say, again reflecting Gibran's belief in the Unity of Being and in the blessings of Universal Love:

> Winds of the East,
> Blow
> And carry me away
> A lover
> Moved by yearning
> For the Beloved's bosom
> Carry me away
> I have long tarried
> Here

This world is only a dream
Pure illusion, a mere mask.

Mounah had recently shown renewed interest in Gibran as the herald of modernity in Arabic literature,[20] agreeing with Adonis in *Ṣadmat al-Ḥadātha* that he was a force of destruction in Arab culture as a prerequisite for construction and progress and a new understanding of the world and a preliminary step to change and continual improvement.[21] In his interpretation of *Lazarus and his Beloved,* Mounah clearly depicts Gibran's view of life in this world as a temporary separation from the spiritual origins to which humans are bound to return in a renewed and ever-improving moral rise to a full union with the Absolute Universal Self. In this understanding, life is a dream and death is a waking, and love is the only principle that unites humans with one another in this life and with God in eternity.

And yet, despite his fascination with Gibran's metaphysical views as expressed in *Lazarus and his Beloved,* Mounah Khouri has his own distinctive philosophical outlook on certain fundamental questions, prompted by his own private experience. This is clearly revealed in two of his most recent poems: "Al-Ṭayr al-Mufāriq" (The departing bird) and "Fī Mawkib al-Riyāḥ" (Sailing with the wind).[22]

In the first poem, Mounah addresses his blue-eyed, five-year-old granddaughter, Tristyn, who had lost her beloved bluebird to death, buried him under a rose tree as all the family attended, and came to Mounah crying, "Grandpa, isn't he going to come back again?" With sorrow in his eyes, Mounah replied, "No, my dear. He has gone forever. He flew to a faraway place, from which no one has ever returned." In the poem, Mounah says in part:

Our singing companion's wings
Have been urged by the winds
To go to the end limits of space
In the journey of existence.
Like an arrow that is shot
And goes to a far place,
He went
And shall not return.

My little blonde,
O tear of fire:
When the lake-blue of the eyes

Is clouded and gone,
Will it ever be bright again?
Will it ever be clear and light?
I called out to Heaven,
As if calling out were of any avail.
I was reminded of immortality,
As if remembrance were of any use.
There's nothing to hope for
In the invisible Beyond
That will spare us our tragedies.
Here, here alone
Is our only existence
There's nothing beyond.

In the second poem, published simultaneously with the "Al-Ṭayr al-Mufāriq," Mounah Khouri is more assertive of his disbelief in the idea of "Eternal Return," with which Gibran was passionately obsessed. It is as though, tired of his long journey and endless wandering, Mounah surrenders himself to his eternally lonely destiny and yearns to anchor his battered sail-boat where he can find, with the gently flowing sea waves, his everlasting repose in the "white tranquillity"[23] of the sandy shore. Because "Fī Mawkib al-Riyāḥ" is his "preferred best poem," as he recently told me, and because it embodies how he envisions his own destiny and reveals it so candidly in his own distinctive poetic voice, I quote it here in full to conclude this essay:

O my faithful sail,
White of wing,
Sailing with the wind:
When, pray tell, when
Is our return
To the shore of calm?
How long will this journey
Continue to take us afar,
Away from a shore
In the distance
Where we can take shelter
In its haven
As the light dies
In the eyelids of sundown?

There, O sail,
In the engulfing abundance of the bottom
We'll wash away from our anchor
This rust
With the ocean waters,
We'll drop its heavy chains
We'll quench its burning thirst
We'll sleep together
In the secure harbor
With nothing in our eyelids
Nothing
No dream, no imagined trace
Of woven uncertainties
Gone by or vanished
In the invisible Beyond,
Nothing but tranquillity in the waves
Quietly sleeping in the lap of the sand.

This is how Mounah Khouri sees his own destiny and frankly voices it in his poetry. Sailing with the wind to anchor his sailboat in a secure and quiet harbor after a long journey is his preferred symbolism for his human existence and its end. The rusty anchor representing the old and weak human body burdened with the heavy chains of life's desires, illusions, and pains can finally be released as it is dropped into the ocean waters to be cleansed and put to rest, when life ends like a light dying in the eyelids of the horizon at sunset. In the security and quietude of the harbor, the tired and lonely sailor hopes to sleep in peace along with his clean anchor and white sail, nothing of the past and its transcendental uncertainties disturbing his everlasting tranquillity in the waves that sleep quietly in the lap of the sand, gently lulling his eternal repose.

This article was completed in February 1996, ten months before Mounah Khouri passed away on December 28, 1996.

Notes

1. For details of Mounah Khouri's publications, see the bibliography prepared by Terri DeYoung preceding this article.

2. Māzin (b. 1961) graduated from the University of California at Berkeley and is a businessman and a certified professional golfer. Mark (b. 1965) graduated from the University of California at Hayward and is a businessman too. He is married and has two little daughters. A collection of his poems in English entitled *Poems of Hope* was published in Walnut Creek, California in 1981.

3. See the bibliography.

4. I also had a long newspaper clipping of an article Mounah Khouri wrote in a well-documented and spirited response to the Egyptian scholar, Dr. Aḥmad Zakī, who, in a lecture in Jerusalem, had discounted the contributions of the Syro-Lebanese writers of Egypt to the literary *nahḍa.* Mounah's article drew a public apology from Dr. Zakī published a few days later.

5. See Kaissar Afif, *Ḥiṣā al-Dhākira: Munaḥ Khūrī Yatadhakkar Mawāsim al-ʿUmr* (Sidon: Dār al Jār al-Jāmiʿa, 1997).

6. Information on this episode was whispered among Mounah's students of the 1940s in Palestine. Later on, he himself gave me details of it on various occasions. It was briefly related in a *malaff,* or special section, of *Al-Ḥaraka al-Shiʿriyya,* 1, no. 1 (autumn 1992): 39–77, entitled "Munaḥ Khūrī: Shāʿiran wa-Nāqidan wa-Muḥāḍiran," containing three articles written respectively by Asʿad Khayr-Allāh, Henri Zughayb, and Maḥmūd Shurayḥ and including some of Mounah's verse.

7. Parts of this poem have been published in *Al-Ḥaraka al-Shiʿriyya* 1, no. 1 (autumn 1992): 46–47 and 65–66.

8. I translate "andā" and "wa-anqāhu" as "the most generous" and "and the purest," because that is what Mounah recited to me. But in his article, Henri Zughayb has "ashhā" and "wa-arwāhu," meaning "the most desirable" and "and the most satiating." See his quotation in *Al-Ḥaraka al-Shiʿriyya,* 65.

9. Jesus Christ was called Teacher by his disciples. See, for example, John 3:2.

10. See *Al-Ḥaraka al-Shiʿriyya,* 66.

11. See *Al-Qāfila* 10 (July 6, 1947): 6.

12. Handwritten copy sent to me by Professor Khouri. It was published in *Al-Nahār* of August 28, 1993.

13. See *Al-Ḥaraka al-Shiʿriyya,* 11–13.

14. Kahlil Gibran, *Lazarus and his Beloved,* ed. Kahlil and Jean Gibran (New York: Graphic Society, 1973).

15. *Al-Ḥaraka al-Shi'riyya* 3, no. 2 (summer 1995): 15–26.

16. "La'āzar wa-Ḥabībatuh: Jadaliyyat al-Mawt wa-al-Inbi'āth fī Ru'yat Jubrān," *Al-Ḥaraka al-Shi'riyya* 3, no. 2 (summer 1995): 9–14.

17. *Al-Ḥaraka al-Shi'riyya,* 13.

18. *Al-Ḥaraka al-Shi'riyya,* 13–14.

19. See *Al-Ḥaraka al-Shi'riyya*, 9–10; and also Alma Reed, *J.C. Orozco* (New York: Oxford University Press, 1956), 102–3, cited by Mounah Khouri in *Al-Ḥaraka al-Shi'riyya*, 14.

20. See his article, "Jubrān fī 'Ālamih al-Fikrī wa-al-Adabī," *Al-Majāl,* 250 (January 1992): 8–11.

21. Mounah A. Khouri, *Studies in Contemporary Arabic Poetry and Criticism* (Piedmont, Calif.: Jahan Book Company, 1987), 17–23.

22. The two poems appeared in *Al-Nahār* (Beirut) October 28, 1994. They both had misprints which, in a personal communication, Professor Mounah Khouri corrected for my benefit.

23. "White tranquillity," the last two words of the former poem, "Al-Ṭayr al-Mufāriq" (The departing bird), refer to the final repose at death.

My Demon and I
(A Poem)

Jabrā Ibrāhīm Jabrā

For Mounah A. Khouri

(In Arabic mythology, every poet has a demon without whose help his inspiration would fail. Poets' demons live in a valley of their own called 'Abqar.)

My demon played hell with me for some time,
Taking advantage of my passions
Running away with me like wild horses
Between the forests and arid plains:
He would invade me at my weakest hours,
Late at night, before dawn, when I was
In most need of sleep and rest,
And provoke me by instilling my five senses
Into my dreams, charging a nocturnal vision
With the look and touch of a body
All too real,

Prompting me with rare selected phrases
Complete with similes and metaphors
Urging me to leave my bed in order
To pour them down on paper somehow,
As he mounted my shoulder, whispering
That what I wrote
Was only a beginning,
That what was to come was even greater
And lovelier, and all I had to do
Was to keep his company in hallucination,
As he chuckled or lamented in my ear,
In an endless trance.

But I rebelled today, rejected
His insistent whispers
And turned him away, telling him he was
Much less important than he thought,
That my experience or my raving was too large
For him to absorb in his ravings:
The explosive pleasure I knew
Was beyond him, nor could he fathom
My torment with all its wounds.
Go to your Valley, I said, and run loose
With your little brother demons,
And leave me to myself, so that
I may write what you could never dream of,
And so it will be you who'll learn
From me, as though from now on
I were your inspiration and your demon!

I had a hunch then what I would write
Could only crystallize in beauty or terror
If words came running to portray,

To escalate, to make what seemed
To shoot through the mind in sudden glow
Like a ghost
Get caught at last on paper
To be retrieved, re-lived, to be drunk
Like a bottle of ancient wine,
As it fluttered and throbbed
With love, abandon and lustful folly.

Words, words!
What's agony like in the heart
As it calls out like a clarion,
What's vanishing
In a white cloud encircling the brain
Elevating one's whole being
Into ecstasy and the impossible?
Shall I shout, shall I sing, shall I
Contort my body in a violent dance,
Or race the wind, fly like fountain water
Into blue space then cascade
On marble floors in rainbow colours?

And the music which used everyday
To unravel me into threads
Then re-weave me shred by shred,
How am I to emulate it now
That I am unravelled thread by thread
All scattered on the floor
With no one to weave it back again,
Waiting for a hand never outstretched,
Waiting for lips always seen
But never embodied,
Waiting for a voice that fills the world

With rejoicing yells, reverberating
Further and further away until
It is heard no more by me
Despite the endless din?

Yes, I said, I shall write.
I shall write what turns madly round
To no final form,
What eddies in stormy waters
Sinking to depths
Which only lead to hell.
I shall write what is beyond all utterance,
Rejects logic, and trembles
Like a butterfly's wings at midday,
Or melts like flecks of snow
Falling on deserts and wasteland.
I shall write what will respond
In loving laughter to the morning sun,
Pants with a profligate's lust,
Or lets itself go with the follies
Of a green night crazed
By the moon which causes
The earth to go mad with moaning
And desire.
How are the innards stabbed
To screaming, turning their blood
Into paintings and sculptures?
How are sounds transformed into tears,
Torrents, cloud-topped mountains
And valleys devouring suns no end?

Is this the aching for a vision
That never surrenders itself,

When tempests rush where nothing
Is left behind but ruined reason?
Is this the lust of the soul
Or of the body?
Is there any difference between them?
Let words articulate,
And let them fashion for my eyes
A face the like of which
God perfects once only in a thousand years.

Is this hell without oblivion?
Those driven down to hell are given
One or two draughts from Lethe,
And they forget:
How many draughts, O lord of hell,
Have you given me, repeatedly,
To no avail?
You've given up, and I've remained
In a torment you would not wish
For your worst enemy.
You knew the terror of memory's serpents
And so created Lethe's waters
To kill them:
But here are serpents that refuse to die
Making fun of all your waters,
Pursuing the torture of their pleasures.

O vaulting blood in black domains
Resplendent in darknesses going naked
Like forests in rain,
Whose call will never cease for a moment.
Night's forests are sheer murder
In agonized love.

The beasts of night are marauding me,
And the beasts of day seduce me
With night's forests and their burning beasts.

◆ ◆ ◆

I turned round and found
My demon, lighter than air,
Had mounted my shoulder, whispering
As was his wont in my ear—
But I knew not this time what exactly
He'd planned for me with his whispers,
And his voice was truly strange:
Was it a new sorrow he had for me
Or a long-absent joy?
Or was it that his laughter tonight
Was more akin to tears?

(Translated from the Arabic by the author)

Note

Jabrā Ibrāhīm Jabrā, the well-known poet, novelist, and literary critic, died in Baghdad on December 12, 1994. A close friend of Mounah A. Khouri's since the middle 1940s when they both taught school in Jerusalem, he was a research fellow at Harvard University in 1952–54, along with the poet Tawfīq Ṣāyigh, when Mounah Khouri was a doctoral candidate there and their friendship became proverbial. Professor Khouri invited Jabrā to the University of California at Berkeley as a visiting professor in the spring of 1974. When invited to contribute to this *Festschrift,* Jabrā sent this poem and wrote the following to Issa J. Boullata in a letter dated December 20, 1993:

> "I would like to participate in this book honouring my beloved brother Mounah Khouri. Yesterday, I wrote to Professor DeYoung in this regard and suggested sending you the enclosed poem, the English translation of which is dedicated to Mounah Khouri. . . . The poem is one of twenty-five I wrote in the second half of last year. It is perhaps the most beautiful poem I have ever written, and I have intentionally put off publishing it in a book."

Gibran's Concept of Modernity

ANTOINE G. KARAM

"To me, Mary, perfection is a limitation and I cannot conceive perfection any more than I can conceive the end of space or time."

—Kahlil Gibran to Mary Haskell, January 3, 1917

There is no unanimity among critics regarding the definition of "modernity." In fact, the term has meant different things, at different times, to different users. However, if we cannot circumscribe the fluctuating meanings of the term, we can at least note certain common tendencies, premises, and aims that designate what may be called "modern." In a broad sense, it is

The basic text of this article was written in Arabic by the late Antoine Karam, professor of Arabic literature at the American University of Beirut, and translated into English by Adnan Haydar. It was intended for inclusion in a book entitled "New Currents in Modern Arabic Poetry" that both Mounah Khouri and his colleague Karam started working on during the latter's stay in Berkeley as visiting professor in 1974–75. Unfortunately, the manuscript was never finished because of Karam's premature death in 1979. Apart from the addition of the introductory and concluding sections, footnotes, and necessary editing, the full credit for writing the article goes to Antoine Karam. Most recently, this revised form of the article was made available to the editors of this book by a mutual friend of both Professors Karam and Khouri with the request that it be included therein in honor of the collaboration and friendship of these two colleagues. The editors wish to express their gratitude to Dr. Haydar for his able translation.]

not a chronological designation, and, however loosely defined, the congeries of characteristics it may suggest are usually marked by a strong and conscious break with the forms and techniques of a certain established tradition. Applied in a more specific sense to twentieth-century Arabic literature, the term "modern" or "modernist" refers to the pre-romantic works of Muṭrān and the "Dīwān" group in Egypt as well as writings of the "Mahjar" (emigrant) poets led by Gibran, in whose works modernity found its most articulate expression.

Before focusing on Gibran's concept of modernity, and without belaboring in great detail the literary history and achievements of the two modernizing schools referred to as the Dīwān and Mahjar writers, it may suffice to outline here briefly some of their objectives, activated fundamentally by a spirit of revolt against the neoclassical tradition which dominated the literary scene prior to the 1930s.

The first modernistic changes manifested themselves in the poetry of Muṭrān, whose individual talent and solid training in both the classical Arabic tradition and French letters and culture combined to inspire his innovations. These involved a series of breaches with the current neoclassical trend and advanced Arabic poetry toward a freer language, richer themes, newer forms and techniques, and a more coherent mode of existence. However, the process of poetic modernization had to be carried out by a younger group of poets.[1]

Partly influenced by Muṭrān and partly by the English romantic poets and critics, particularly Hazlitt and Coleridge, three Egyptian modernists known as the Dīwān Group—Shukrī, al-'Aqqād, and al-Māzinī—set out on a new path. Their objective was, in essence, to consolidate the romantic trend generated by Muṭrān which was destined to be reinforced by a similar current being developed simultaneously by their contemporaries, the Mahjar or Syro-American group.

Despite differences in character and temperament which, among other factors, led to the rift between the Dīwān poets, it is quite evident that both al-'Aqqād and al-Māzinī shared Shukrī's ideas and that their thinking remained within the general framework of his concepts of poetry. Chief among Shukrī's views are the rejection of the unity of the *bayt* (line of verse) and the emphasis on the organic unity of the poem; the insistence on clarity, simplicity, and quiet beauty of the poetic language; and the necessity of drawing upon all sources of inspiration, traditional and foreign, which might broaden and deepen the poet's perception and sensibility. But more important than these concepts, already advocated by Muṭrān, was Shukrī's redefinition of poetry as *wijdān* (emotions or inner feelings).[2]

Much of what the Egyptian modernists were doing in the second and third decades of this century was also being explored by Arab Mahjar poets in the Americas. This group consisted of Syrians and Lebanese who had emigrated to the New World and who then found themselves caught between two cultures: that of the West, which proved extremely influential on both the forms and content of their works, and their original Arab culture, which they sought to both preserve and modernize. Their position as emigrants, immersed in Western culture and freed from the strains and doubts which assailed their fellow Arabs in their homeland, meant that they were best suited to revitalize Arabic letters and shape Arab sensibility.

In general, their ideas may be characterized as romantic, humanistic, and often mystical. They shared the belief that they lived in an age with its own sensibility and its own expectation of literature and function. They agreed on the need for adopting a new concept of language, neither sacred nor profane, but rather a living medium of expression subject to changes and developments. Consequently, they emphasized the need for reviving the Arabic language and restoring to it the simplicity and vitality that centuries of stagnant conservatism had destroyed. In addition, they stressed human experience and subjective feelings as the basis and source of all true literature.

The better educated writers from among the Mahjar group of North America, Gibran, Nu'ayma, and al-Rīḥānī, were in general influenced by the romantic literature of the West, by the American transcendentalists, especially Emerson, and by such poets as Longfellow, Whittier, and Whitman. Apart from a common background, experience and literary taste, and the pursuit of common objectives, they had no specific ideology and showed in their works individual tendencies.[3]

It is generally agreed that Gibran was the leading and most influential figure of the Mahjar writers. His work, which, besides painting, includes poetry, criticism, essays, novels, short stories, and books of meditations, is primarily characterized by a strong, conscious break with the traditional values and assumptions and their forms and techniques of expression. He not only rejects historical continuity by turning away from the tradition, but also from the society whose modes of existence and guiding institutions history records.

In his perception of the ideal world, he envisioned and aspired to create a new world in place of the old one he demolished. Gibran, imbued with a genuine romantic and mystical attitude towards existence, exalts life; glorifies "nature"; elevates the individual and his inner being over social man and his corrupt human society; and celebrates imagination, passion, and the freedom of the human spirit as more trustworthy than reason, logic, religious dogmas, codified laws, and scientific postulates in guiding mankind to the right path. This, as revealed in his vision, is the path to the romantic mythopoeic, transcendental world where all the antinomies, conflicts, and complexities of civilized life, as well as of man's anxiety and bewilderment in the face of ultimate questions, are resolved.

Gibran's biographers (like Nu'ayma and Jean and Kahlil Gibran),[4] editors of his diaries and personal letters (such as Tawfīq Ṣāyigh and Virginia Hilu),[5] and authors of scholarly works on him like Khalīl Ḥāwī and Adūnīs ('Alī Aḥmad Sa'īd)[6] provide illuminating findings about several aspects of his life, work, and achievements.

These references alone, not to mention many other valuable works, leave very little to be explored further in the field of Gibranic studies. However, notwithstanding such limitations and the belief that Gibran's own work, like all great works of art, remains an inexhaustible source of interpretation, I turn now to his concept of modernity.

To begin with, Gibran's work, however complex its sources may be, whether it was influenced by Nietzsche, Blake, Rodin, the romanticism and transcendentalism of American literature, or the Bible and Eastern mysticism, has never lost its own unique and original character. This is how Zarathustra, the superman and the symbol of historical mysticism, metamorphoses into a transcendental mystic and a symbol of infinite love which merges the individual soul (the microcosm) with the universal soul (the macrocosm). This is how Christ becomes the embodiment of the idea of the superman and how the clash of opposites in Blake's visions reverts to a peaceful harmony in *The Prophet* or to a wedding of the heavenly and the natural in Gibran's *The Earth Gods.* Similarly, this is how Gibran blends neo-Platonism with Emerson's romanticism and Eastern mysticism and produces out of the admixture his own visions of the ascension of perfected humanity toward the infinite Absolute.[7]

Without any doubt, Gibran's Arabic compositions revealed some innovation in *Al-Mawākib* (1919), but they reached their best form in *Al-'Awāṣif*

(1920) and in some portions of *Al-Badā'i' wa-al-Ṭarā'if* (1923). On the other hand, *The Prophet* (1923) has been heralded as his best work in English despite the visions and fresh dimensions found in *Jesus, the Son of Man* (1928) and *The Earth Gods* (1931).

The second point to be stressed is that the romantic movement which reached its height in the Arab world in the 1930s received its directive force from Gibran's romanticism in its broad and fundamental dimensions: romantic individualism with its emphasis on imagination and emotion and romantic transcendentalism with its organic view of nature.

At the root of Western romanticism was the belief—or, more precisely, the religious enthusiasm for the idea—that man, the individual, is an infinite reservoir of possibilities and that if society can be rearranged by the destruction of all oppressive orders then these possibilities will be realized and progress will be achieved. Romanticism was basically a comprehensive revolt against the established order in all fields of thought, taste, and expression. Its social, intellectual and literary aspects were for the most part blended together in full harmony. Transplanted into Egyptian soil, the European equation of romanticism with comprehensive revolt was changed into a much narrower one of romanticism as a literary revolt against the formalism of neoclassical poetry. Thus, the poetical productions of the Egyptian modernists are far more valuable and interesting as literary achievements than as the embodiments of a more comprehensive romantic revolutionary philosophy.[8] The link between the social and literary aspects of most of their compositions is indeed very tenuous.

On the other hand, the romantic philosophy held by Gibran and the spirit of romanticism which permeated his works were not only very radical and comprehensive, but also fundamentally those of a visionary writer. Like a mystic, he aspired to unveil the world of the unseen and discover the unknown. It is this mystical approach that led some critics (Adūnīs) to compare his visionary experience with that of Ibn al-'Arabī, who conceives of vision as a state of unity with the unknown creating a new image of the world or rather creating the world afresh. Thus the visionary is totally unconcerned with the sensory realm in all its monotony and habituality. Instead, he is completely preoccupied with the transcendental, perceiving it to be in a state of continual change and renewal and aspiring to unveil it uprooted from his old world; alienated in his new one; shocked by what he has experienced and has seen around him in terms of corruption, conflicts, and despair; and struggling to free himself and mankind from all man-made chains and fetters. Gibran's romantic attitude to life and existence manifested itself in the framework of a destructive-constructive scheme or dialectic, a process by which he revolted against the church and the state and their oppressive religious and political authorities.[9] Instead, he prescribed a new mode of existence freed from all conventional rules and dogmas and guided by the ideals of a new humanism which conceived of man as being at the very center of all life and all experience and conceived of his freedom, happiness, and unity as one great brotherhood.

These are, in broad strokes, the distinctive features of Gibran's romanticism. If we now turn to the manifestation of his revolutionary romantic philosophy in the literary sphere, the following contributions to modernity may be noted.

He was the only author among the moderns who practiced two complementary art forms. The painter in him took his inspiration from the poet's vision, and the poet in him learned from the painter the nature of form, the music of line and color, the power to penetrate the crust of the material world, and the desire to discern the spirit beyond. This unique combination found its articulation in his prose style, particularly in his two short story collections, *Nymphs of the Valley* (1906) and *Spirits Rebellious* (1908), and in his novel, *Broken Wings* (1912), where he retained his lyrical quality and made his stories the vehicle of his literary commitments and the outlet for the emanation of the spirit while it suffers in love, yearns for life, or languishes before death. Many were those who imitated Gibran's prose style, which became the inspiration of all the Arab romantic poets between the two World Wars.

Secondly, the very high level he attained in handling internal rhythm and in exploiting the allusive quality of words made him proclaim in one of his letters to Mary Haskell in 1920 that he had created "a language within the language."[10] Indeed, the most distinguishing quality of his art is his ability to capture "poetic images." He saw the whole world fraught with the symbols of hidden truths and with fleeting moments within the totality of life. His handling of metaphor enabled him to create a world above this world. His "soul" metamorphoses into a "tree" and the tree metamorphoses into a "universe"; the cloud materializes as "a city" that disappears, in turn, into "the sunset"; the morning nymphs of the sea revert to dancers tripping upon the waves and over the hills; the birds of prey sink their beaks into the poet's heart while crows flutter around his deathbed and carry in their claws pieces of his flesh, as in the paintings of Goya or Hieronymus Bosch. Or he is al-Khiḍr charging on a white horse from the recesses of history in order to kill a dragon and save the crucified world. With such visions he changes the poetic image from naive simile into metaphor, symbol, and mystic illumination.

Thirdly, while the neoclassicist's main preoccupation was with rhetoric and the classicists' had been in distinguishing form from intellectual content, Gibran welded poetry to thought in a fashion unprecedented, except perhaps in the prose of the "rational" Ṣūfīs. When his writings in English, which reveal his genuine Eastern style and which are fraught with images and thoughts, were translated into Arabic they did not seem to come from a foreign literature. It was as if the East found itself again in his work. After him, Arabic literature sought new depths, and Arabic poetry revolved in the orbits of abstract thought and introspection. In particular, Gibran's *Madman* (1918), *The Prophet,* and *Jesus, the Son of Man* educated the public in a new literary sensibility which savored the glimmers of distant contemplations and disliked the shallowness of the neoclassical poem. In due course, neoclassical poetry was identified with a manifestation of degradation and backwardness.

Fourthly, Gibran did not write lengthy books because the poetic mode was dominant in his work. His meditations in *The Prophet,* his various portraits of Jesus in *Jesus, the Son of Man,* and his portrayal of the tense dialogue between the gods in *The Earth Gods* all made it possible for him to express truth in a few tight, transparent allusions that are hard to fathom. Often he expressed himself in parallels or used metaphors to encompass the invariable truths of life, as he does in *Sand and Foam* (1926) or in the comprehensive summaries which are, in effect, his dicta.

Gibran has also distinguished himself with his "poèmes en prose," which during the last three decades have become the distinguishing feature of modern Arabic poetry. It is possible to suggest that he felt more at ease in giving shape to his visions in this form than in the old prosodic forms. The rhythm of carefully molded prose was more immediately capable of embodying his inner feelings. Nevertheless, we still find thirteen poems in his collected works in which he emulated the rhythmic structure of the Andalusian *muwashshaḥ*. His poems are thus short, often consisting of shorter lines and with a changing rhyme scheme. The intellectual elements in these poems acquire transparency and power of suggestion from their simplicity and gentle, flowing rhythm.

Gibran's major work in verse, however, is his book *Al-Mawākib (The*

Procession). He devoted this work to a series of meditations on metaphysical questions with which he was preoccupied in all his works, such as the duality of good and evil, body and soul, freedom and predestination; the problems of man-made laws; religious institutions; the unity of the universe; and the question of transcendental reality. To each of these questions he devoted an independent ode, constructing the odes as dialogues between two symbolic characters: an old man and a youth who represent the dualities which form the essence of the book. The meeting-point between the two is the area separating nature from culture. It would seem that the old man embodies the dislocation suffered by human societies and the defective nature of the codes of morality and value systems. The old man's statements represent the fixed values evident in reality, compressed into the form of aphorisms. These meditations are imbued with a tone of metaphysical agony. As a result, the old man's statements become sorrowful elegies revealing the defects inherent in man's nature ever since he came into existence. The meter chosen for them is *al-basīṭ,* and each of them has a particular rhyme. By rendering all of his themes in the same metrical form, the poet seems to be trying to reflect the monotony of the fixed, absolute values which he is exploring. The youth, on the other hand, is a symbol of virgin nature, the suppleness of primitiveness, and the longing for renewal and the eternal return where good and evil melt into each other, contradictory forces meet, and all times, past, present, and future fuse, life thus being complemented by death in the law of survival which embraces all opposites and by the bliss of eternal joy being realized. The youth's meditations have the metrical form of *al-ramal* (in its shorter, four-foot version), and the rhyme scheme is varied, as if to communicate the joy of optimism, in contrast with the dark pessimism of the old man's words.

A third symbol appears in *The Procession,* namely, the flute, which provides the musical response for each ode and which the poet intends, perhaps, to be a transformational element unifying the opposites by referring them back to nature, to the wholeness of life which is both older than the past and younger than the future. On this optimistic note, Gibran ends his book with the melodic tune of the flute, which echoes his overall view of life when he says: "the Ensemble of life is sweet and good, and everlasting."[11]

Gibran's final major contribution to modern Arabic literature is his use of myth. He certainly was not the first Arab writer to incorporate myth into his own work, but several factors, including his familiarity with Western writers and his own romantic outlook, rendered his use of myth more compelling and influential on later generations of Arab poets than anyone who preceded him.

In order to appreciate the significance of Gibran's innovative use of myth, it should suffice to describe very briefly the role myth has traditionally played in both Western and Arabic literature. It is generally agreed that myth has been an important part of Western literature since the Middle Ages. However, of particular significance to Gibran would be the role of myth in the works of Blake and other romantic writers with whom he clearly felt strong bonds. The romantic period saw two important developments in myth. First, the ambivalence that earlier writers and philosophers had felt towards myth gave way to the romantic's complete embrace of myth as a creative force in poetry. Poets began to reshape myths to fit their works, rather than relying solely on their allegorical potential as fixed tales. Secondly, the romantics were the first to perceive that myth was inextricably bound to the human mind and, thus, a necessary component of literature. Although Gibran makes no overt use of myths in his poetry, his extensive use of them in his prose works leaves no doubt that he recognized the creative power of myth in literature.

In the sphere of Arabic literature, classical Arab poets used allegory, legends, and mythicized tales in their works.[12] However, it was not until the beginning of the twentieth century that Arab poets, led by Sulaymān al-Bustānī in his monumental translation of *The Iliad* (Cairo, 1904) came to realize the importance of myth as a literary device. Several of the Dīwān poets wrote about the role of myth in literature, but few attempted to incorporate it into their works. By the 1930s, a new generation of poets, the Apollo group, led by Aḥmad Zākī Abū Shādī, made extensive use of myth, but they concerned themselves exclusively with classical—and more specifically, Greek—myths, which were largely unknown and hence inaccessible to an Arab audience.[13] Thus, myth played a marginal role in contrast to the central position it occupied in the works of Western writers who could count on audiences well acquainted with classical literature and mythology.

Gibran, writing well before the Apollo group, obviated this problem by relying on myths that were indigenous to his own culture, such as biblical stories, ancient Near Eastern myths, and Arab folklore. In addition, it is a measure of his literary creativity that he succeeded in using myth as an integral part of the structure of his work rather than as mere external scaffolding. In this, he anticipated and surpassed the works of the mythopoeic Arab poets of the 1950s.

We can, perhaps, best appreciate Gibran's use of myth by briefly examining one of his pieces. Gibran's only play, *Lazarus and His Beloved,* published posthumously in 1973, is an excellent example of his manipulation of myth.[14] Although Gibran apparently did not write *Lazarus and His Beloved* until two years before his death (1929), the idea of the play came to him quite early in his writing career. Gibran's nephew, Kahlil Gibran, indicates that at least as early as 1914, his uncle was thinking of writing an Arabic poem on Lazarus and his only love.[15] Thus, the play is of particular importance since, from conception to execution, it spans most of Gibran's writing career.

As the title implies, the play is based on the biblical story of Jesus's resurrection of Lazarus. The play opens after Lazarus has returned home, but rather than the rejoicing that one might expect at such an occasion, the atmosphere is one of foreboding; Lazarus is wandering in the hills, while his sisters and mother wonder about his gloominess. Most of all, one is acutely aware that the natural order has been disrupted:

> Mary: (turning to Martha) You do not work. You have not worked much lately.
>
> Martha: You are not thinking of my work. My idleness makes you think of what our Master said. Oh, beloved Master!
>
> The Madman: The day shall come when there will be no weaver, and no one to wear the cloth. We shall all stand naked in the sun.[16]

When Lazarus returns from walking in the hills, he tries to explain his anguish to his sister Mary:

> I was a stream and I sought the sea where my beloved dwells, and when I reached the sea I was brought to the hills to run again among the rocks. I was a song imprisoned in silence, longing for the heart of my beloved, and when the winds of heaven released me and uttered me in that green forest I was recaptured by a voice, and I was turned again into silence. I was a root in the dark earth, and I became a flower and then a fragrance in space rising to enfold my beloved, and I was caught and gathered by a hand, and I was made a root again, a root in the dark earth.[17]

He describes the eternal union with his beloved which he experienced in death and which was sundered by Jesus's call:

> We were in space, my beloved and I, and we were all space. We were in light and we were all light. And we roamed even like the ancient spirit that moved upon the face of the waters; and it was forever the first day. We were love itself that dwells in the heart of the white silence. Then a voice like thunder, a voice like countless spears piercing the ether cried out saying, "Lazarus, come forth!" And the voice echoed and re-echoed in space, and I even as a flood tide became an ebbing tide, a house divided, a garment rent, a youth unspent, a tower that fell down, and out of its broken stones a landmark was made. A voice cried "Lazarus, come forth!" and I descended from the mansion of the sky to a tomb within a tomb, this body in a sealed cave.[18]

But Lazarus does not succeed in convincing Mary, who continues to implore him to remain among the living, and Lazarus, in a complete rejection of his resurrection, refuses the food offered by his mother (a dish of lentils, which is curiously reminiscent of the porridge of lentils and rice for which Esau sold his birthright), and flees once more to the hills, as the Madman says:

> Now he is gone, and he is beyond your reach. And now your sorrow must seek another. *(He pauses.)* Poor, poor Lazarus, the first of the martyrs, and the greatest of them all.

The use and, even more importantly, the alteration of a Christian story in *Lazarus and His Beloved* quite fully illustrates Gibran's personal philosophy. Although raised a Maronite Christian, Gibran rejected much of the traditional teachings of his mother church in favor of the Protestant view of personal interpretation of the Scripture. Through this freedom of interpretation, he was able to accommodate religion to his own beliefs, especially the one explored in this play, the all-encompassing importance of love. Indeed, he saw love, and especially the eternal union of lovers after death, as man's means to God; Lazarus speaks with Gibran's voice when he says:

> Then death, the angel with winged feet, came and led my longing to her longing, and I lived with her in the very heart of God. And I became nearer to her and she to me, and we were one. We were a sphere that shines in the sun, and we were a song among the stars.[19]

Perhaps this shift from Maronite Christianity to a mysticism with clear ties to Eastern religions like Hinduism and Buddhism[20] is what allowed Gibran to alter biblical tales in his own works. His retelling of the story of Lazarus here is particularly powerful in that he has Lazarus reject what is clearly the ultimate gift from God, the gift of life on this earth, for the sake of satisfying his passionate longing for the reunion of his soul with the Greater Universal Soul.

It is also important to note the implication of secularism in Gibran's approach to the biblical stories. Especially in the context of Arab society, altering the Bible was a very daring act, indicating the approach of a free thinker. Subsequently, Gibran was in the vanguard of a secularizing trend which became the hallmark of modern Arabic literature.

Finally, *Lazarus and His Beloved* is an important work in that it illustrates Gibran's complete mastery of the myths he uses. He has not simply retold the myth or made allegorical references to it, he has successfully built his work around the myth. He expects his audience to know the biblical story of Lazarus and the resonances it has in the cultures that are familiar with it, and upon that understanding he has built something new which rests on the characters and plot of the original story but which conveys his own vision of Jesus as a Superman, of his crucifixion as an absolute necessity so "that the Kingdom of Heaven that is in us may be preached, and that man might attain that consciousness of beauty and goodness and reality within himself,"[21] of his belief in Eternal Return, in the healing power of Universal Love, and in the Unity of Being.

These, then, are, in broad strokes, the new directions Gibran provided in his works that left a deep impact on his contemporaries and eventually were able to effect a radical transformation in the entire sphere of Arabic letters. Recognized in his lifetime as the foremost creative writer in the Arab world, Gibran was recently honored, sixty years after his death, by the United States Congress's dedication in May 1992 of the Gibran Memorial Garden in Washington D.C., which stands as a landmark to his international fame and most remarkable contribution to the world literary legacy.

Notes

1. See Mounah Khouri, *Poetry, and the Making of Modern Egypt, 1882–1922* (Leiden: E. J. Brill, 1971), 134–72.

2. Khouri, *Poetry,* 173–95. For further readings on Muṭrān, al-'Aqqād, al-Māzinī and Shukrī, see M[uḥammad] M[uṣṭafā] Badawi, *A Critical Introduction to Modern Arabic Poetry* (Cambridge: Cambridge University Press, 1975), 68–116.

3. See Mounah Khouri and Hamid Algar, introduction to *An Anthology of Modern Arabic Poetry* (Berkeley: University of California Press, 1974), 1–20; see also Badawi, *A Critical Introduction,* 179–203.

4. Mīkhā'īl Nu'ayma, *Jubrān Khalīl Jubrān* (Beirut: Maktabat Ṣādir, 1934); Jean and Kahlil Gibran, *Kahlil Gibran: His Life and World* (Boston: New York Graphic Society, 1974).

5. Tawfīq Ṣāyigh, *Aḍwā' Jadīda 'alā Jubrān* (Beirut: Al-Dār al-Sharqiyya, 1966); and Virginia Hilu, *Beloved Prophet, the Love Letters of Kahlil Gibran and Mary Haskell and Her Private Journal* (New York: Alfred Knopf, 1972).

6. In addition to Antoine Karam, "La vie et l'oeuvre de Gibran Khalil Gibran" (Ph.D. diss., Sorbonne, 1958), see Khalīl Ḥāwī, *Kahlil Gibran, His Background, Character and Works* (Beirut: the American University in Beirut Press, 1963) and Adūnīs, *Ṣadmat al-Ḥadātha* (Beirut: Dār al-'Awda, 1978), 159–211.

7. See Antoine Karam, *Malāmiḥ al-Adab al-'Arabī al-Ḥadīth* (Beirut: Dār al-Nahār, 1980). See in particular the essay entitled "Al-Ṣūra al-Shi'riyya fī Adab Jubrān Khalīl Jubrān," 97–122.

8. See Khouri and Algar, *Anthology,* 9–12.

9. See Adūnīs, *Al-Thābit wa-al-Mutaḥawwil,* 3 vols. (Beirut: Dār al-'Awda, 1974–1979). For a lengthy commentary on this work see "A Critique of Adonis's Perspectives on Arabic Literature and Culture" in Mounah Khouri, *Studies in Contemporary Arabic Poetry and Criticism* (Piedmont, California: Jahan Book Co., 1987), 13–44.

10. Quoted in Ṣāyigh, *Aḍwā',* 33. See also the third volume, entitled *Ṣadmat al-Ḥadātha,* of Adūnīs, *Al-Thābit wa-al-Mutaḥawwil,* 205.

11. Hilu, *Beloved Prophet,* 364.

12. Terri DeYoung, "And Thereby Hangs a Tale: A Study of Myth in Modern Arabic Poetry," (Ph.D. diss., University of California, Berkeley, 1988), 65.

13. DeYoung, *And Thereby Hangs a Tale,* 76.

14. Gibran, *Lazarus and His Beloved,* eds. Jean and Kahlil Gibran (Greenwich: Graphic Society, 1973). See also the Arabic version of this play as rendered into

verse and introduced by Mounah Khouri, in *Al-Ḥaraka al-Shiʿriyya* 3, no. 2 (summer 1995): 9–26.

15. Gibran, *Lazarus and His Beloved,* 19.

16. Gibran, *Lazarus and His Beloved,* 38.

17. Gibran, *Lazarus and His Beloved,* 48.

18. Gibran, *Lazarus and His Beloved,* 50–52.

19. Gibran, *Lazarus and His Beloved,* 48.

20. Ḥāwī, *Kahlil Gibran,* 229.

21. Hilu, *Beloved Prophet,* 363.

The Greek Cultural Heritage and the Odyssey of Modern Arab Poets

As'ad E. Khairallah

Adūnīs (b. 1930), a leading Arab poet of Syrian origin, lived the second half of his life in Beirut, and since 1986 has been living in Paris. A cornerstone of his poetry is the vision that life and art are a permanent, external and internal journey. Addressing Ulysses, he says in one of his poems:

This article was originally a lecture delivered at the Second International Congress on Greek and Arabic Studies (Delphi, July 1985) in the presence of Adūnīs, al-Bayātī, Ḥijāzī, and Rifqa and dealt mainly with the poetic worlds of these poets. It was later slightly expanded for a lecture at the University of Oslo (1990). I should like here to thank the European Cultural Center of Delphi and the Norwegian Oriental Society as well as the Semitic Department of the Institute of East European and Oriental Studies of the University of Oslo for their generous invitation. In the meantime other poets have been treated within the framework of the present theme. On Khalīl Ḥāwī, for example, see Mohammad Shaheen, "Sindbad: The Other Voyage," in his *The Modern Arabic Short Story* (London: Macmillan, 1989), 26–70. Also the special issue of the *Revue de Littérature Comparée* 68, no. 1 (janvier-mars 1994) on the theme of "Le voyage dans la littérature arabe moderne." Of particular relevance to the present subject are the articles of Jacques Berque, "Le voyage d'Adonis," 81–88 and Issa J. Boullata, "Between East and West: Search Journeys of Ḫalīl Ḥāwī," 89–96.]

Even if you return O Ulysses
. . . .
You remain a history of departure
You remain in a land of no promise
You remain in a land of no return[1]

On the other side of the Mediterranean, in Alexandria, lived C. P. Cavafy (1863–1933), a descendant of Ulysses and the father of modern Greek poetry. In his poem "Ithaca" he says:

As you set out for Ithaca
hope your road is a long one,
. . . .
May there be many summer mornings when
with what pleasure, what joy,
you enter harbors you're seeing for the first time;
may you stop at Phoenician trading stations
to buy fine things,
mother of pearl and coral, amber and ebony,
sensual perfume of every kind—
as many sensual perfumes as you can;
and may you visit many Egyptian cities
to learn and go on learning from their scholars.

Keep Ithaca always in your mind.
Arriving there is what you're destined for.
But don't hurry the journey at all.
Better if it lasts for years,
so you're old by the time you reach the island,
wealthy with all you've gained on the way
not expecting Ithaca to make you rich.[2]

Here Cavafy makes it clear: it is not Ithaca that counts so much, it is the journey itself. Ithaca is like the philosopher's stone, which we never acquire, yet makes us wise through our long search for it.

If, for Cavafy, Ulysses is still the Greek obtaining wealth and knowledge at the eastern shores of the Mediterranean, what this article will emphasize is the journey of the Arab poets through Western culture and on European shores. It would need more than an article to cover the impressive presence of the Greek cultural heritage in modern Arabic poetry. It would take books. All I should like to do is to cast a glance on the resurgence of this heritage, showing how it helps shape and express the modern Arab consciousness, then concentrate on three central figures, namely, Heraclitus, Orpheus, and above all Ulysses.

In my attempt to explain how Arab poets adopt these figures to their creative needs, I shall cite extensive samples, hoping to render my analysis more concrete, while allowing the reader a closer acquaintance with some of our poets. These are by no means the only ones who conceive their whole work as a sea journey expressing their main quest, be it nationalist, religious, political, aesthetic, existential, or a combination of all these. The frame of this paper confines me, however, to a few poets and to short excerpts from their work. Yet I hope to present the most important aspects of their journey, keeping in mind that their use of classical Greek figures deeply reflects their very good acquaintance with modern European poetry and thought. For they have all studied modern Western literature and most of them have lived or are still living in Europe. In this sense, rereading classical mythology and thought has been heavily influenced by the modern European perspective.

In order to make this clearer, it may be useful to remember two phenomena: the first is that traditional Arabic poetry was either not suited for narrative or shunned it, and that outside some mystical circles, symbolism and allegory were not welcome. Thus we rarely find legends or myths extensively developed in poetry, except for those stories anchored in the Qur'ān or the Bible, but not of the heathen, Greco-Roman tradition. So, compared with the extremely rich borrowings in the intellectual and scientific fields, classical Arabic poetry remained strikingly refractory to any Greek impact of note.

The second curious feature of this poetry is that, despite the Arabs' experience at sea, their traditional poetry showed relatively little interest in the sea and sailing. The famous Sindbad travels, heavily influenced by Ulysses's wanderings, remained confined to folk literature in prose.

These two facts make it all the more essential to point out that it is precisely in the field of poetry that a fundamental change takes place in modern times: on the one hand, classical Near Eastern as well as Greek mythologies play a central role in modern Arab consciousness and poetic expression; on the other hand, the theme of sea and sailing becomes by far the most important framework of modern poetic imagery. Thus, Badr Shākir al-Sayyāb, a major pioneer of the New Poetry, says about the end of his life that he is giving up the use of myth, "except for the mention of two mythical personages and what pertains to them, namely, the Arab Sindabād and the Greek Odysseus."[3] It is striking to find here a poet who made use of so many mythical figures not only planning to limit himself to the mythical framework of sea and sailing but finding it necessary to associate Ulysses with the most famous Arab sailor, Sindbad! So why this development and how does it manifest itself?

Intensive cultural contacts with the West started with what the Arabs call the *nahḍa,* that is, their cultural renaissance, which began in the last century and opened their doors to Western civilization, from which many literary forms and genres were introduced. Yet, more important than the literary borrowings themselves was the overwhelming socio-political and cultural shock that threw them off their axis and triggered their deep identity crisis, which is far from having been overcome.

The poets, the sensitive consciousness of the nation, were the avant-garde of those who set sail, so to speak, in search for the lost self. Indeed, with the collapse of faith in one's own nation, cultural traditions, and beliefs, it is quite difficult to keep faith in one's individual self. And in the absence of prophets, the modern Arab poet had to reassume the visionary task of the pre-Islamic poet, namely, to guide the whole tribe on their journey through the desert, and to accomplish the missionary role of simultaneously finding and creating their promised land.

This prophetic function of the modern poet, revived with the Romantic movement in the West, reached the Arab world at the turn of the century with a strongly convinced visionary poet, Kahlil Gibran (1883–1931), whose major work is tellingly entitled *The Prophet* and whose persona is called Almustafa, the Chosen One, which is an attribute of the Prophet Muḥammad. Therein Almustafa reveals the secrets of life to the people of Orphalese, a city called after Orpheus, then sails serenely into death, for he is sure to be reincarnated in another prophet, when mother-life feels the need for it.

In Egypt, 'Abbās Maḥmūd al-'Aqqād (1889–1964), 'Abd al-Raḥmān Shukrī (1886–1958), 'Abd al-Qādir al-Māzinī (1880–1949), and above all Aḥmad Zakī Abū Shādī (1892–1955)[4] and his literary Apollo group played an important role in introducing Greek mythology into Arabic poetry. Thus many poems were published on Icarus, Prometheus, Sisyphus, Orpheus, and others, endowing them with symbolic meaning, especially as personae for the poet and his mission.[5]

But despite this widespread interest in Greek myth, it is first in the second half of the century, with what is called the New Poetry, that the use of mythology becomes, for many, a constituent element of poetic composition. Earlier, we found separate, mostly narrative poems, re-telling the story of a Greek hero, god, or mythic figure with clear hints at what they were supposed to symbolize. This approach persisted at the beginning of the New Poetry, but with time these myths became familiar enough that the poet was able to integrate these archetypes as personae and to use them freely. This means that the poet may decide to use only one or a few aspects of the figure, depending on his own need. It also means that he could resort to mixing the different figures, whether from his own, or from Greek, tradition, thus transforming them into objective correlatives that function as parts in an organic whole, expressing his individual, symbolic, and mythopoetic world. As an example, let us consider the way Fu'ād Rifqa (b. 1930) addresses Orpheus:

> Your hymn is a glitter,
> Panting of roads, directions
> Your hymn is river-wild land.[6]

Here we find a multireflective combination of our three archetypes fused under the title Orpheus, the poet-singer whose hymn is the glittering fire and running water of Heraclitus as well as the Ulyssean panting travels on water and land, and in all directions.

Such condensation of complex imagery is not the only capital development with the New Poetry, for it is coupled with much freedom and flexibility in using traditional meter and rhyme. Both acquisitions were an expression of a fresh sensibility originating in a new ontological outlook, itself expressed in symbolic terms, thus pregnant with poetic imagery. This outlook is the Heraclitean principle of eternal change. Thus the traditional Platonic ideal of immutable forms and the religious belief in immortality or reincarnation of the soul are shattered by the Heraclitean symbols of ever-changing fire and ever-moving water.

So the pearl of immortal harmony, union, youth and perfect love in a perfect society becomes an impossible dream and is permanently chased by the poet-prophet, who chants his incantation for the return to permanent union and for rebirth.

Thus 'Abd al-Wahhāb al-Bayātī (b. 1926) chases Lara, his Eurydice, from the North Pole, to Paris, to Alhambra, to the Black Sea, but whenever he is about to unite with her, a hand extends and separates them:

> I draw her image on the snow—
> The green in her eyes and the honeybrown are enkindled,
> Her cherry-red, warm mouth draws near my face;
> Our hands joined in an eternal embrace
> But a hand is extended
> Blotting out her image.
> . . . .
> The world's heart is made of stone
> In this exile-realm.[7]

Here, Kahlil Gibran's trust in a divine wisdom that governs the whole cycle of death and rebirth gives way to a bitter sense of frustration in the face of whimsical fate and to helpless anxiety before the river Styx.

But the poet cannot give up. He should remain attentive to what may sparkle in his depths, hoping with Rifqa that

> Perhaps a lightning voice
> Prophetic
> Of warm accent, would drive away
> The dagger of blind death.[8]

and with Adūnīs always seeking and creating what he calls "the land of visions and longing," and with al-Bayātī asserting that

> Out of poetry's fire came sacred verses
> and prophets of revolution.[9]

In short, our poets are obviously caught in the paradox of not giving up Plato's dream of a Republic or a Utopia, while being sharply conscious of the Heraclitean Flux. Whence the tragic sense that dominates this modern Odyssey, where the poet is always facing the winds of Time, driving him away from his Ithaca.

Nonetheless, Utopia remains a cornerstone of our Odyssey. It is not equivalent to Ithaca, yet it overlaps with it. In 1948, Utopia is nostalgically recalled by a pioneer of the New Poetry, the Iraqi poetess Nāzik al-Malā'ika (b. 1923). Her poem, "The Lost Utopia,"[10] expresses her dream of a lost paradise:

A lost echo, like a distant mirage,
    attracts my soul day and night.

For her, Utopia is a land where chains dissolve and thought is free, where the sun never sets, and where people enjoy everlasting youth and eternal spring. But she suddenly awakes:

In the bottom of my soul I felt madness
    and deep yearning like a deep sea
I want the strange road to lead
    to that coveted faraway land
To that eternal horizon
    where tender Apollo lives
I walked and walked and nothing appeared
    before me, save the road stretching out
. . . .
With a crying thirst, I finally
    woke up and saw no Utopia.[11]

The harsh disillusion after the long travel towards Apollo's land, or Paradise Lost, is further illustrated by the contrast between a type of natural Arcadia and the actual human misery in the village. In another poem, called "Utopia in the Mountains,"[12] she sings of the play of water and light over a mountain village:

Burst out, O springs
With water and melted rays
Burst out with light and colors above the pale village
. . . .
Burst out with beauty
And, in the mountains, build Utopia.[13]

Yet, again, the poetess cannot forget reality, for as she says:

The Village has always been
A tale mingled with pain
Whose sorrow is told by the winds.[14]

• • •

The point I am trying to make is that Ithaca often has two faces. One face is Arcadia, the lost Ithaca of the past, of childhood, youth, mother, family, village, and complete harmony with nature. The other, perhaps more adult, face of that Ithaca is Utopia. It is our ancient human dream both religious and Platonic, of a society where freedom, justice and dignity help the individual and the group (the captain and the crew) to realize their creative communion with the true, the good, and the beautiful.

Needless to say, with most poets these two faces of Ithaca closely interact and feed off each other and are difficult to separate. They naturally acquire different names, depending on the poet's background and imagination. But whether blended or separate, and under whatever name, these two faces of Ithaca remain the lost or impossible land of longing and of coveted salvation from the suffering of loss and exile.

In the modern, bad Arab times, disillusion is the rule. After the Palestinian disaster, Arab poets longed for the rise of a savior, hero, or god who would not exploit or oppress but be loving enough to go through death in order to rejuvenate national and human culture. Consequently, about two decades were dominated by what has been called Tammūzian Poetry, with the Mesopotamian god, Tammūz (i.e., Adonis) and with Christ and the phoenix as heroes of death and rebirth. In moving incantations, the poets identified themselves with these symbolic figures, praying for rebirth, that is, a return to a creative reunion with Ithaca. But most often, actual history and its modern heroes let their poets down.

A major symbol for al-Bayātī's utopia is Nīsābūr (i.e., Nishapur), the city of the Persian poet, Omar Khayyām (d. 1123). Both western Arcadia and oriental Nīsābūr are raped then thrown down by human wickedness and greed:

"Arcadia" after "Nīsābūr"
The sorcerer hung it with a pin on the world map
Shut it in behind walls
. . . .
Made love to it, took out the pin
And turned off the light
So who's knocking on the door?
The Magians went back home under
the shadow of palm trees, crying
And the wind cries
"Arcadia" after "Nīsābūr"[15]

So for this Iraqi Marxist, both Ur-communism (Arcadia) and the future Paradise on Earth (Nīsābūr) lie behind walls imprisoned by evil, despotic forces, against which the poet must invest all his Orphic, Tammūzian potential of self-sacrifice as well as his Orphic, artistic vision in the creation of a more beautiful world. Yet despotism is not exclusively Oriental. Even Greece, the original land of democracy, can be dominated by dictators, and can have its poets thrown into jail. On such an occasion, in 1959, al-Bayātī protests against Greek dictators and pseudogods in a poem called "Greetings, Athens":

> The sun is in a detention camp
> Guarded by dogs and hills
> Perhaps a thousand nights have passed
> And still
> Penelope waits
> Weaving the garment of fire,
> Or Ulysses still in chains
> On the island of the impossible
> Perhaps on Mount Olympus
> Greek gods are still begging
> The barren lightning on the mountains
> Their food is wine and bread
> And the suffering of millions of men.
> I said: "Greetings"
> And my heart wept
> And in the ruins, the dawn
> Lit the new face of the world,
> The face of a poet breaking his chains.[16]

This poem shows how Ulysses becomes metamorphosed into a poet who breaks his chains and returns, like the phoenix rising from his ashes. By now the pattern is clear: the lost pearl of human justice and love, Ithaca (call it Granada, Shīrāz, or Nīsābūr) where Penelope waits (Lara, 'Ā'isha, Eurydice) is a city walled in by the monstrous, oppressive forces of both gods and men. And the poet is more than a Sindbad who embarks on individual adventures, caring only for his health and wealth and having neither wife nor kingdom to save. He is a Ulysses, who goes out for a cause and has to lead his men back to Ithaca.

When al-Bayātī sings the revolution of the poor, he is torn between the attraction of hope and powerful disillusion, but never gives up his Ulyssean tenacity:

But we remain steadfast
Standing we die
Standing we sail
To the cities of the far future
We rape the world with death, revolution, and departure
We die away from home, but we are born anew
. . . .
And anew we fall in the traps of kings and despots
We carry our wounded on our foreheads and we bury the dead
With no dates and no names
We dwell, alive, in their tombs
We continue the great procession from death to birth
We remain in all the ages of misery and light
Hung with the black threads of hope
Awaiting fire and flood.[17]

Of central importance here is the association between death, revolution and departure. The wretched of the earth and their revolutionary herald, the poet, die in exile, but they are born again, undergoing an almost eternal procession of death and rebirth on their seaway to Utopia, which lies far off in the future.

The same sense of being robbed of both past and future Ithacas is painfully expressed by the Egyptian poet, Aḥmad 'Abd al-Mu'ṭī Ḥijāzī (b. 1935), a socialist, with particular commitment to the rebirth of Egypt and of the Arab culture. In his poem "Elegy for the Beautiful Life,"[18] the poet-singer, let down by his savior-hero, airs his commitment to his leader and his nostalgia for old harmony and justice:

O my Lord!
How thirsty we've been for times that seize the heart
We told you: "Do what you like!
But bring back to our city the pearl of justice,
The unique pearl of the impossible."
Someone shouted: "Don't support him!"

But I was beating the strings of my guitar
Searching for an old refrain![19]

Ḥijāzī's longing for this impossible pearl of justice, this city of God, this ideal Granada, Palestine, or Ithaca, is frustrated by the death of his hero, a father or god-image. So the singer-poet buries him and, like a lost Ulysses, resumes the quest:

It is time for me to go back to my guitar
To continue my odyssey and crossing
There Granada disappears
. . . .
And I go back to my fate and destiny.
Who knows now in what land I shall die!
    In what land my rebirth will be!
I am lost between the lands,
Lost between my two histories:
    the impossible one
    and the one I recall
Carrying my calamity in my blood
Carrying my fault and my fall
Shall I ever remember my old voice
    So that, from my ashes, God might revive me?
Or shall I vanish as you vanished
And, in the ocean, Granada would fall?[20]

This is the expression of a very faint hope, indeed, that this Atlantis would be saved. Yet, the poet remains alert to any sign of life from home. Thus an Egyptian popular rebellion in 1977 fills him with great exaltation and gives birth to his poem entitled "Resurrection and the Lost Child,"[21] in which the poet has a vision of the Nile rising towards heaven carrying with it cities, villages, people, animals, and birds, like a new fountain of life. He remembers the idyllic harmony in his lost Arcadia, and implores: "Who will take me back!" to that

Village of green limbs
Drunk with intense fragrance
Lying down with its intimate history
Exalted,

Exchanging sweet laments.
"Who will take me back!"[22]

Then our poet, exiled in Europe, describes his lost journeys and his yearning for his Mother Egypt:

And I see you in wretched cities.
I had thought I was the only one who lost
  his face on their roads
And that one day I'll shake off their yoke and return.
But I saw the river as lost as I was
Sickly, seeking shelter under their walls
I saw you O mother.
. . . .
And I keep running away
Lost between the trains, that spread their rails over my body
And tore me out in the cities
Traveling in another life than mine
Carrying my naked roots
From snow to snow
And when I look again behind me
You come.[23]

But the poem ends on a hopeful note, repeating a previous incantation to the life cycle:

O swing of birth don't stop!
Turn round
Sink into the veins of the thirsty clay
Then rise again,
Flutter
And beget the one whose birth you've been promising for ages
Tear out for him your stubborn soil
And bleed![24]

• • •

With the Lebanese existentialist poet Fu'ād Rifqa, this odyssey is directed totally inwards, and very little is left for immediate social concerns. Rifqa seems too haunted by the oppressive running of Time to see any use in social utopia. But this does not stop him from sailing constantly after an Orphic vision.

Rifqa's poetry revolves around the adventure of the poet as a journey undertaken into the depth of the soul, where he hopes to discover reality and incarnate it in a poem that he brings as a new vision of himself, his culture, and man. This adventure is conceived by our poet as a binary opposition between, on one hand, the static house with its connotations (garden, fence, hearth, etc.) and on the other, the unlimited temporal and spatial distance that lures, but in which death lurks. The poem is an adventure of ship travel inside the self. In this respect, Rifqa's existentialist, and specifically Heideggerian outlook constitutes the framework of his poetry. For him man is temporal, earthly, and rooted. "His rootedness is the house implanted in a country, a country is walls, and walls are protection." But a protected, rooted being "likes to make adventures; adventure is travel in search of poetry, and poetry is song."[25] Such an outlook gives us the key to the way Rifqa faces the Heraclitean river:

Only once, just once we throw
Into the earth of the field the efforts of the years
Then we raise around them the wall of yearning
And we sing
The season that is coming and its tender bunches
Only once, we come, we go
Once, no more, we come and go.

> It is strange not to step into the river twice, strange to be and not to be, strange that we die: we, the more dying, more than the fruits.[26]

Thus, the dialectic of rootedness and adventurous travel leads the ship inwards. Yet since the real struggle is against destructive Chronos, it is the creative poet this time who raises protective walls around his visionary sprouts, so that Time may not destroy but help them flourish. Like al-Bayātī's and Ḥijāzī's voyages, Rifqa's travels are continuous cycles of Orphic death and rebirth. In his earlier poetry, Rifqa often went back full of joy and riches to Damascus, his Ithaca:

I am coming back, O Damascus, to awaken my days
To stretch out and unfold, like a ladder, for the clouds

In your lands. I'm coming, my face has become
Ripe fruits, opening its door
For bells. My face is now a loaf of bread
And in my garments there is light.[27]

But Rifqa's later poetry seems to accentuate the devouring aspect of Phrygian time and carries quite a sad tone in such a poem as "Curve":

You come to the last curve
Then the crossing
To the shores of wind and *defeat*
Then goes round whatever goes round
And the banquet is *ended*
You come to the last curve
You *tremble* a while
You become part of all things
You become, between earth and heaven
A ship, and water.[28]

Had his poem lacked the accent put on the terms "defeat," "ending," and "trembling," then it could have also expressed the outlook of Adūnīs, who has been most fertile in experimentation and breaking new ground. His world view was a combination of existentialism and Marxism, which drove him for a while on a search for a sociopolitical utopia. But the more he traveled, the more his Ithaca became "the inner Andalus," as he calls it.

The distinguishing characteristic of Adūnīs is his completely positive attitude towards flux and fire as the essential course and texture of life, while always keeping faith in the permanent resurgence of a new god, a new axis and mover of human life. Only when we have an insight into this basic vision of his, are we able to enter the world of such poems as "Loss":

I get lost, I throw my face to dawn and dust
I throw it to madness
My eyes are of grass and of burning
My eyes are flags and travelers
God how beautiful that my face leads me with it to my loss,
Full of fire
O grave, O my end at the beginning of spring.[29]

Here we realize that the mixture of the idea of loss with that of burning transposes loss into the world of the phoenix which the poet often sings.

This willingly lost phoenix, seeking his end and reborn with the spring, is another variation on Orpheus, the "Magician of Dust," who, through his death, transforms all things into song. Similarly Sisyphus functions as another persona for the poet and becomes a visionary singer:

> I accept what you wish: my songs
> Are my bread, my kingdom is my words—
> O my rock, make my steps heavier
> I carry you as a dawn on my shoulders,
> I draw you as a vision on my features.[30]

In this Adūnīs affirms life to the extreme and with no reserve. His loss is beautiful; he carries his rock as a dawn. All suffering is welcome to him as a step nearer to his inner Ithaca. He identifies himself with the Arab mythical bird, the phoenix, who burns and is reborn from his ashes:

> Phoenix is the secret of my heart.
> He is one with me; in his name I know the form of my present
> In his name I live the fire of my present.[31]

Then he implores the phoenix to guide the way and burn:

> Phoenix, die! Phoenix, die!
> Phoenix! O Christ, O cross
> In a strange world.[32]

Commenting on a poem by Badr Shākir al-Sayyāb (1926-1964) entitled "The River and Death," Adūnīs says:

> Death in the river is a life which goes beyond: it redeems, it creates and re-creates. Death in the river is a double journey within the self and outside the self, in the cosmos. And death in the river is a cosmic narcissism that becomes one with the cosmic water.
>
> Water is motherhood. So death in water is a return to the mother.[33]

In this analysis we find at its best the image of man, life, and the whole cosmos as a running river, where life and death are so intimately interwoven as to make the harmony with this flux the highest poetic and human achievement. In this permanent movement, the "inner Andalus" lies deeper and deeper; that is why the poet must keep going, never tiring, never looking back, losing and rediscovering himself and his world. He must totally identify himself with the river in order to become like the poet's persona, Mihyār, who "is the wind that does not go back and the water which does not return to its spring." Mihyār is not rooted, for "his roots are in his steps."[34]

Thus, Mihyār looks for Ulysses:

I run wild in the sulfur caves
I embrace the sparks
I surprise the secrets
In the cloud of incense, in the demon's nails

I search for Ulysses
He might raise his days for me like a *mi'rāj*
He might tell me, tell what the waves ignore. . . [35]

The central image here is that of the *mi'rāj,* the name for the Muslim Prophet's journey to the heavens. The Prophet's guide was Gabriel, while the poet's guide is Ulysses, whose life becomes the *mi'rāj,* the ladder, and whose knowledge is deeper than the waves of life.

The ever-changing fire and ever-running water enjoy the full acceptance of our poet. Not without a tragic sense, the poet knows that he must give up the search for a past Arcadia, the land of return, as well as for any external future land of promise. He must keep sailing within himself, to the inner land:

Even if you return O Ulysses
Even if distances become narrow for you
And the guide burns out / In your tragic face
/ Or in your intimate terror
You remain a history of departure
You remain in a land of no promise
You remain in a land of no return
O Ulysses!—Even if you return![36]

Of course, the Lebanese civil war shattered everybody's dreams. (The destruction of Beirut, with its immense impact on the poetic mood, deserves by itself a whole discussion, which I hope to do elsewhere.) On the one extreme, we have someone like Khalīl Ḥāwī (1919–1982), for whom the *coup de grâce* came with the Israeli invasion: he chose to put an end to his life. On the other, we have poets who went on living in Lebanon, but under great hardships, such as Fu'ād Rifqa, Unsī al-Ḥājj (b. 1937), and Shawqī Abī

Shaqrā (b. 1935) among the pioneers, and many younger poets of the second generation.

But in the middle, we have many important poets who had to leave, like Adūnīs, Maḥmūd Darwīsh (b. 1942), and Buland al-Ḥaydarī (1926–1996), who have been added to the long list of Arab pioneer poets and intellectuals (such as al-Bayātī[37]and Ḥijāzī[38]) who found themselves for a long time on the western shores of their Odyssey. Freedom and democracy being the haven, without which they cannot function, these poets have carried their message from the various points of their journey; for whether they call it loss or exile, the European haven has kept alive their faith in a homecoming.

In conclusion, it is true that in the inner sphere of the human search for more light, the Odyssey will go on forever, and we may repeat with Adūnīs:

> You remain in a land of no return
> O Ulysses!—Even if you return!

For in the journey after the farthest psychic and spiritual depths, any land remains a land of no return in an ocean without shores. And this is a fortunate thing. Yet, on the social and cultural level, one would hope that open minds and generous hearts would succeed in bringing the Arab and European shores so close together that any Arab, or Western, Ulysses would always feel at home.

Notes

1. Adūnīs, *Aghānī Mihyār al-Dimashqī,* 3rd. ed. (Beirut: Dār al 'Awda, 1971), 80.

2. C. P. Cavafy, *Collected Poems,* trans. Edmund Keeley and Philip Sherrard, ed. George Savidis (Princeton: Princeton University Press, 1975), 35–36. I am grateful to Michael Beard for drawing my attention to this poem and for many helpful remarks.

3. Interview with Kāẓim Khalīfa, *Ṣawt al-Jamāhīr* (Baghdad), October 26, 1963. The passage is quoted and translated by Issa J. Boullata, "The Poetic Technique of Badr Shākir al-Sayyāb," *Journal of Arabic Literature* 2 (1971): 113.

4. For a general bio-bibliographical and critical discussion of these poets as well as of the poets mentioned elsewhere in the present article, see M[uhammad] M[ustafa] Badawi, *A Critical Introduction to Modern Arabic Poetry* (Cambridge: Cambridge University Press, 1975); S[hmuel] Moreh, *Modern Arabic Poetry, 1800–1970* (Leiden: E. J. Brill, 1976); Salma Khadra Jayyusi, *Trends and Movements in Modern Arabic Poetry* (Leiden: E. J. Brill, 1977); M. M. Badawi, *Modern Arabic Literature* (Cambridge: Cambridge University Press, 1992); and Abdullah al-Udhari, ed. and trans., *Modern Poetry of the Arab World* (London: Penguin Books, 1986).

5. For a perceptive discussion of this subject see Muhammad Abdul-Hai, *Tradition and English and American Influence in Arabic Romantic Poetry: A Study in Comparative Literature* (London: Ithaca Press, 1982), especially chapter seven, "The Pagan Gods: Greek Mythology in Arab Romantic Poetry," 126–63. See also Jayyusi, "The Myth and the Archetype" in *Trends,* 720–52.

6. Fu'ād Rifqa, *Anhār Barriyya* (Beirut: Dār al-Nahār li-al-Nashr, 1982), 92.

7. Abdul Wahab al-Bayati, *Love Under the Rain* (Madrid: Editorial Oriental, 1985), 18: from a poem entitled "I am Born and Burnt in Love," translated by George Masri.

8. Fu'ād Rifqa, *Al-'Ushb Alladhī Yamūt* (Beirut: Dār al-Nahār li-al-Nashr, 1970), 68.

9. 'Abd al-Wahhāb al-Bayātī, *Mamlakat al-Sunbula,* 2nd ed. (Cairo: Al-Hay'a al-Miṣriyya al-'Āmma, 1985), 96–97.

10. Nāzik al-Malā'ika, *Dīwān,* 2nd ed., vol. 2 (Beirut: Dār al-'Awda, 1981), 37–46. The Arabic title is "Yūtūbiya al-Ḍā'i'a."

11. Al-Malā'ika, "Yūtūbiya al-Ḍā'i'a," 42.

12. Al-Malā'ika, "Yūtūbiya fī al-Jibāl," 154–60.

13. Al-Malā'ika, "Yūtūbiya fī al-Jibāl," 154–55.

14. Al-Malā'ika, "Yūtūbiya fī al-Jibāl," 159–60.

15. 'Abd al-Wahhāb al-Bayātī, *Qaṣā'id Ḥubb 'Alā Bawwābāt al-'Ālam al-Sab'* (Baghdad: Wizārat al-I'lām, Mudīriyyat al-Thaqāfa, 1971), 82–83.

16. 'Abd al-Wahhāb al-Bayātī, *Dīwān* vol. 2 (Beirut: Dār al-'Awda, 1972), 465–66. The poem is dated "Baghdad, May 10, 1959."

17. Bayātī, *Qaṣā'id Ḥubb,* 54–55.

18. Aḥmad 'Abd al-Mu'ṭī Ḥijāzī, *Dīwān* (Beirut: Dār al-'Awda, 1973), 546–49.

19. Ḥijāzī, *Dīwān,* 551–52.

20. Ḥijāzī, *Dīwān,* 558–59.

21. Aḥmad 'Abd al-Mu'ṭī Ḥijāzī, *Kā'ināt Mamlakat al-Layl* (Beirut: Dār al-'Ādāb, 1978), 59–69.

22. Ḥijāzī, *Kā'ināt,* 62–63.

23. Ḥijāzī, *Kā'ināt,* 63–65.

24. Ḥijāzī, *Kā'ināt,* 69.

25. See Rifqa's preface to *Anhār Barriyya,* 5.

26. Rifqa, *Anhār,* 9.

27. Fu'ād Rifqa, *'Alāmāt al-Zaman al-Akhīr* (Beirut: Dār al-Nahār li-al-Nashr, 1975), 28.

28. Rifqa, *Anhār,* 36 (italics are mine).

29. Adūnīs, *Aghānī,* 48.

30. Adūnīs, *Aghānī,* 54.

31. Adūnīs, *Awrāq fī al-Rīḥ* (Beirut: Dār Majallat Shi'r, 1958), 76.

32. Adūnīs, *Awrāq,* 78.

33. Adūnīs, *Zaman al-Shi'r,* 2nd ed. (Beirut: Dār al-'Awda, 1978), 218.

34. Adūnīs, *Aghānī,* 14.

35. Adūnīs, *Aghānī,* 78.

36. Adūnīs, *Aghānī,* 80.

37. After over thirty years of chosen or imposed exile, al-Bayātī went back to Iraq in 1990, but the Gulf War forced him to leave again. At present, he lives in Jordan.

38. Ḥijāzī had to leave Egypt for about ten years, which he spent in Paris. Since 1991, he is back in Cairo, writing in *Al-Ahrām* and editing the literary review *Ibdā'.*

Nasser and the Death of Elegy in Modern Arabic Poetry

Terri DeYoung

The elegy (*marthiya* or *rithā'*) has been a central part of the "public business" of poetry in Arabic since very early times. In a courtly society, elegy on the occasion of death becomes a paradigmatic situation where the poet emerges as most crucially visible to the society around him in the function of mediator: the one who will retrieve a discourse of power in the face of an event that would seem to render discourse radically powerless. This view of elegy as an indispensable part of the impersonal social ceremonial of mourning (exemplified in the expectation that the poet would elegize those who were related to his patron rather than himself) had become solidified in Arabic literature at least by the early Abbasid period.[1]

Even earlier than this, however, there exists a competing configuration of Arabic elegy as "private business," carried out within the social structure of the family, or that family writ large, the tribe. The most well-known elegies of the pre-Islamic period, for example, were almost without exception composed by close relatives of the deceased. Here the names of al-Khansā' the famous poetess who lived long enough to become a Muslim,[2] and Mutammim ibn Nuwayra who mourned his brother, killed by Khālid ibn al-Walīd in the Wars of Apostasy after Muḥammad's death, spring to mind.

This structuring of elegy as an "originally" private business transferred later to the public arena leaves its trace on the contours of the genre within the narrative of Arabic literary history, giving it an inherent ambivalence both toward its subject, the deceased, and toward the position assumed by the poet within that discursive space. This becomes especially clear when it is compared with other courtly genres like *madīḥ,* or panegyric (an unproblematically public genre), and *ghazal,* love poetry (a genre unproblematically private). One sign of this ambivalence can be discerned in the unusual prominence of women as both producers and subjects of elegy, as women are normally the absent signifier in Arabic literary genres defined as public: there are few, if any, panegyrics written to or by women. Another instructive example is the dominant reading of the career of the most highly regarded early Abbasid poet, al-Mutanabbī that makes his most important elegy the one he wrote for his own grandmother, despite the fact that, as court poet for the Syrian prince Sayf al-Dawla, elegy was an integral and constant part of his "public voice."

This ambivalence about elegy and its cultural role has continued into the modern period. Beginning in the late nineteenth century, the "public voice" of elegy received an impressive boost from the new perception of it as an ideal vehicle for contesting colonialism. Shawqī Ḍayf makes this point quite explicitly when he says:

> Perhaps the most important [new] tonality that entered modern elegy was contributed by political and patriotic movements [which developed] once colonialism had settled upon the Eastern nations. It was not long before freedom fighters and leaders appeared in every country, who well deserved the honors accorded them by their homelands. Whenever the telegraph would announce the death of one of them, our poets would immediately pick up their lyres to accompany the sorrows and distress of their fellow citizens. In the works of Ḥāfiẓ and Shawqī we find elegies for Sa'd Zaghlūl, Muṣṭafā Kāmil, Muḥammad Farīd and other political leaders, and [by their poems] they put pressure on the colonizer as far as they were able in their homelands.[3]

This appears to be a very early example of the category of "resistance literature" so usefully described by Barbara Harlow in her book of the same title, where she points out that the "relationship to the inherited past and its cultural legacy has been rendered problematic by the violent interference of colonial and imperial history."[4]

It may be no coincidence, once circumstances changed and colonial rule was expressed through more covert institutional structures following World War I, that this public elegy found itself the object of unrelenting attacks by the "Arab romantic" literary schools (the Dīwān School in Egypt and the Mahjar School in North and South America). These groups emerged not long after the turn of the century to articulate a counter-discourse to that of their predecessors, one which valorized sincerity, originality, emotional authenticity and the idea of individual (as opposed to national) freedom.[5] In the name of these values they privileged the private voice of elegy over the public one. For them, elegy could only be effective, could only fulfill completely its generic pattern, if it concerned someone with whom the poet had had an intimate and long-standing relationship: either a family member or a close friend. The success the Arab romantics had in imposing this view of elegy meant that public elegy, while it did not disappear by any means, was forced into a defensive position. It constantly had to justify and make a case for its rhetorical strategies and even for its very existence.

So, although *rithā'* survives into the twentieth century, it finds itself seemingly obliged to recreate itself in modern Arabic literature in terms of a poetic that privileges the private voice over the public one. In effect, during this period, at the same time that the Arabic elegies are seeking to retrieve the presence of their absent subjects, they become involved in a project to take the place of those subjects and find a way to be themselves remade and in effect *reborn* as a discursive practice. Although one path to this kind of rebirth might have been through simple abandonment of the authoritative public voice entirely, this would have entailed also abandoning the undeniable power of a public voice to shape the direction of the culture's discourse, something that Arab poets naturally were hesitant to do, if only in the name of resisting an already long-dominant Western discourse minimizing the relevance of Arabic literature for the modern world. In order to more clearly map the actual trajectory of *rithā'* in modern Arabic literary history, then, it might be worthwhile to examine an occasion where the public and private voices were seen as coinciding in the creation of a cultural space where life and literature might symbiotically and symbolically intertwine. Such an examination may very well allow us to interrogate how these constructs could be used—and were used—to organize an aesthetic representation of self and other at a moment of intense subjective epistemological crisis.

In this respect, the death of the Egyptian president Jamāl 'Abd al-Nāṣir in the early autumn of 1970 functions as a case unto itself. Nasser[6] suffered a fatal heart seizure literally in the midst of one of the most serious challenges to the ideal of Arab unity in that decade, a crisis second in importance only to the June 1967 war itself. This was the destructive and deadly civil war that had erupted earlier in September in Jordan between the *fidā'iyyīn* forces of the Palestinian leader Yāsir 'Arafāt[7] and the regular-army units of Jordan's King Ḥusayn. Most observers at the time recorded the impression that it was only through the extraordinary negotiation efforts of Nasser and the power of his undeniable personal prestige that a shaky and provisional truce between Arafat and Husayn was engineered in Cairo during the last week of September.[8]

According to the minute-by-minute account published in *Al-Ahrām,* in the early evening of the twenty-eighth, on the tarmac of Cairo airport, just after having bid farewell to the Emir of Kuwait, last of the departing heads of state who had been in attendance during the anxious days of the truce negotiations, a drained and obviously fatigued Nasser suffered a heart attack that would ultimately prove fatal. Barely able to move, he called for his limousine, which carried him directly to his modest villa on the outskirts of the city where his wife, their five children, and his two young grandchildren were waiting. He was able to summon the strength to go inside, mount the stairs to his second-floor bedroom, change into pajamas, and get into bed, but he soon lost consciousness and later that night, despite the best efforts of the heart specialists who had been quickly summoned to his bedside, he died at the relatively young age of fifty-two.[9]

Few events in twentieth-century Arab political history have been read as more fraught with symbolic implications than this one. In a sense, this was merely the continuation of trends obvious throughout the course of Nasser's active political life. More than once in the succession of dramatic episodes that filled those years—from the Suez Crisis in 1956, to the union with Syria in 1958, to the 1967 war with Israel—his actions had been compared to those of a number of heroic figures drawn from the annals of Arab-Islamic history. He himself at times, for instance, encouraged the drawing of parallels between his own career, centered as it was upon opposition to European colonialism, and that of Ṣalāḥ al-Dīn, hero of the resistance to the Crusader invasions in Egypt and Syria.[10] In addition, he was also less directly identified by writers, poets and essayists with a series of other famous figures out of the Arab past, including 'Antara ibn Shaddād, the pre-Islamic poet and warrior; Ṭāriq ibn

Ziyād, the conqueror of Islamic Spain; and 'Abd al-Raḥmān al-Dākhil, nick-named Ṣaqr Quraysh, the founder of the Umayyad dynasty in Andalusia.[11] The extension of this historic grid into Egypt's more distant past, its Pharaonic heritage, also occurs but with less frequency and with more ambivalence than Arab-Islamic allusions—Pharaonic imagery had as often been used to criticize Nasser for behaving like a tyrannical Pharaoh as it had been to praise his heroism and achievements.[12] Such identifications can be seen as a crucial element in the successful construction of teleologically powerful narratives that would underwrite the reversal of the narrative of a necessary and benevolent Western hegemony used by the colonial powers to dominate the shape of Egyptian public discourse for more than a century.

Such symbolic troping was deflected into two new arenas of teleological coding with Nasser's passing. The first was a heuristically powerful narrative that compared Nasser's end with the Prophet Muḥammad's death in somewhat similar circumstances. Its lineaments would seem first emergent in Luwīs 'Awaḍ's tribute to Nasser where he briefly alludes to the expression of a popular sentiment that "th[is] man would rise upward [after death] like the prophets *(ka-al-nabiyyīn)* on the Night Journey *(isrā')* and Ascension *(mi'rāj)*."[13] The metaphor is then notably extended and consolidated by the first lines of Nizār Qabbānī's controversial poem, "Qatalnāka" (We killed you), published in the October 10 edition of *al-Ahrām:*

> We killed you, last of the prophets,
> We killed you
> This is nothing new for us, the slaying of Companions and Friends [of God],
> How many prophets we have killed
> How many imams have we slaughtered, as they performed the evening prayer.

By the following month, the comparison would be even more fully and strikingly set forth in the review of a play, "Ḥijjat al-Wadā'" (The farewell pilgrimage), by Ẓāfir al-Ṣabūnī:

> We should be aware of the great resemblance between [the circumstances surrounding the Prophet's death] and the circumstances surrounding the President's death. The Prophet had performed the Farewell Pilgrimage after delegations of Arabs from the Bedouin tribes *(al-'arab)* had professed Islam in his presence. Then he said: "Have I not

> truly delivered [the message]—yes, I so witness," and passed away, leaving the Byzantines in possession of Jerusalem and Galilee. And the President performed the final ceremonies *(marāsim)* of farewell, after having delegations of Arabs make peace with one another *(taṣāluḥ)* in his presence. Then he said "Thank God, now I will take a rest," and he passed away, leaving the Zionists in possession of Jerusalem and the Sinai.[14]

In a sense, this is simply the extension of the "heroic" discourse found during Nasser's lifetime. But it also subjects that discourse to a refashioning within a religious frame that would have been considered highly dubious if applied to a living person and thus suggests a new departure as well.

The second set of metaphors may perhaps best be approached through a return to the interrupted narrative of Nasser's death as reported in the newspapers. When the news had first been broken to the unsuspecting Egyptian masses, they—as well as millions of ordinary people throughout the Arab world—spontaneously went out into the streets in mass processions, and the cry "Nasser is not dead, Nasser will not die" ("'Abd al-Nāṣir lā yamūt") spread like wildfire everywhere. This refusal by the people to accept the reality of their beloved leader's death matches many paradigmatic portrayals of the stages of grief in descriptions of mourning as a process, where the initial step is one of denial.

Perhaps less expected is the swiftness with which the media used this denial of death to link the Nasserist experience to the myths of fertility gods of ancient times, like Tammuz, who had died or been sacrificed to give life—and in a sense be reborn—in the seasonal renewal of nature. Allusions to these myths of death and rebirth had indeed formed a staple of Arabic poetry, at least since the early 1950s when the spokesmen for Arab nationalism, including Nasser himself, had proclaimed the imminent regeneration of the Arab world under the aegis of their ideology. There has, however, always been a debate among literary critics as to how deeply these narratives can be said to have penetrated—or reflected—popular consciousness beyond intellectual circles.[15]

The content of the editorial pages of *Al-Ahrām* in the days immediately following Nasser's death, however, would seem to indicate that such mythic frames were in fact expected to be rhetorically effective in reaching a broader range of the populace than the literary elite. The first significant evidence of this can be seen in Ghālī Shukrī's tribute to Nasser:

> Few are the men in the course of time whose lives are transformed after their death into a myth *(usṭūra)* that can stir the hearts of generations to come, until they seem to be a part of the eternal human spirit, beyond the reach of time.
>
> Nasser was not just the embodiment of the spirit of Egypt, nor of just the spirit of Arabism; instead he was a beacon burning with the human spirit and its eternal essence. It chose a young man . . . as its embodiment for a short time—that is the period of time during which Nasser lived among us. He brought together there the loveliest plants from the farthest corners of the earth and built for us a well-furnished nest upon a branch whose coat of verdure had never known the withering of age. Then, once the phoenix *('anqā')*—as the myth goes—has burned itself up and become ashes, the divine fire will raise up from them a new phoenix to build a new nest.
>
> Indeed the resurrection of Christ, the rise of Osiris and the return of Tammuz have all been symbols of the return of the spirit *('awdat al-rūḥ)*[16] to the burned-out ashes, they have been symbols of that minority of men whose lives after their death are transformed into a myth. . . .[17]

Significantly, though Shukrī is an influential literary critic and therefore quite at ease with the idiom and features of the ancient Semitic death-rebirth myths, he is also something of a popularizing writer who has made a successful career of writing in the media. For him to assume that his symbolism here would be familiar enough to a mass audience to be immediately understandable is probably a surer indication that it actually was than would have been the case had this quotation been culled from the writings of, for instance, the avant-garde poet Adūnīs.

If we need further evidence for the role such "death-rebirth" discourse was able to play in shaping the public perception of Nasser's death, we need look no further than the same page of *Al-Ahrām* the next day, where we find the following poem:

> The hero is dead
> He walks on still
> He walks on no longer
> Walking still, walking no longer—here he is
> In our hearts
> Here he is, created anew
> Created anew in every moment

Within the sugar canes
From yellow fields of wheat
From gold
From the rich brown earth
From stone.[18]

Here, even though the grid associated with death-rebirth has not precipitated into a particular mythic form, the traces of the narrative of the heroic figure dying and being reborn—being embodied—within the frame of the natural cycle of the seasons are quite visible. Even more compelling as evidence of the power of this discourse to penetrate beyond the elite is the fact that this poem written in colloquial, the language of the "people of Egypt," not the standard, universal literary Arabic of the intellectuals.

To give final shape to such a rich field of crisscrossing symbolic associations taken from a number of radically heterogeneous discourses for the teleological purpose of finding meaning in Nasser's death would seem to be a task ready-made for the sophisticated formal treatment that can best be provided through the convention-rich and highly disciplined patterning available in Arabic poetry, in particular the *rithā'*, and this proved to be the case. The early, tentative efforts to give voice to the mourning of a nation, found —as we have seen—largely on the editorial pages of *al-Ahrām* quickly gave way to more considered works by some of the most talented and famous poets then writing. These appeared in a number of forums, perhaps most notably in the pages of the Lebanese literary magazine *Al-Ādāb,* noted at the time for its support of the Arab nationalist cause.

Then, starting a little more than a year after Nasser's death, two volumes of elegies appeared whose significance, both together and singly, should not be underrated. The first of these consisted of twelve elegies collected in a single slim volume, introduced by the well-known Egyptian poet Aḥmad 'Abd al-Mu'ṭī Ḥijāzī. Given the evocative and somewhat enigmatic title *Kitābāt 'alā Qabr 'Abd al-Nāṣir* (Some writings on the grave of Nasser), this book was published in 1971 by a private printing house, Dār al-'Awda, in Beirut. Two years after this, a second work—with very little crossover from the first set of elegies—was published by the Egyptian government. The elegies in this volume (over sixty in number) had been selected by the members of the Egyptian Ministry of Culture's Poetry Committee, an arm in the Supreme Council for Guidance of the Arts, Letters and Social Sciences, in order to "gather together the widest possible number of selected pieces in a memorial record that will mark the date of this occasion *(munāsaba)* and is in accordance with its solemnity . . . as one witness among others to the glorious memories everyone harbors of the great departed one."[19] Collectively, these two anthologies form the most widely distributed and easily available body of work on which evaluations of Nasser's representation in Arabic literature might be based.

Of the two, *Kitābāt,* because of its earlier date of publication, is perhaps best viewed as the initial frame for the discourse about Nasser, with the official volume constituting, at least to an extent, the response to that frame. Although *Kitābāt* contains the writings of many stellar names who were even then well known throughout the Arab world, and whose fame would only spread with the passage of time—names like Adūnīs, Maḥmūd Darwīsh, Amal Danqal, Samīḥ al-Qāsim, Fadwā Ṭūqān and Hijāzī himself, it exudes an air of being fugitive, perhaps even oppositional, to the official "business of mourning" for a revered public figure. Such an impression is confirmed by the fact that few from this group were involved more than marginally in the ceremonies surrounding Nasser's funeral. A good number were not even in Egypt at the time. Most of their elegies comprise part of that larger group of poems which first saw the light of day on the pages of *Al-Ādāb* in the months following Nasser's funeral.

With the exception of two of the Egyptian poets, Ṣalāḥ ʻAbd al-Ṣabūr and ʻAbd al-Muʻṭī Ḥijāzī, who were actually members of the ministry's Poetry Committee, only two of the elegies from *Kitābāt* also appear in the official volume. The presence of the first of these two elegies, a highly conventional work by the minor Lebanese writer Ḥabīb Ṣādiq, is easily explained by the fact that it was actually recited at Nasser's memorial service and the fact that it closely mirrors the traditional structure and style of the other elegies included in the official collection. Its admission into the group, then, appears quite unproblematic.

The other poem, Maḥmūd Darwīsh's "Al-Rajul Dhū al-Ẓill al-Akhḍar" (The man with the green shadow), is less naturalizable in the context of the official volume than its companion, for several reasons. First, it is unlikely that Darwīsh's poem, like most of the others in *Kitābāt,* had any direct connection with the Egyptian memorial ceremonies for Nasser.[20] Second, the poem itself is in the form known in Arabic as *"al-shiʻr al-ḥurr"* (free verse). Although the Poetry Committee had somewhat softened its initial opposition to this untraditional form after 1964[21] and by 1968 the younger poets

Ṣalāḥ 'Abd al-Ṣabūr and Aḥmad 'Abd al-Mu'ṭī Ḥijāzī, who wrote most of their poetry in the new form, had become members of the committee, in the official volume of elegies commemorating Nasser's death, containing more than sixty poems, only three are demonstrably in free verse: 'Abd al-Ṣabūr's, Hijāzī's, and Maḥmūd Darwīsh's. The inclusion of the first two was probably inevitable, given the fact that their authors were actually on the Poetry Committee at that time, but this would not have been true of "The Man with the Green Shadow." Darwīsh was Palestinian and the committee apparently had no compunction about excluding the free-verse elegies from *Kitābāt* by the Palestinian poets Samīḥ al-Qāsim and Fadwā Ṭūqān in favor of a more traditional piece by Hārūn Hāshim Rashīd, which companions Darwīsh's work in the official volume. No doubt the fact that "The Man with the Green Shadow" ended up being included in both the traditionalist and oppositional anthologies was the result of a combination of elements, both intentional and accidental, but I believe that a closer examination of the poem itself will reveal that a good deal of its appeal may have had to do with how it directly confronts the question posed at the beginning of this discussion: How can *rithā'* recreate itself to speak with both public and private voices? That Darwīsh's exploration of this problem was an especially thoughtful one that gave due consideration to the concerns of both the traditionalists and the reformers in this respect was no doubt important in the positive evaluation accorded it by critics.[22]

Before, however, proceeding to an analysis of exactly how Darwīsh interrogates the elegy and develops strategies to open it up as a site both of social myth and personal engagement, it is imperative to examine more closely exactly how *Kitābāt* seeks to subvert the dominant discourses about elegy, and elegies for Nasser in particular. For this, Ḥijāzī's introduction to the volume functions as an important touchstone.

A certain ambivalence about Nasser and a desire to distance him is apparent even in the first sentence of this introduction where Ḥijāzī says "Nasser had one thing in common with poetry: Both of them always addressed themselves to the nation." Here, Nasser is not linked to—and implicitly, therefore, admitted as one of—the producers (that is, the poets) of the discourse under discussion. He is instead coupled with the discourse itself (the poetry): both acknowledging his power to influence the Arab masses and at the same time denying him a role in consciously shaping that discourse as a thinking and speaking subject.[23]

That this "objectification" of Nasser is a deliberate rhetorical strategy on Ḥijāzī's part is revealed more clearly a short time later when he comes much closer than authors had generally dared during Nasser's lifetime[24] to accusing him directly of being a major moving force in the marginalization of literature within Arab social and political life and, through this, of derailing—however unintentionally—the power of his own revolution to change what many perceived as the disheartening reality of the Arabs' powerlessness over their own destiny in the contemporary world. Though Ḥijāzī speaks only of "the revolution" and refrains from explicitly naming Nasser himself when he condemns the revolution as having been "corrupted by the exercise of power and virtually strangled by it," the trope does not entirely conceal Ḥijāzī's implication: that the ones who exercised this power became corrupted by it and thereby dealt a fatal blow to the revolution were Nasser and his Free Officers.

According to Ḥijāzī, it was only in death that Nasser again became a figure with whom Arab poets could identify:

> It was [the poets] who had been the guardians of the revolution. And some of them persisted in keeping their distance [from those in power] and continued to show their hostility both to the power *(sulṭa)* of the state and to the revolution.
>
> But now that Nasser has passed away, the tears of the Arab poets for him have been released, just as their songs about his victories flowed freely in earlier days.
>
> Thus Nasser has returned in the form of a dream, as he was in the days of his first glorious, sweet victories. He has returned as a revolutionary untouched by power. The revolution will dissolve the soul of the revolutionary in molten flame within the crucible of the nation *(umma)*, so that it will not return seeking to exercise power *(mutasalliṭ)*. In fact, the revolution in its deepest sense is always at war with authority *(sulṭa)* even when it is incorporated into it, because it can only be true to itself by repudiating everything that is part of the established order. . . . Likewise, death liberates the hero from the noose of worldly power and makes him again a citizen among his fellow citizens.[25]

That Ḥijāzī is here giving voice to a very real dissatisfaction with Nasser's policies, one which was especially widespread among the generation of modern poets who came to maturity in the 1950s and 1960s, can be confirmed by a careful perusal of their writings—and the writings of those who sympathized with them—about the relations of the state and the literary establishment in those years.[26] Most observers who have written after the dust settled from these literary battles also agree that, after his accession to power, Nasser ended up following a cultural policy which largely privileged those who had attained their standing under the compromises of the old regime, those who already controlled access to avenues for recognition and publication and continued to use this access as a weapon to reinforce the strength of their own position.[27] The government gave very little voice, in turn, and almost no power to the postwar generation, which saw itself as consisting of the ones who had truly responded to Nasser's revolutionary message. Yet the very power of the Egyptian state institutions for the promotion of culture which were ultimately controlled, at least theoretically, by Nasser through the medium of artists and writers coming from the generation of the 1920s and 1930s—in particular poets like 'Abbās Maḥmūd al-'Aqqād and Ṣāliḥ Jawdat—meant that the younger poets could only express their disappointment and hostility covertly as long as they received support from the state, as most did.

Thus, when these same poets were called upon to elegize Nasser, the ambivalence that commonly imposes itself upon the one left to mourn—the sense of an overwhelming and paralyzing loss coupled with relief (and therefore guilt) at having survived—combined itself with an even more powerful set of ambivalences that were generated for these poets by Nasser's unusual rhetorical gifts (which allowed him to dispense—at least to an extent—with the mediating function poetry had assumed in public life as a means to arouse the populace to political action), on the one hand, and the unparalleled power he had exercised over their institutional and intellectual lives, on the other. This created a situation uniquely suited to the production of great elegies, provided the poets were willing to confront their ambivalent feelings of admiration and betrayal head-on. Probably never again would they have a figure of Nasser's stature to write about nor one who shared so many characteristics with them as poets (though this meant that, for Nasser, they were also at least to a degree redundant since he had less need than most of their mediating voice). In the sense, then, that never again would it be likely that such a set of circumstances would be found, Nasser's death both created an opportunity for poets to use their elegiac talents to the fullest and made it difficult, if not impossible, for them to duplicate their efforts at a later date. Thus, Nasser's death could be said to have decreed the death of elegy (at least as a public, politically focused genre) in modern Arabic poetry.

With this contextual framework in mind, it should now be possible to return to Darwīsh's "The Man with the Green Shadow." This poem focuses primarily on this tension between the poet-speaker as producer of a discourse —one of whose intentions could be to influence the public—and his subject, a political leader who was particularly famed for his ability to produce discourse that was demonstrably effective in doing just that. Darwīsh's manipulation of the deictic pronouns (when a change is made from one form to another, and to which groups or individuals they refer) becomes the central strategy which he deploys to explore this tension. His use of "you" and "I," and most especially "we" becomes an opportunity to observe the drama of poetic composition at its best and most dynamic.

The question of pronouns is problematized right from the poem's outset. In the first three lines, "we" and "you"[28] are situated in positions that syntactically front their polarity while at the same time asserting rhetorically a relationship of identity: "*Na*ʿīshu maʿ*aka,*/ *na*sīru maʿ*aka,*/ *na*jūʿu maʿ*aka.*" Here, the "we" (as the subject of the active present tense verb) is placed at the greatest possible physical distance in the sentence from the "you" (as the object of the preposition), which undercuts rather than reinforces the propositional force of the sentences: We are *all* doing these actions *together.* The syntax suggests, instead, that "we" and "you" may be doing these things at the same time, but there is also an undeniable ontological gap between this "us": a gap as wide as that between subject and object.

In and of itself this structure might justly pass unremarked—were it not for the fact that in the third and fourth lines the whole question of the separation and identification of "we" and "you" is thematized and made the focus of both the expressive meaning and its representation in the syntax of the language itself: "Wa-ḥīna *ta*mūtu/ nuḥāwilu allā *na*mūta maʿaka." Here the structure, with "you" and then "we" the subject of the same verb, "to die," underscores rather than contradicts the surface message, one that warns of the danger inherent in too great an identification with an "other" (in this case the "you") since this may ultimately lead to the extinction of self: to a real or figurative death. Thus the "we" and the "you," it follows, should strive in their referential function rather for exactly the kind of separation we saw them enjoying structurally in the preceding lines.

These latter two lines also begin to give us the contextual clues that will eventually permit us to identify the referents for these deictics. The "you" is dying, or is in danger of doing so, and it is precisely this attribute which separates the "you" from the "we." The reader, therefore, is impelled at least provisionally to tag the "we" as "the living." The increasingly specific series of predications tied to the "you" in lines six through thirty-one eventually allow the reader, even one with no knowledge of the immediate context of the poem's utterance, to narrow the referent for "you" to Nasser, and for "we" by implication to "the people of Egypt" or—given the allusion in line sixteen to one of the great victories in Arab military history, the battle of Qādisiyya in 642 C.E.—to "the Arab people" or even simply "the people" without any qualifier.

But, having established a fairly stable field of referents for the two pronouns, the speaker almost immediately moves to decenter this process of naturalization by changing the relationship—beginning with line thirty-five—from the public one of "we" and "you" to the private one of "I" and "you." Once the speaker becomes an "I" (or more precisely a "my") and detaches himself from any identification with the "we" of the "people," he also virtually at the same time begins to develop a strong identification with the "you" that had just before, in line thirty, been depersonalized and objectified as "a window on a train receding into the distance." Now, conversely, the "you" and the "I" are once again linked by a verbal action as they were at the beginning of the poem. But, even more tellingly, the "you" is now the subject, the actor, and the "I" is present in the sentence only as a possessive pronoun attached (in the Arabic) to the end of the direct object, almost an afterthought rather than a participant. Thus, the separation of the "I" is to its detriment rather than its benefit.

Then, in line forty-six, there is a return to the "we" pronoun, but the propositional meaning no longer gives clear evidence about just exactly whom this "we" includes and excludes. The "we" that will "buy that pharmacy" is radically inclusive, absorptive of almost any combination of the poet-speaker, Nasser, and "the people" that the reader might care to make, but is it the same "we" who will be "resurrected" by the Aswan Dam? Since to be resurrected presupposes a death, this would simultaneously point to the inclusion of Nasser in the "we" and to an implicit admission on the speaker's part that the initial attempt at separation from the dying "you" was unsuccessful.

Thus, the next strategy deployed, the repetition of the initial lines at the end of the poem would seem to indicate, not a gesture toward closure, but an almost desperate attempt to recapture that initial impulse toward separation and distancing from the deceased so necessary to the process of mourning.[29] And this time it seems to work because the poet asserts in the supplementary postscript (beginning with line sixty-three) that the "you" will be in the grave—the position of the detached, passive observer to others' actions—and "we" will be doing the "moving."[30]

How is this transformation accomplished? How are the questions of indeterminacy introduced by attempts to accommodate the public and private voices of elegy contained and controlled here, at least according to the internal logic of the poem? The answer would seem to hinge upon lines sixty-three and sixty-four. Somehow the introduction of an allusion to a poetic convention tied to pre-Islamic elegy—an appeal made by the poet for the heavens to send showers of rain down upon the deceased's grave so that grass will grow upon it—seems to make the gesture of closure possible (whether it is actually achieved is of course another matter).

At first this allusion would seem to be no different from other appeals in the poem to those extrapoetic discourses that had emerged in the days following Nasser's death, as writers had attempted to shape and channel the psychic mechanisms for coping with the event. For example, the two lines repeated several times in the poem "You are not a prophet/But your shadow is green," would seem to originate in those comparisons of Nasser's death to, respectively, the Prophet Muḥammad's and the ancient fertility gods', which we saw earlier so dominated the pages of *Al-Ahrām* in the early days of October 1970. The assertion that Nasser was not a prophet would seem to be a rejection of those who, like Nizār Qabbānī, had read Nasser's death as directly attributable to the tensions generated by the September fighting between the Jordanians and the Palestinians and thus the fault of the Arab people, who could not maintain their unity—the killing of the "last of the prophets."[31] Instead, the speaker appears to embrace, at least provisionally, the alternate reading of Ghālī Shukrī and Khalīl Muḥammad Fāḍil, who did not focus on fixing blame for the death, but emphasized the rebirth (or continued presence) of Nasser's principles in the hearts and minds of the people. The metonymic allusion to green, the color of vegetation and growth, is especially felicitous in this regard because it brings the circle back, in a sense, to Muḥammad himself who has long been identified in Islamic symbolism with this color.[32] Thus, while rejecting the negative aspects of Qabbānī's discourse and refusing to let it dominate his own reading of Nasser's death, the speaker-poet seems to be suggesting here that it might be possible to reread this metaphor, equating Nasser and Muḥammad through a different perspective that would allow itself to be seen as imbricated and mutually reconcilable with the rebirth tropes.

In the sense that the invocation asking for rain to fall on the deceased's grave also suggests an echo of ancient fertility rituals, Darwīsh's allusion to it would seem to be merely a supplement to the line declaring Nasser's shadow to be green. There is, however, an addition to the meaning of the first metaphor—a supplement in the Derridean sense of the word[33]—which is of importance here, for this line alludes to a convention that is specifically literary and traditionally most often appears at the end of poems to mark their final close. It is thus the assertion of literature's power—in more personal terms, of the poet's power—to usefully channel the direction of discourse through an alliance with the power of tradition, for times of mourning and grief are paradigmatically situations where closure must somehow be found. One must detach oneself from the dead, in order to continue living, and if that closure can only be achieved sometimes through resort to a fiction, then what better provider of fictions can one find than the literary tradition?

Darwīsh's strategy of first dramatizing the speaker's and people's closeness to Nasser and then appealing to a literary tradition that permits him to picture Nasser in his grave—an inspiration, but one which belongs to the past and can no longer speak—allows the poem to articulate both registers, the public and the private, of elegy. But it does this only by registering some very important elisions concerning the power over discourse we find in that very compelling poet's "other," Nasser, whose legacy still continues to resonate in so much of the social and cultural discourse being produced in the Arab world today.

The Man with The Green Shadow

We live with you
We move onward with you
We hunger with you
And when you die
We try not to die with you!

But
Why are you dying far from the water
When the Nile fills your hands?
Why are you dying far from the lightning
When the lightning resides upon your lips?
And you promised the tribes
A summer's journey from the Jāhiliyya.
And you promised th[ose in] chains
Mighty arms poised to fire.
And you promised the warrior
A battle: one to bring back Qādisiyya.

We see your voice now, filling every throat
Storms
Following
Storms.
We see your broad chest now a revolutionary's barricade
A sloganed banner for the streets
We see you
            We see you
                        We see you
Standing tall
            Like a stalk of wheat in Upper Egypt

Beautiful
        Like a steel mill
Free
        Like a window on a train receding into the distance.

You are not a prophet
But your shadow is green
Do you remember
How you made the features on my face
How you made my brow
How you made my exile and my death
Green
Green
Green?

Do you remember my face as it was of old?
A face mummified in a British museum
Fallen in the mosque of the Umayyads
When, my comrade?
When, my dear friend?
When will we buy that pharmacy
With the wounds of Ḥusayn and Umayya's glory?
When will we be resurrected as bread and water by the Aswan dam,
Or as a million kilowatts of electricity?
Do you remember?
Our civilization used to be a beautiful Bedouin
Trying to study chemistry,
Dreaming in the palm tree shade
Of an airplane
Or a dozen women.
You are not a prophet
But your shadow is green.

We live with you
We move onward with you
We hunger with you
And now that you are dying
We try not to be with you.
Then new wheat will grow above your tombstone
And fresh water will come down
And you will see us
Moving
Ever onward,
Ever on.

(Translated by Terri DeYoung)

Notes

1. Shawqī Ḍayf, in his short overview of the genre, *Rithā'* (Cairo: Dār al-Ma'ārif, n.d.), gives a good summary of how the institutionalization of elegy proceeds and develops new strategies of presentation during this period. See especially pages 100–101.

2. She was best known for her elegies on her brother Ṣakhr, but she also composed verses mourning her other brother Mu'āwiya and her father. See Ḍayf, 14–15 and the selection of her poetry in the medieval anthology by Ibn Qutayba, *Kitāb al-Shi'r wa-al-Shu'arā'* ed. by Aḥmad Muḥammad Shākir (Cairo: Dār al-Ma'ārif, 1966), 343–47. Her inclusion in this highly selective early anthology is indicative of the high regard in which her work was held among classical poets and critics.

3. Shawqī Ḍayf, 85.

4. Barbara Harlow, *Resistance Literature* (London: Methuen, 1987), 19.

5. See Muḥammad Mandūr, *Fann al-Shi'r* (Cairo: al-Hay'a al-Miṣriyya al-'Āmma li-al-Kitāb, 1974), 162 for a summary of the principles of poetry espoused by the Dīwān School. See also 'Abbās Maḥmūd al-'Aqqād and Ibrāhīm al-Māzinī, *Al-Dīwān* (Cairo: Dār al-Sha'b, n.d.), 12–13. Interestingly, of the five poems by the neo-classical poet Aḥmad Shawqī which were the focus of the Dīwān School's initial attack, the first two were elegies.

6. I have decided to adhere to the generally prevalent way of referring to the Egyptian president that has been adopted in and from Western media discourse, precisely because of its familiarity to English readers, even though it is technically incorrect: his last name should be rendered as 'Abd al-Nāṣir (literally, "servant of the 'One Who Grants Victory'"—the latter being an epithet of God) and "Nasser" is a semantically distorting truncation of this.

7. For the names of individuals who are familiar from the Western press, I have given their names full diacritical marks the first time they are mentioned and thereafter used the same spelling without diacritics, for simplicity's sake.

8. For an account of these perceptions, see Muḥammad Ḥasanayn Haykal, "Bi-Ṣarāḥa," *Al-Ahrām,* 30 October 1970, p. 3.

9. For the details of this event (as well as a cogent example of its nascent rhetorical shaping), see Muḥammad Ḥasanayn Haykal's column, "Bi-Ṣarāḥa: 28 Sibtambir, al-Arba' wal-'Ishrūn Sā'a al-Akhīra," in *al-Ahrām,* 16 October 1970, p. 1. It is illuminating to compare this with the account in *al-Ahrām* on the day following Nasser's death.

10. A biased (but perhaps even more illuminating for that) account of the details of how one incident, the 710th anniversary (on May 7, 1960) of the defeat of Louis IX at Manṣūra by one of Salāḥ al-Dīn's Ayyubid successors, was used to shape this "resistance narrative" may be found in Nissim Rejwan, *Nasserist Ideology: Its Exponents and Critics* (New York: John Wiley and Sons, 1974), 21–22. See also the text of Nasser's speech on this occasion, *Al-Ahrām,* 8 May 1960.

11. See the short, apparently anonymous reminiscence published in *Al-Ahrām* 5 October 1970, p. 10. The poetry of Amal Danqal and Adūnīs also is a particularly rich field for cataloguing the range of "historical" allusions used with regard to Nasser. In particular, I would argue that Adūnīs's series of poems about Ṣaqr Quraysh are based on his own dialectical reading of his ambivalent relationship with the Nasserist revolution. Ḥusayn Muruwwa, in his article "'Thawrat 23 Yūliyū' wa-al-Adab al-'Arabī," in *Al-Ādāb* 19 (February 1971): 26, suggests much the same point (though he does not explicitly make the equation between these poems and an Adūnīsian meditation on the relationship between the poet and the hero).

12. For examples of typical Pharaonic allusions see *Al-Ahrām,* 5 October 1970, p. 10; and *Al-Ahrām,* 11 October 1970, p. 10. In Islamic discourse, Pharaoh was the Qur'ānic archetype of the tyrant, primarily based on the narrative in Sura 26 ("The Poets") of his confrontation with Moses.

13. Luwīs 'Awaḍ, "Ṣadīq al-Fuqarā'," *Al-Ahrām,* 30 September 1970, p. 5.

14. See Fatḥī al-'Asharī, "28 Sibtambir wa-Ḥijjat al-Wadā'," *Al-Ahrām,* 6 November 1970, p. 10.

15. For a brief, but useful discussion of this debate, one which manages to foreground most of the important elements of its various dimensions, see Salma Khadra Jayyusi, *Trends and Movements in Modern Arabic Poetry,* vol. 2(Leiden: E. J. Brill, 1977), 739.

16. This is an allusion to Tawfīq al-Ḥakīm's famous novel of the 1930s, which was often cited by Nasser as a work that highly influenced his thinking when he read it as a young man. The novel is structured through symbolism that is based on ancient Egyptian myth.

17. *Al-Ahrām,* 3 October 1970, p. 7.

18. Khalīl Muḥammad Fāḍil, "Al-Balad wa-al-Baṭal," *Al-Ahrām,* 4 October 1970, p. 5.

19. The Supreme Council for the Guidance of the Arts, Letters, and Social Sciences, *Min Marāthī al-Shu'arā' al-'Arab fī Dhikrā al-Za'īm al-Khālid Jamāl 'Abd al-Nāṣir* (Cairo: Al-Hay'a al-'Āmma li-Shu'ūn al-Maṭābi' al-Amīriyya, 1973), 1.

20. He was apparently in Moscow during the time of Nasser's death and funeral ceremonies. See Mu'īn Bisīsū, "Awwal Ḥadīth Ma'a Maḥmūd Darwīsh—Shā'ir al-Arḍ al-Muḥtalla—fī al-Qāhira," *Al-Ahrām,* 11 February 1971, p. 5.

21. For an account of the unsuccessful attack led by the Poetry Committee, under the leadership of 'Abbās Maḥmūd al-'Aqqād, on free verse in 1964, see Ghālī Shukrī, *Dhikrayāt al-Jīl al-Ḍā'i'* (Baghdad: Wizārat al-I'lām, Mudīriyyat al-Thaqāfa al-'Āmma, 1972), 87–94. Shukrī also discusses the changed composition and role of the Poetry Committee by Nasser's death in 1970 in this same work, 212–17.

22. For early evidence of this poem's impact, see Ḥusayn Muruwwa's speech about it at the First Poetry Conference, as reported in Muḥammad Dakrūb, "Al-Shi'r al-Ḥadīth, wa-al-Thawra, wa-al-Jumhūr fī al-Multaqā al-Shi'rī al-Awwal," *Al-Ādāb* 19 (January 1971): 84.

23. It should be noted, however, that this kind of "depersonalization" of Nasser was a well established convention in writings about him. One can find, for example, Ḥusayn Muruwwa referring to Nasser as an "issue *(qaḍiyya).*" Probably the most interesting example of this rhetorical strategy can be found in one of the installments of Muḥammad Ḥasanayn Haykal's column "Bi-Ṣarāḥa" shortly after Nasser's death (*Al-Ahrām,* 23 October 1970, p. 1) where Nasser's close friend and apologist starts out to subvert this strategy but ends in inadvertently underwriting its use: "I was certain that Nasser was not rule *(al-ḥukm)* nor power *(al-sulṭa)*; rather, he was the living embodiment of Egyptian patriotism and Arab nationalism." This does not obviate the importance of Ḥijāzī's use of the strategy here, as he goes on to underscore the proposition that Nasser has become "a dream," thus making the central theme of his essay this depersonalization and transference of Nasser into the realm of something more than (and also less than) human.

24. For a revealing example of the "constrained approach" used during Nasser's lifetime, see Adūnīs's essay "Jamāl 'Abd al-Nāṣir wa-al-Muthaqqafūn," *Al-Ādāb* 16 (June 1968): 4–5. Adūnīs, more than most of his contemporary poets, had the reputation of being oppositional to Nasser while the latter was alive, primarily because he published a number of essays critical of the July 1952 Revolution in a special issue of his literary magazine *Mawāqif* (November-December 1969). Yet, in the 1968 *Al-Ādāb* article, he never says anything negative about Nasser himself, confining his criticism to the "politics in the Arab world," and he concludes the essay by saying: "reassurance, in circumstances like our current ones comes from above—from the political leadership. And President Nasser, in his words about this reassurance, teaches freedom before he teaches anything else. He is confirming our right to dream, to be free, to discuss and be uneasy; this is his confirmation of our right to bread and work. And in this

is the beginning of the revolution. . . ." The contrast of tone with Ḥijāzī's introduction to *Kitābāt* is marked.

25. Aḥmad 'Abd al-Mu'ṭī Ḥijāzī, "Al-Shi'r wa-'Abd al-Nāṣir," introduction to *Kitābāt 'Alā Qabr 'Abd al-Nāṣir* (Beirut: Dār al-'Awda, 1971), 10.

26. I should emphasize here that I am not saying that Nasser can be objectively shown to have oppressed literary figures as a systematic state policy or that his regime was not relatively benign in comparison with others in the Middle East, especially in more recent times. What I am referring to, instead, is a perception among the younger poets themselves, *at the time of Nasser's death,* that their experience of literary life after the 1952 Revolution was not all that it could have been. For discussions of specific incidents that engendered this sense of frustration and disappointment, see Muḥammad Mandūr, *Qaḍāyā Jadīda fī Adabinā al-Ḥadīth* (Beirut: Dār al-Ādāb, 1958), 88-89 (for an account of the incident in the late 1950s where al-'Aqqād had all the free verse poems submitted for a poetry prize sent instead to the Prose Committee); Ghālī Shukrī, *Dhikrayāt al-Jīl al-Ḍā'i',* 87–94 (discussing the manifesto attacking free verse published by the Egyptian Ministry of Culture's Poetry Committee (under the Supreme Council for the Guidance of the Arts, Letters and the Social Sciences) in 1964); and Sāmī Khashaba, "Wizārat al-Thaqāfa: Mushkilatuhā wa-Mushkilatunā," *Al-Ādāb* 19 (January 1971): 95–96 (for specific examples of individuals who had trouble getting their works published or distributed by the Ministry of Culture in the years directly before Nasser's death).

27. For overviews of these policies and varied assessments of how they were perceived, see Muḥammad Dakrūb, "Al-Shi'r al-Ḥadīth, wa-al-Thawra, wa-al-Jumhūr . . . fī al-Multaqā al-Shi'rī al-Awwal," *Al-Ādāb* 19 (January 1971): 11–13; Ḥusayn Muruwwa, "'Thawrat 23 Yūliyū' wa-al-Adab al-'Arabī," *Al-Ādāb* 19 (February 1971): 26–31 and 78–81; Sāmī Khashaba, "Durūs min 'Aṣr 'Abd al-Nāṣir: Fī Dhikrāhu al-Rābi'a," *Al-Ādāb* 22 (October 1974): 5–6; as well as the special issue of *Al-Ādāb* devoted to the assessment of the impact of the 1952 Revolution on its fortieth anniversary (40 (September–October 1992)).

28. It may be worth noting here that in Arabic (unlike English) there are five forms of "you," each explicitly marked for gender and number: a masculine singular form, a feminine singular, a dual (used for both genders), a masculine plural, and a feminine plural. Darwīsh uses a single form, the masculine singular, throughout his poem. The Arabic "we," in contrast, is equivalent in markedness to the corresponding English pronoun—there are no gender indices, and the same form is used for dual and plural.

29. Ever since this point was made by Sigmund Freud in his influential 1917 essay, "Mourning and Melancholy," (*Collected Papers,* vol. 4 [London: The Hogarth

Press, 1925], 154), practicing therapists and cultural theorists alike have emphasized that denial of the reality of a death is often supplemented by the insistence of the survivor on behaving as though the dead person is still alive in order to continue to keep everything just as it was and avoid the consequences the death would normally entail—the mother who tidies her dead child's room and changes the sheets every week is only one of the most common and least disruptive manifestations of this form of behavior. Others are much more severe and harmfully obsessive. It is worth noting that Freud finds resemblances between mourning and the mental condition he calls melancholia (manic-depressive illness), and observes that the chief difference between them is that mourning does not involve necessarily a loss of self-esteem or an increase in feelings of guilt and self-blame. When such emotions do appear in grief, we are on the border, according to Freud, between mourning and melancholia. For him, then, "healthy" mourning focuses primarily on separating the mourner from his "libido-object," the deceased.

30. Note that this is an exact reversal of the statements beginning in line seventeen, where the "we" occupies this passive position.

31. One might note that such a reading comes very close to Freud's melancholia, where grief is turned into self-reproach and blame.

32. His battle flag was green, for example, and people who claim descent from him often wear turbans of this color, especially on ceremonial occasions.

33. Derrida frequently plays with the two senses of "supplement" (in both French and English): to add something extra which is not necessary (and therefore trivial and superfluous) to the original discourse and to add something that remedies a lack in the original discourse. See Jacques Derrida, *Of Grammatology,* trans. Gayatri Chakravorty Spivak (Baltimore: The Johns Hopkins University Press, 1976), 141–64 and Jacques Derrida, "Structure, Sign and Play in the Discourse of the Human Sciences," in *A Postmodern Reader,* ed. Joseph Natoli and Linda Hutcheon (Albany: State University of New York Press, 1993), 223–42, and especially 236–37.

Ibrāhīm Ṭūqān's Poem "Red Tuesday"

Issa J. Boullata

Ibrāhīm Ṭūqān (1905–1941) is the most important poet of Palestine in the first half of the twentieth century.[1] Strongly based on the Arabic classical tradition, his poetry has innovative dimensions that give it a particular modern flavor totally its own. In this regard, he may be considered one of the leading innovative poets of his generation in the Arab world. The major themes of his poetry include love, which he celebrated with all the ardor that youth could impart and with all the anguish that the death of his beloved later added.[2] His major themes also include politics related to the Palestinian national cause, and these were treated by him with no less ardor and anguish,[3] given his perception of the unjust policies of the British mandatory government of Palestine, the ineptitude of the Palestinian Arab political leadership, and the constant Zionist threat to the very existence of Palestine and its Arab population.

This paper offers a literary study of his long poem, which he composed in 1930. It is entitled "Al-Thulāthā' al-Ḥamrā'" (Red Tuesday).[4] It commemorates three Palestinian men who were sentenced to death and hanged by the British mandatory authorities for their participation in the revolt of 1929.[5] It also expresses the indignation of the Palestinians at their harsh and unfair treatment by the British. The revolt was triggered by an unprovoked breach of the status quo at the Wall of al-Burāq, the Western Wall of the al-Ḥaram al-Sharīf compound in Jerusalem where on August 15, 1929, militant

Zionists held an unprecedented political demonstration and Jewish worshipers introduced equipment and flags that were not traditionally used or allowed in that location. The Muslims considered this act to be an aggression against the sanctity and integrity of the Islamic Holy Places, and bloody clashes between Arabs and Jews occurred in the country, mostly between August 23 and 29, 1929, especially in Jerusalem, Hebron, Jaffa, Haifa, and Safad. As a consequence, 133 Jews were killed and 339 injured; furthermore, 116 Palestinians were killed and 232 injured, mostly at the hands of the British army.[6] Among the many Palestinian Arabs arrested and tried for taking part in the revolt were three men: Muḥammad Jamjūm and ʻAṭā al-Zīr from Hebron and Fu'ād Ḥijāzī from Safad. The underlying causes of the revolt, exacerbated by the incident at the Wall of al-Burāq and by the creation in August 1929 of the enlarged Jewish Agency in Jerusalem to represent world Jewry, were the continuing rejection by the Palestinians of the Zionist plans for Palestine, their objection to the Balfour Declaration of 1917, and their resistance to the British policy bent on implementing this declaration and the League of Nations mandate and on creating in Palestine a "national home" for the Jews at the expense of the Palestinians and their historical rights to the land of their ancestors.

Despite appeals by the Palestinians to the British High Commissioner in Jerusalem to commute the death sentence of the three men,[7] the British authorities chose to ignore Palestinian feelings and hanged the three rebels in the prison of Acre on Tuesday, June 17, 1930, in three successive hours beginning at 8:00 A.M. First to be hanged was Ḥijāzī,[8] then Jamjūm,[9] and lastly al-Zīr.[10] It had been officially scheduled for al-Zīr to be second, but Jamjūm broke his fetters and asked to replace him. His request was granted so that al-Zīr could spend one more hour with his wife and children.

The emotional atmosphere in the country was mournful and tense. Ten days later, on June 27, 1930, while Palestinians were still smarting from grief and indignation, Ibrāhīm Ṭūqān recited his poem "Al-Thulāthā' al-Ḥamrā'" at the annual graduation ceremonies of Madrasat al-Najāḥ, a high school in his hometown of Nablus, where he was teaching Arabic language and literature after his graduation with a B.A. from the American University of Beirut in 1929. The poem galvanized its immediate audience and, on publication, the whole Arab population of Palestine. It was a new departure for Ṭūqān, with its artistic sophistication, dramatic effect, and powerful symbolism presenting the historic even in a truly impressive manner. Ṭūqān wrote a few other poems of this caliber before he died in 1941 at the young age of thirty-six.[11]

"Al-Thulāthā' al-Ḥamrā'" is a complex *muwashshaḥ* consisting of nine stanzas, after the eighth of which three strophes are interpolated. The stanzas follow a specific rhyme scheme and the strophes another, but both stanzas and strophes are based on the *mutafā'ilun* (˘ ˘ - ˘ -) foot of the *kāmil* meter and its variations.

Every stanza has five lines, the first and the second of which rhyme with each other and are equal in length, having six feet each divided into two equal and internally rhyming hemistichs; the third and the fourth lines are shorter by half, having three feet each, and they rhyme with each other, not with the first two lines, and contain an agreeing internal rhyme before the last foot of each; the fifth line is equal in length to the first but ends with a different rhyme and has no middle rhyme at the caesura. All the stanzas follow this rhyme scheme, but the rhyme sounds are not identical except for the one ending the last line of each stanza, that end rhyme being identical throughout all nine stanzas.

On the other hand, the three strophes have ten lines each. Each strophe has its own monorhyme different from the other two strophes and begins with a line having an internal middle rhyme at the caesura. Each line has four feet (following the *majzū' al-kāmil* meter) with an additional syllable appended to the last foot of each line (*muraffal:* ˘ ˘ - ˘ - -) as well as at the caesura of the first line only.

This complex pattern of rhymes and rhythms parallels the complex pattern of themes and motifs which the poet treats in his poem. To dramatize the historic national event, Ṭūqān resorts to the use of multiple voices in the poem. There are three sets of voices: the first is that of the narrator and it is a single voice; the second is that of history and it has three personified "days" of the past speaking in succession; the third is that of the time in which the three men were hanged and it has the three personified hours of the hanging speaking in succession.

This polyphony is carefully distributed between the stanzas and the strophes: the narrator and the personified "days" of the past using the stanzas, and the three personified hours of the hanging using the strophes.

The narrator begins the poem by describing the ill-fated day when the three men were hanged, when "[m]inaret calls and church bells lamented," and when the atmosphere in the country was grim while death roamed and snatched three lives away. Looking back on past ages, the personified day asks whether humanity has ever seen the like of it. The first day of the past to answer is that of the "iniquitous Inquisition courts"; but, on comparing the injustice of those with that of the British courts in Palestine, it admits it has never seen worse injustice than that resulting in the hanging of the three Palestinians. The second day of the past to answer is that of slavery, when human beings were bought and sold; but it admits that the day of the hanging is worse because those who have forbidden the "purchase and sale of slaves / Are now hawking the free"—a pointed reference to the British who, in the perception of the Palestinians, have sold Palestine to the Zionists and robbed it of its freedom. The third day of the past to speak is one from Ottoman history when, after a military court trial at 'Aley (Lebanon) during the First World War, many young Arab nationalists were hanged under orders from Jamal Pasha (the "Butcher") for plotting against Ottoman rule and seeking national independence for the Arab people; but this day of injustice and mourning admits that the day of the hanging of the three Palestinians is worse, its terrible character being like that of the "Day of Resurrection."

The narrator then returns to comment on the day of the hanging and on Palestine, which he perceives as a country going to perdition through the injustice of the British; and he advises the Palestinians to resist their enemies with pride in order to remain morally undefeated.

He says how everyone had hoped that the British High Commissioner in Jerusalem would pardon the three men, heeding the petitions submitted to him by the Palestinian people and their leaders. The narrator's tone is sarcastic as he describes the British lack of sympathy and clemency, and he advises the Palestinians not to humiliate themselves any further by "supplicating and begging." The British are heartless, he concludes, and Palestinians should not seek favors from them but should rather preserve their own dignity.

At this mention of dignity in the poem, the three personified hours intervene, one at a time. The first hour, representing Ḥijāzī, prides itself on being the hour of the "dignified soul" that has the "virtue of priority," but it asserts that all three hours "symbolize the ardent zeal" of the Palestinians. It says it has a "significant effect" on the national cause by inspiring young men with "steadfast faithfulness" so that they will inevitably overcome the enemy one day. Then it swears by Ḥijāzī's soul as it enters heaven that immortality can be achieved only by sacrifice; and it hails all souls that sacrifice themselves for their homeland.

The second hour, representing Jamjūm, voices its pride in being the hour of the ready and courageous man, who broke his fetters as a symbol of seeking freedom and vied with the preceding hour to obtain immortality. It asserts that it has kindled the spark of determination in young men so that they will not be deceived by false promises regarding the fate of the homeland. Then it swears by Jamjūm's soul facing death and by his mother singing a national anthem and consoling herself with her son's "good repute" that there is "[n]o nobler reward" for serving the homeland than that of martyrdom.

The third hour, representing al-Zīr, expresses its pride in being the "[h]our of the patient man" and the "symbol of resolve to the end," for its hero faces death with firmness and joy and wins the hearts with his fortitude. The hour then warns the enemy of an "impending evil for them" and swears by al-Zīr's soul, by Paradise, and by al-Zīr's weeping children that only brave and patient men can save the homeland.

To end the poem, the narrator's voice returns in a final stanza to comment that the three men's bodies now "lie in the soil of the homeland" and "[t]heir souls rest eternally in the Garden of Bliss." He says that they are now beyond all oppression and enjoy a divine pardon—an allusion to the British oppression and to the British pardon that was withheld from them. The narrator then terminates by advising everyone not to "hope for forgiveness from anyone but God," whose "power is above those deceived / By their own power on land and sea"—this being a final barb thrown at the British, whose power on land and sea extended over a vast empire on which, in those days, the sun never set.

Ibrāhīm Ṭūqān's achievement in this poem establishes a turning point in his poetry. Not only does he depart from the traditional classical form of the Arabic poem and even from the common form of the Andalusian *muwashshaḥ,* but he also transcends his own previous poetic ventures. His earlier exquisite poems "Malā'ikat al-Raḥma" (Angels of mercy),[12] or "Fī al-Maktaba" (In the library),[13] or "Al-Fidā'ī" (The commando)[14] and a few others had drawn critical attention and popular acclaim by their freshness and new style. But his innovation in "Al-Thulāthā' al-Ḥamra'" was more significant and lies basically in his effective dramatization in an unprecedented manner of the historic national event. He gives voice to the day of hanging, to the three personified days of history, and to the three personified hours of hanging, while, at the same time, keeping his own voice concealed behind that of the narrator posing sometimes as an objective observer, more subtly as a critic of British policies in Palestine, and as an experienced moral adviser well-informed about British duplicity and the ways of the world and the values of a better life. In this poem, Ṭūqān frees himself of the classical form by adopting a dramatic mask and abandoning the lyrical and emotional rhetoric of declamatory oratorical verse. Furthermore, he uses the powerful suggestiveness of religious symbols as well as that of popular myths and national lore to heighten the effect of his dramatization. With a very economical language that borders on starkness and a very simple diction that verges on the conversational, Ṭūqān enlivens his poem with images that leave a lasting imprint on one's mind and a continuing vibration in one's soul.

The structural form of the poem and its semantic content combine into an organic unity in which sounds, rhythms, words, ideas, and images maintain a symbiosis of rare subtlety. The regular alternation of long and short verses, the schematic variation of rhyme sounds, the pounding repetition of the identical recurring rhyme at the end of each one of the nine stanzas, the monorhyme of the three strophes with an extra syllable assertively added to the last foot of each line, and the pervading prosodic versification based on the *kāmil* meter throughout the poem all help to create a haunting rhythm. On the other hand, the distribution of voice functions between stanzas and strophes, and between narrator, personified days, and personified hours, helps to create a sort of musical counterpoint in the poem as the voices are all interwoven into a harmonic whole. Each voice retains its linear quality as an independent melody while it tells its part of the drama, but all the voices combine into a single texture in the totality of the poem. The narrator's voice with his mournful but dignified tone and with his ironic but worldly-wise attitude underlies them all as the base melody, and so does the *mutafā'ilun* (˘ ˘ – ˘ –) foot which constitutes the base rhythm underlying the whole poem. The identical single rhyme that recurs regularly at the end of each of the nine stanzas enhances the harmonious structural and semantic unity of the poem as though to signify a certain inevitability about life and death that cannot be helped but also a certain inexorability about the detestable British policy in Palestine. In the final analysis, the organic unity of the poem arises from the successful fusion of thought and emotion, from the effective congruence of form and content, and from the subtle interplay of the various elements of poetic structure.

"Al-Thulāthā' al-Ḥamra'" is a unique poem in modern Arabic literature. Ibrāhīm Ṭūqān has been able to rise to the peak of his poetic potential and, and by doing so, to open the way for further achievements for himself and for Arabic poetry. It was not altogether a coincidence in his poetic career, for it was followed by a few other poems of a similar quality such as "Al-Shāhid" (The martyr),[15] "Ghādat Ishbīliya" (The lass of Seville),[16] "Al-Ḥabashī al-Dhabīḥ" (The slain turkey),[17] and "Maṣra' Bulbul" (Death of a nightingale).[18] But "Al-Thulāthā' al-Ḥamra'" stands alone as the poem that has successfully captured the magnitude of the historic national event and the mood of the Palestinians in a most memorable way and has recorded them for future generations in a uniquely artistic manner.

Red Tuesday

by
Ibrāhīm Ṭūqān (1905–1941)

INTRODUCTION

When your ill-fated star rose
And heads swayed in the nooses,
Minaret calls and church bells lamented,
Night was grim, and day was gloomy.
Storms and emotions began to rage
As death roamed about, snatching lives away,
And the eternal spade dug deep into the soil
To return them to its petrified heart.

It was a day that looked back upon past ages
And asked, "Has the world seen a day like me?"
"Yes," answered another day. "I'll tell you
All about the iniquitous Inquisition courts.
I have indeed witnessed strange and odd events.
But yours are misfortunes and catastrophes,
The like of which in injustice I've never seen.
Ask then other days, among which many are abominable."

Dragging its heavy fetters, a day responded,
History being one of its witnesses:
"Look at slaves, white and black,
Owned by anyone who had the money.
They were humans bought and sold, but are now free.
Yet time has gone backwards, as far as I can see . . .
And those who forbade the purchase and sale of slaves
Are now hawking the free."

A day wrapped in a dark-colored robe
Staggered under the delirium of suffering
And said, "No, yours is a much lesser pain than mine.
For I lost my young men on the hills of Aley
And witnessed the Butcher's deeds, inducing bloody tears.
Woe to him, how unjust! But . . .
I've never met as terrible a day as you are.
Go, then. Perhaps you're the Day of Resurrection."

The day is considered abominable by all past ages
And eyes will keep looking at it with dismay.
How unfair the decisions of the courts have been,
The least of which are proverbial in injustice.
The homeland is going to perdition, without hope.
The disease has no medicine but dignified pride
That renders one immune, and whoever is marked by it
Will end up dying undefeated.

Everyone hoped for [the High Commissioner's] early pardon,
And we prayed that he would never be distressed.
If this was the extent of his tenderness and kindness,
Long live His Majesty and long live His Excellency!
The mail carried details of what had been put in a nutshell.
Please, stop supplicating and begging.
The give-and-take of entreaties is tantamount to death.
Therefore, take the shortest way to life.

The mail was overloaded with pleading, but nothing changed.
We humbled ourselves and wrote in various forms.
Our loss is both in souls and in money,
And our dignity is—alas—in rags.
You see what's happening, and yet ask what's next?
Deception, like madness, is of many kinds.

A humiliated soul, even if created to be all eyes,
Will not be able to see—far from it.

How is it possible for the voice of complaint to be heard,
And for the tears of mourning to be of any avail?
The rocks that felt our plea broke up in sympathy.
Yet, on reaching their hearts, our plea was denied.
No wonder, for some rocks burst with gushing fountains,
But their hearts are like graves, with no feeling.
Don't ever seek favors from someone
You tried and found to be heartless.

THE THREE HOURS

The First Hour

I am the Hour of the dignified soul
And have the virtue of priority.
I am the firstborn of three Hours,
All of which symbolize ardent zeal.
I am the daughter of the [Palestinian] cause
And have a significant effect on it:
That of sharp swords
And light lances.
In the hearts of young men I've inspired
The spirit of steadfast faithfulness.
They will inevitably have a day
That will deal the enemy the cup of death.
I swear by Fu'ād's pure soul
As it leaves his ribs
On its way to the welcome of heaven
To abide in its lofty paradise:
No rank of eternity is reached

Without an acceptable sacrifice.
Long live the souls that die
In sacrifice for their homeland.

The Second Hour

I am the Hour of the ready man,
I am the Hour of extreme courage.
I am the Hour of death that honors
Everyone performing a glorious deed.
My hero has broken his fetters
As a symbol of seeking freedom.
I've vied with the Hour preceding me
To obtain the honor of eternity first.
In the young men's hearts I've kindled
The spark of strong determination
That can never be deceived by promises
Or numbed by pledges.
I swear by Muḥammad's soul
As it meets with sweet death,
I swear by your mother
As she sings an anthem at your death
And finds consolation for bereavement
In her son's far-reaching good repute:
He who serves the homeland receives
No nobler reward than that of martyrdom.

The Third Hour

I am the Hour of the patient man,
I am the Hour of the big heart.
I am the symbol of resolve to the end
In all important matters.

My hero faces death with the firmness
Of solid rock.
He joyfully looks forward to dying.
Wonder, as you may, at dying with joy.
He meets God with dyed palms
On the Day of Resurrection.
His is the fortitude of youth in calamity.
He is my trust and fills all hearts.
I am warning the enemies of the homeland
Of a day of impending evil for them.
I swear by your soul, O 'Aṭā',
And by the paradise of the Almighty King
And by your young cubs weeping
For their lion with abundant tears:
No one saves the dear homeland
But a brave, patient man.

CONCLUSION

The Three Heroes

Their bodies lie in the soil of the homeland,
Their souls rest in the Garden of Bliss
Where there is no complaint of oppression
But there is an abundance of pardon.
Don't hope for forgiveness from anyone but God.
He it is whose hands possess all glory.
His power is above those deceived
By their own power on land and sea.

—*June 27, 1930*

(Translated by Issa J. Boullata)

Notes

1. For a short notice on him, see "Ibrāhīm Ṭūqān (1905–1941)" in *Al-Mawsū'a al-Filisṭīniyya* (Damascus: Hay'at al-Mawsū'a al-Filisṭīniyya, 1984), 1 (Alif-Thā'), 39–40. For a general study of his life and poetry, see 'Abd al-Laṭīf Sharāra, *Ibrāhīm Ṭūqān* (Beirut: Dār Ṣādir/Dār Bayrūt, 1964), and Ya'qūb al-'Awdāt, *Ibrāhīm Ṭūqān fī Waṭaniyyātih wa-Wijdāniyyātih* (Beirut: al-Maktaba al-Ahliyya, 1964).

2. For his love poetry, see Ya'qūb al-'Awdāt, *Al-Ghawānī fī Shi'r Ibrāhīm Ṭūqān* (Beirut: Dār al-Riḥānī, 1957).

3. For his nationalist and politically inspired poetry, see Zakī al-Maḥāsinī, *Ibrāhīm Ṭūqān, Shā'ir al-Waṭan al-Maghṣūb* (Cairo: Dār al-Fikr al-'Arabī, 1955) and especially Ya'qūb al-'Awdāt, *Al-Waṭan fī Shi'r Ibrāhīm Ṭūqān* (Amman: al-Maṭba'a al-Waṭaniyya, 1960).

4. See *Dīwān Ibrāhīm: A'māl Shā'ir Filisṭīn Ibrāhīm Ṭūqān* with an introduction, "Akhī Ibrāhīm," by Fadwā Ṭūqān and a study by Iḥsān 'Abbās (Beirut: Dār al-Quds, 1975), 97–100; and *Dīwān Ibrāhīm Ṭūqān* with a preface by Aḥmad Ṭūqān and an introduction, "Akhī Ibrāhīm," by Fadwā Ṭūqān (Amman: Maktabat al-Muḥtasib / Beirut: Dār al-Masīra, 1984), 42–49. See also my English translation of the poem appended to this article.

5. For information on the 1929 revolt, see "Thawrat 1929" in *Al-Mawsū'a al-Filisṭīniyya,* 1: 614–17.

6. Walid Khalidi, *Before Their Diaspora: A Photographic History of the Palestinians 1876–1948* (Washington, D.C.: Institute for Palestine Studies, 1984), 90.

7. There were twenty-six Palestinians sentenced to death, the sentence of twenty-three of whom was commuted to life imprisonment. See "Thawrat 1929" in *Al-Mawsū'a al-Filisṭīniyya.*

8. Born in Safad, Fu'ād Ḥasan Ḥijāzī was educated there at the Scottish College (commonly known as the Semple School) and later graduated from the American University of Beirut. For more on him, see "Fu'ād Ḥijāzī (1904-1930)" in *Al-Mawsū'a al-Filisṭīniyya,* 3 (Ṣād-Kāf): 478–79.

9. Jamjūm and his two companions met their executioner with dignity and joy, dressed in the red prison attire of those sentenced to death; they had spent the night singing "Yā Ẓalām al-Sijn Khayyim" (Reign, prison darkness). For more on Jamjūm, see "Muḥammad Khalīl Jamjūm (1902–1930)" in *Al-Mawsū'a al-Filisṭīniyya,* 4 (Lām-Yā'), 145–46.

10. Born in Hebron, al-Zīr and Jamjūm were given henna at their request, and they dyed their hands with it in accordance with Hebronite custom on weddings

and other joyous occasions. For more on al-Zīr, see "'Aṭā al-Zīr (1895–1930)" in *Al-Mawsū'a al-Filisṭīniyya*, 3: 283.

11. For further studies on Ṭūqān, see 'Umar Farrūkh, *Shā'irān Mu'aṣirān: Ibrāhīm Ṭūqān wa-Abū al-Qāsim al-Shabbī* (Beirut: al-Maktaba al-'Ilmiyya, 1954); and Walīd Ṣādiq & Sa'īd Jarrār, *Shā'irān min Jabal al-Nār: Ibrāhīm Ṭūqān wa-'Abd al-Raḥīm Maḥmūd* (Amman: n.p., 1985). For general studies on Palestinian poetry, including Ṭūqān's, see 'Abd al-Raḥmān Yāghī, *Ḥayāt al-Adab al-Filisṭīnī min Awwal al-Nahḍa ḥattā al-Nakba* (Beirut: Dār al-Āfāq al-Jadīda, 1968); Kāmil al-Sawāfīrī, *Al-Ittijāhāt al-Fanniyya fī al-Shi'r al-Filisṭīnī al-Mu'āṣir* (Cairo: Maktabat al-Anjlū al-Miṣriyya, 1973); and Nāṣir al-Dīn al-Asad, *Muḥāḍarāt fī al-Shi'r al-Ḥadīth fī Filisṭīn wa-al-Urdunn* (Cairo: Ma'had al-Dirāsāt al-'Arabiyya al-'Āliya, 1961), For English translations of Ṭūqān's poetry, see *Anthology of Modern Palestinian Literature,* ed. Salma Khadra Jayyusi (New York: Columbia University Press, 1992), 317–19.

12. *Dīwān Ibrāhīm,* 29; *Dīwān Ibrāhīm Ṭūqān,* 143–44.

13. *Dīwān Ibrāhīm,* 42–43; *Dīwān Ibrāhīm Ṭūqān,* 98–99.

14. *Dīwān Ibrāhīm,* 94; *Dīwān Ibrāhīm Ṭūqān,* 69–70.

15. *Dīwān Ibrāhīm,* 145; *Dīwān Ibrāhīm Ṭūqān,* 40–41.

16. *Dīwān Ibrāhīm,* 118–19; *Dīwān Ibrāhīm Ṭūqān,* 127–29.

17. *Dīwān Ibrāhīm,* 104; *Dīwān Ibrāhīm Ṭūqān,* 146–47.

18. *Dīwān Ibrāhīm,* 149–52; *Dīwān Ibrāhīm Ṭūqān,* 184–90.

Conflicts, Oppositions, Negations: Modern Arabic Poetry and The Fragmentation of Self / Text

KAMAL ABU-DEEB

I.

I.

The struggle of the modern, to borrow a phrase from the British poet Stephen Spender,[1] has been tragic; and this statement applies to both the modern in the world at large and the modern in Arabic culture. Modernity, like Modernism, has been an incomplete project. This phrase also is not mine, but that of Jürgen Habermas.[2] In what follows, I do not hope to be

---

This paper was written in 1988 and published in *Poésie du Proche-Orient et de La Grèce* (Paris: Asfar, 1990). I would like thank the publishers for permission to reprint this slightly modified version here. A more comprehensive version is to appear in a forthcoming book entitled *Culture Between Fragmentation and Multiplicity,* in which the phenomena considered here are traced in more recent works in both poetry and fiction.

able to present a faithful picture of this modernist project or of its incompleteness, but only to capture that moment in time when the project began to crumble and to depict some of the developments and transformations in Arabic poetry which can be attributed to the fact that the project of modernity has reached that specific juncture which I have described elsewhere as embodying the fragmentation of the organic world of Arab political, social and cultural life.[3] I shall consider some manifestations of this process of fragmentation on the level of the poetic text itself, and try to reveal the conflicts, oppositions, and negations which permeate its structure. Needless to say, my discussion cannot be comprehensive or fully satisfying. Due to the very nature of the material, as well as to the limitations imposed by this volume, my own project will have to remain, like its subject matter, incomplete.

2.

Some years ago, at a point when fragmentation was still nascent, I suggested that Arabic poetry would develop in two opposing directions: 1) a contemplative, abstract, metaphysical line and 2) a worldly, down-to-earth line, preoccupied with daily life, personal experience, the world of things, and the intimate presence of the poet as an individual in the world.[4]

The change came sooner than I had anticipated. Nothing can depict this more eloquently than to look at what has happened in the poetry of a master like Adūnīs, who had shaped his world over thirty-five years of crea-tive activity in such a manner as to make it difficult to expect any sudden shifts in his poetic world. Yet, as I will show presently, such a shift is exactly what has taken place. Simultaneously, we can examine the works of a younger generation of poets and compare their language and poetic sensibility with those of their seniors. Quite naturally, the process of change is an ongoing one; therefore, we can expect a certain amount of activity to represent a continuation of the main currents of the past decades. This is especially true as far as the involvement of poetry in ideology, authority, political indoctrination, et cetera is concerned. But the change is so widespread and deep that even the "typical" ideological voices of the sixties and early seventies have been undergoing a process of transformation, if not comprehensively, then at least in the sense that you can now hear them breaking outside their circles and attempting to explore virgin forests, uttering a different language with a truly different accent, all of which brings them close to one or the other of the two main currents I identified above.

In order to illuminate the first current, I shall first discuss aspects of Adūnīs's latest work, *Iḥtifā'an bi-al-Ashyā' al-Ghāmiḍa al-Wāḍiḥa* (In celebration of things obscure and clear),[5] concentrating particularly on the dominant role played in it by a striking phenomenon: namely, its use of the language of paradox, conflict, opposition and negation. And for the purpose of illustrating the second current, I shall discuss a number of pieces by poets who began to attract wider attention as the eighties drew to a close.

3.

Out of time and out of place, positioned ethereally in space, unbound by contingencies, and at the very height of his creative power, Adūnīs holds language in his fingers as a shaman's or sorcerer's magic pipe. And through it he utters his tantalizing pronouncements. Like the old man of the mountains, the contemplative hermit, Adūnīs distills the world, divine and human, into crystal-clear, oppositional statements. In a true sense, he actually transcends experience, leaving it behind like the sediments of grapes after ages of fermentation. The pure spirits he ultimately offers us to taste are liqueurs, subtle and exquisitely smooth. Here is his celebration of time as embodied in what in our minds stand out as oppositions: day and night; winter and summer; sun and moon; life and death:

Daylight closes the fence of its garden
washes its feet and wears its robe
in order to receive its friend, the night.

Quietly dusk progresses
a stain of blood on its shoulder
and in its hand a rose on the point of withering.
In fury dawn moves forward
its hands opening the book of time
while the sun turns its pages over.

On the threshold of the evening
daylight breaks its mirrors
in order to be able to sleep.

Days are letters which time writes to people
but without words.

Each day the sun gives birth to a child
which she names 'morning,'
But it doesn't live long.

Time is a wind
which blows from the direction of death.

Night buttons up the shirt of the earth
and daylight undresses it.

If daylight were to speak
it would herald the night.

Winter is loneliness.
Summer is migration.
Spring is a bridge between them.
Only Autumn permeates all the seasons.

Time is a mountain inhabited by daylight and night.
Daylight ascends, and night descends.

Daylight knows how to sleep
only in the lap of night.

Dusk is the only pillow
over which embrace daylight and night.

The dreams of night are yarns
with which we weave the garments of daylight.

Finally, this wonderful image of time:

The past is a lake
for a single swimmer: memories.[6]

4.

At the very height of his maturity, Adūnīs acquires that most tantalizing of visions: the paradoxical. Writing, creativity, poetry, language, man and woman, society, individual and collective, life and death, time, nature, physical being, as well as metaphysical space, all enjoy an existence distinguished not by its unitary structure, its similarities and symmetries, or by its one-sided perfection—no, but by presence in the state of an oppositional structure. Everything acquires value and the power of being from embodying in its very essence its very opposite. From being both itself and its opposite, it derives its reality; and from yearning for its opposite it derives its power of movement. This paradoxical language is not new to Adūnīs. I discussed its role in his poetry as far back as 1970. But here it is elevated to the position of singularity: it is the singular way in which he views the world. This in itself is of course paradoxical: while negating singularity, Adūnīs asserts it in the strongest possible fashion. While "celebrating things vague and clear," he produces a Newer Testament for the worshippers of the world as a paradoxical space—as being and nothingness all entwined in one entity. Yet, while discovering that the nature of things hides a process of fusion between opposites, producing a new totality in which (-) and (+) are two facets of the same reality, at times his recognition of oppositions implies an acknowledgment of their independence and separateness. Both aspects of this vision are evident in the following examples:

> Marvel at paradoxes which alone are logical,
> at contradictory things outside of which we can see no unity.[7]

> I murmured: Nothing fills me with clarity
> like this obscurity;
> or maybe I murmured: Nothing fills me with obscurity more than
> this clarity.[8]

Quite naturally, perhaps, but no less interestingly for that, this divided consciousness applies also to the poet's very creativity. His ultimate battle is seen by Adūnīs as being:

> With language you have wanted to know yourself
> and know the world.
> Therefore you have separated things from their
> names. You instigated the object against its name
> and the name against the object.
> And here they are still fighting; each searching

and not finding.
Why, after all this,
do you appear as if you have only known
those things which have no names.[9]

5.

The features which I have been discussing merit some further elaboration. The language of paradox operates in three distinct ways. Firstly, it reveals an antithetical relationship between two entities which, on the surface, appear similar or identical. Secondly, it reveals the oneness, the inner identity, of two entities which appear widely different. The third and more striking way is the revelation of the inner tensions within one entity. The latter way acquires great significance in the poetry of Adūnīs, Maḥmūd Darwīsh, and a few other poets, where it takes the form of discovering the multiplicity of the One and realizing that such multiplicity is underlined by difference, opposition, contradiction and destructive negation. In Adūnīs's poetry, this is revealed on both the level of the individual being (especially in the fact of the Other) and the level of collective being, that is, society. I shall consider briefly some manifestations of these conflicts in his poetry before discussing the manner in which they appear in the poetry of Darwīsh. And I shall deal in particular with a fundamental relationship in poetic language, especially in cultural contexts where poetry acquires a role which goes beyond the purely personal and confessional. By this I am referring to the I/Other relationship wherein the Other embodies the group or society as a whole.

The I/Other relationship in Adūnīs's latest work is of a paradoxical nature. When the Other is singular, it often complements the I and represents the missing being without which the I remains incomplete.

A single man: a single wing;
a single woman: a broken wing.

In the beginning was the couple; then came the first error which was named the one, the individual. Thus I'll write the word "couple" as if I were digging up a spring; and I'll pronounce it as if the water were on the point of gushing forth.[10]

Thus, the nuclear unit of man's existence is not the singular or the individual, but the pair, the couple. Singularity is an error, indeed, the first error or the first, original, sin. But when the Other is plural (more than the couple), group, society, et cetera, things are different. A split arises; an abyss stands out between the I and the Other. All virtues belong to the I, although they might appear as if they belonged to the Other. The I—the individual self—is the real force of history. Difference, contradiction, and negation become the essential properties of the relationship between the I and the Other. And this split between individual and group is now given as a fact of life, of history, as valid as saying: "The sun rises in the East." For decades, Adūnīs's relationship with the Other had been tense. But there had been times when a total identification took place: (I/You-They) embodied a perfect resolution of tension between poet and world. At that point he wrote his poem "Singular in the Plural Form." But in his latest testimony, the split is back in a more acute form. It is now stated in absolute terms as individual/group (rather than as I/You) the latter being the historical self representing stagnation and ossification or oppression and tyranny. Here are some statements:

> The group writes history,
> but the individual is the one who reads it.
>
> The individual is a unit of infinity
> and the group is an infinity of loneliness.
>
> O.K., I'll emerge out of my isolation
> but, where to?
>
> I open a lake for forgetfulness
> and in it I sink my history.[11]

Thus, conflict, struggle, and violence explode at the very heart of Adūnīs's vision. While revealing the essential oneness of opposites, he comes up against the imperative necessity of conflict, of the violence which one entity has to exercise against its opposite in order to free life, to create a better world:

> The sky itself cannot be the only mistress
> unless it kills the earth.
>
> Your homeland, O poet
> is where it is impossible for you not to be exiled.[12]

And in all this, Adūnīs has brought to its full flourish what had always permeated his poetry, but in a less powerful fashion, namely, the language of paradox: the fusion of contradictions and the fission of the One. I have devoted an independent paper to the study of this most poignant and seductive of poetic language in his recent work.

6.

I shall now consider briefly those aspects of paradoxical language most relevant to the I/Other relationship in the recent poetry of Maḥmūd Darwīsh. Darwīsh's vision of the contradictions within the One seems to operate mainly on the level of identity, "national" cohesion, and homogeneity. Arabic culture appears to him to be fragmenting its own body, exploding its own structure through the relations of negation between its constituents. Identity, as an oppositional entity, is a source of much pain and tragic energy—but of much beauty too—in his poetry especially after 1976. His poem "Aḥmad al-Za'tar"[13] is a landmark in the development of this tone in his work. But in view of the limited space available to me, I shall content myself now with shorter quotations from other, more recent, poems of his. In these pieces, we see how an interwoven process of conflict and fragmentation takes place on two different levels. First, the conflict tears apart the collective self; then it tears apart the individual self. The poet is the victim of both shattering conflicts:

> We are spoils of war in these slimy times.
> The invaders have handed us to our folks.
> And no sooner had we bitten the earth than our
> protector attacked the weddings and the memories,
> so we distributed our songs to the guards,
> from a king on a throne
> to a king in a coffin,
> spoils of war we are, in these slimy times.
> We could find nothing to mark our identity
> except our blood.[14]

But this collective "we," which is asserted in the face of both enemies and brothers, soon crumbles and gets shattered by its own inner conflicts:

1. We are as we are.

We are the generation of the massacre.
A nation which severs the breast of her mother
A nation which kills the shepherd of her dreams
on moon-lit nights
without weeping over him.

Where is the shade of the tree?

A knight stabs his brother in the chest
in the name of the homeland
and prays for forgiveness.

Where is the shape of the tree?[15]

2. And can I reach the peak of the difficult
mountain, when the slope is an abyss
or a siege, and the middle of the path
is a crossroad . . .
Woe to a journey in which
martyrs murdered martyrs.[16]

Ultimately, the individual self falls apart:

I walk to myself but it dismisses me from
al-Fusṭāṭ. How often I enter the mirrors.
How often I break them, they break me.

I wake up and ask in the clothes of my corpse
about me. It laughs: we are still alive . . .

My soul has gotten broken, I'll throw my corpse
so that the raids may strike me again
and the invaders may hand me to the poem . . .[17]

How tragic it is that this tormented, fragmented voice is the same pure, cohesive voice which only a few years earlier had sung with all the faith, certainty, and sense of oneness that a poet in total unison and harmony with the collective self could possibly master. Just recall such famous earlier poems of his as "A Lover from Palestine" and "Register, I Am an Arab," and you will realize the extent of the agony I am trying to crystallize here.

7.

In the time of organic growth, poetry created an imaginative geography, an ecstatic fairyland inhabited by the dream. Only one place existed: the space ahead. The "behind" was a long history of darkness; a heavy burden. Ḥāwī and Adūnīs depicted this past in frightening images. Poetry conceived of motion as being possible only in one direction: forward. The voyage became the symbol of longing and searching for a new world, a world of the heroic, creative, humane, free, progressive, et cetera. The language of transcendence, of the There, the Beyond, flourished. The movement forward strove to transcend the wasteland and the dark cave-symbols which dominated the poetry of the period completely. The future was identified with progress (in the European sense) in a fashion reminiscent of Europe in its Renaissance.

Then fragmentation struck. Of its many manifestations, I shall concentrate for the time being, on one: the fragmentation of the subject, the "I" which views the world and experiences its presence in it in a tormenting fashion never before witnessed in Arabic writing.

8.

Early in the seventies, a young poet had written, "He had walked towards his eyes but never arrived."[18] The self was just beginning to experience what was to become a shattering process of splitting. Quite consciously, a language of division has come to be employed by poets portraying the self as being split into two or more—a sort of schizophrenia proclaimed by that part of the schizophrenic that remains "unified." One of its earliest manifestations occurred back in 1975 in a poem I wrote entitled, "The Incarnation of Kamal Abu-Deeb in His Last Centuries."[19] But the poetry of other poets became also packed with such divisions and splittings. Here is Adūnīs suffering this fate:

> Here I am as Jāsim moves further . . .
> my body separates itself from me
> and my head hurries to catch up with it.
>
> My senses travel and are almost ahead of me
> And here is my voice almost
> emanating from the larynx of the wind.

I am still walking behind the child
who continues to walk in my limbs.[20]

In fact, as it happens, one of the finest expressions of this process of splitting comes from Adūnīs in a major recent poem:

What is it that separates myself from myself?
What is it that negates me, eradicates me?
Am I a crossroad
and my path is no longer my path
at the moment of revelation?
Am I more than one person, my history is
the cliff of my fall
and my rendez-vous is my fire?
What is it that rises in a giggle that rises
from my suffocating limbs?
Am I more than one person, each asking the
other:

Who are you? And where from?
Are my limbs forests of war
in a blood which is a wind
and a body which is a leaf?[21]

9.

As I pointed out earlier, the time of organic existence witnessed a yearning for unity with the Other, this being nature, man, society, the world at large, depending on the ideological orientation of the individual poet. "I am not alone," was Adūnīs's cry after 1967, in the face of defeat and tragedy. Darwīsh's voice was ringing aloud: "Register! I am an Arab,"[22] in the face of the Zionist occupier who has constantly aimed at uprooting the Palestinians and wiping out their identity. As the winds of fragmentation blew, however, not only the sense of oneness with the Other was shattered, but also the feeling of oneness of the One itself. Conflicts, oppositions, and fragmentation have struck the I of the poet as a human being and as a creative being. War shifted from the outside to the inside; the old harmony came to be destroyed. Language itself embodied this fragmentation in some (critically) fascinating ways. The fragmentation of the subject or the object, as well as the fragmentation of the sentence, either actually—that is, on the level of its syntactic structure —or, in some types, on the level of its physical appearance on the page. Here are some instances of this latter phenomenon:

He did not complete

the twelfth
month.
            Out of the year fell
            a heavy
            window.[23]

The single cypress
is split
by its shade.

The jasmine
sheds
its
white

            time.[24]

Furthermore, even when on the semantic level the movement is towards gathering or oneness, the sentence is fragmented physically, that is, in its presence on the page.

The poppies
join
their
first
blood.[25]

suggesting a fundamental split within the very process of conceiving and enunciation, a split which goes much deeper than the power of conscious control as an organizing principle possessed by the creator. Everything undergoes the fragmentation which has struck the I of the subject as a conceiving agent, as enunciator and linguistic creator. He is no longer a structuring animal (or in Roland Barthes's phrase "a structuralist animal"); he is nonstructuring producer. His production now displays the same property: it is destructuralized. Even the air he breathes is so:

The air
is
the first
falling
word.[26]

One of the most significant forms that this fragmentation has taken is that which embodies a split within the sentence on both the semantic and the syntactic levels, as it occurs within the horizontal, linear, forward movement of the sentence. The sentence suddenly opens up in two directions (which are at times related by opposition, but are often unrelated). The splitting of the subject into two distinct I's, which I have discussed extensively in a recent paper, is thus transformed into a split within the predicate or the world. A self which has thus been completely struck by this divisive force is now incapable of resolving the conflict or reestablishing its coherent oneness. It is incapable therefore of producing a unified or integral statement. Sentences are formulated, consequently, as follows:

Your beautiful (m.f.) voice said to me
follow me
I lead you
to the forest of → the treasure
→ light.[27]

(And may I take this opportunity to draw attention to the title of this paper and the way in which the sentence splits into "self" and "text" after the words "fragmentation of.")

As you will note here, the phrase "to the forest of" splits at this point in two directions, one selects "the treasure"; the other selects "light," creating these two lines of selection (and making it difficult for Jakobson's theory[28] concerning the two lines of composition to apply). Moreover, the quoted passage splits in two directions in a much more drastic way: within the single element itself. In the position I used the "m.f." symbols, namely, after the words "your voice" (denoting masculine/feminine), a subtler, more dramatic split has taken place on the level of identity. The pronoun *k* (your) in the Arabic is vocalized simultaneously with a *fatḥa* and a *kasra,* making it both feminine and masculine at the same time and rendering the identity of the voice ambiguous or undetermined. In a culture where the pair "f./m."

form a fundamental opposition on all levels, the double nature of the voice acquires dramatic oppositional significance. Needless to say, the context (our old-fashioned means of granting significance to ambiguous words) does not possess this power here. Neither the context, nor the total structure of the poem helps to resolve the conflict or pin down the identity of the voice. It remains forever undetermined and undeterminable.

II

1.

Having thus identified fragmentation as the dominant force shaping Arabic poetry today and having described and illustrated some of its manifestations on a number of levels, especially on the level of the poetic text as a linguistic structure, I would like now to pose what seems to be an obvious question. Regardless of what fragmentation entails as a social, political, and economic phenomenon and despite all the disastrous consequences it seems to be having on the level of the nationalist dream or project and without in the least wanting to sing its praises as it takes on these levels, is the fragmentation I have been describing a negative process as far as literature in general and poetry in particular are concerned? Has fragmentation deprived poetry of its major sources of strength, of its communicability, and of its role as a force in the process of change and search for a better future which still stamps Arab life in all its aspects? And if so, is this a loss, and how much of a loss is it, for poetry? My answers will be clear, although they might not be stated forcefully. And in order to present them, I shall embark on a discussion of some of the finer qualities of the poetry written today in the space which has been created as a direct consequence of the process of fragmentation that I have been trying to depict.

As it fragments, Arabic poetry is also emerging from the thick shrouds of ideology and authority; and in this process it has been acquiring new qualities and characteristics. New attitudes to reality and the poet's relationship to it; new attitudes to the poet's relationship to his own art; as well as a more subtle, penetrating language (at times distilled like the morning dew) are beginning to take shape. In all its types, progressive or reactionary, as the political jargon goes, poetry had been, and to some extent still is, a poetry of ideas—and huge ideas for that matter. Symbolic, mythic, socialist, nationalist, revolutionary, and whatever else it has been, it has exhausted all the possibilities of utopia (a purely abstract, cerebral utopia) including the role of the poet as creator, seer (voyeur), prophet, redeemer, semigod or demigod, victim, as well as spokesman for the collective self (a highly abstract entity—if an entity at all) with all its hopes and frustrations. Admittedly, even in this sphere, its achievements have been remarkable. Adūnīs, Bayyātī, Ḥāwī, ʻAbd al-Ṣabūr, Ḥijāzī, Qabbānī, al-Khāl, al-Māghūṭ, al-Qāsim, Saʻdī Yūsuf, Darwīsh, al-Maqāliḥ, to name only a few, form a galaxy of creative beings which many other cultures would envy Arabic culture for producing almost contemporaneously in a period when poetry was at the helm and the poet was a powerful public figure. Poetry and ideology were the two shining stars of Arab life for a whole quarter of a century—the years of organic growth, faith, certainty, and confidence in the future. Oil, by then, had not even managed to light a lantern, although seas of it were flowing all across the deserts. The desert was a distant landscape, a wasteland in the literal sense as well as in the metaphoric sense of T. S. Eliot. The desert was the embodiment of all that was dead; all that poetry and ideology had come in order to destroy in the process of inventing a new life and a new geography.

Now the tide has ebbed. Poetry withdraws into a more enclosed, limited, and intimate space, limited at times to a man's bedroom or kitchen with the windows closed (Bassām Ḥajjār is an instance). It begins to stare questioningly and skeptically, to say the least, at the world, at what it had often hovered over, touching only slightly. It had been, with few exceptions, in flight across the oceans of the spirit and the world, but high above them. Now, at least in one of its types, it flutters within the sticky mud. It is down-to-earth. In its "worldliness," it opens new horizons for the human eye, the human heart and the human spirit, all of which had been rather subdued before. And in the process it acquires a degree of freedom, untypicality, and difference which it had lost for centuries. The One has exploded into Many. And the fragments are, on the whole, truly beautiful and seductive. The world is multiple and complex, language is at its freshest and lightest. It has shed the weight of history and is getting truly re-born. The beholding eye now sees things afresh. Indeed the Eye has taken over from the I, which is perhaps the most fundamental change since the emergence of modernist consciousness in the twenties and thirties.

2.

The range of experience and the aspects of reality which poetry now explores have no parallel over the past ten centuries. For reasons that I cannot now elaborate, poetry has often displayed a tendency to fall victim to ideology and authority and to develop stereotypes which quickly dominate it and erect high barriers between it and the world. Whenever this has happened, and it has happened at critical junctures in Arab history, there has been formed a poetic world constituted rigidly and economically, by which I mean that a process of reduction led to a limited set of constituents forming an artificial and clearly defined structure. This poetic world became self-generating, producing stereotypes and imitations.

Even modern poetry, after the first two decades immediately following its initial outburst, fell victim to this mechanism. Adūnīs sensed the stagnation as early as the late seventies and expressed this too strongly to be applauded by his fellow poets.[29] His contemporaries interpreted his views as meaning that they were no longer relevant; while younger poets thought that he was negating them altogether. His basic assumption was, however, valid, although it tended to hide the other side of the coin, namely, that something new was in the making, something which had not yet blossomed into a recognizable and distinct poetic climate. It is a lot easier now to see the trees and to summon the courage to talk about a new forest.

The most impressive thing about this new forest is that its trees and bushes are of such great variety. Many trees belong to identifiable species, but most do not. Some may yet prove to have the potential to generate new species altogether. Some will, no doubt, wither away and die, while others may prove to be no more than old trees which have been subjected to grafting. In certain cases, this grafting is performed in order to produce a truly new kind of tree, but in other cases it is done for reasons that do not go beyond the cosmetic. However, the process of formation and growth is truly fascinating and deserves watching and nurturing.

3.

Thus, the fragmented self is not necessarily an impoverished self. Quite the opposite, fragmentation has been, in a certain sense, identical with liberation. The fragmented self is definitely a freer self. It is, in a way, as if an iron encasement has been blown up and shattered, creating a feeling of panic and a certain degree of loss of direction and orientation. But in this state of dispersal and loss, the soul suddenly breathes the fresh breeze from virgin forests and distant, unknown lands. Its singing powers are still there; so it begins to sing more quietly, serenely, cautiously, but also more intimately and personally. The voice is imbued with sorrow, fear, uncertainty, and hesitation. Yet, in all this (maybe because of this), it is far more human; it is richer, closer to the heart and gentler (in its rhythms) on the ear. Whatever the truth is, however, one thing is certain: the voice is one of discovery and exploration, though not in the heroic, missionary, grandiose fashion of the explorers of the North Pole. It is more like a pale figure feeling his way around by touching everything gently, working out its shape, sniffing its smell, as if to make sure it is there. We do not have now a Khalīl Ḥāwī sailing with Sindbad on these frightening oceanic voyages and ending up in the river of ashes. We have poets discovering the mystery of the world right around them, or those intimate, vague, innermost emotional corners and holes inside themselves. And they do all this in the gentlest, least pompous and least emotional of ways. The great poets of vision, the poets as seers, voyeurs, prophets, demigods, are all things of bygone grandeur, glory, and elemental tragedies. Here is 'Abbās Bayḍūn "criticizing pain" (the term itself is highly significant as a title of a book of poetry)[30] and writing about it in a totally controlled, unemotional, but still rich and humane, way. In memory of a friend who died in the south of Lebanon, he writes:

> When they killed the friend they took him back. Thus, they will send me back to my family. Memories are aunts preoccupied with moistening their mirrors, making them suppler and resembling nothing but them. I used to await his visits. His light or silence or smell; his gaze also used to meet my face many times as we stared from two directions in the darkness. When we go back we do not fear formlessness. Many can jump from one station to another. In continuous insomnia there is no need or no end to lanterns. Only one equal light. Sometimes I think that peasants have blown the earth ahead of us.[31]

Note the striking absence of sentimentality (a characteristic of much poetry over the previous half century), lamentation, the rhetorical tone. Note how the poem calls the victim "the friend," not even "my" friend, erasing the I completely (the I which had dominated the poetry of the previous half century); but note especially the total fragmentation of the poem—no center, intellectual or emotional, no organic form. Indeed, quite out of the blue, the poem itself speaks of formlessness: "we do not fear formlessness," in what appears to be a sentence unrelated to anything else in the poem. It is as if formlessness has become a force filling the poet's subconscious and exploding into his text in a powerful, inorganic way in order to assert its presence. It is inorganicity uttering itself inorganically. Here is another such piece, also by Bayḍūn, also in memory 'Ayn Sīn:

Regret is the Job of Others

> They killed their children with the same brutality with which they killed their enemies. Nevertheless, the whole family is putting on its make-up inside. Sometimes I do not believe that the larger piece causes fury. All this left no ghost. Regret is truly the job of others.[32]

The last piece from Bayḍūn is this unique, detached, unemotional, physical image which is, nevertheless, full of absence and very powerful:

The Hands

> We were looking at a few blindfolded prisoners moving forward stretching their hands into the emptiness. They were surely searching for their hands.[33]

Note the total preoccupation with the external outlines and physical shapes, and the lack of any attempt to penetrate into the inner psychological states of being. Note also the total absence of the I as an active subject or as a center of action. The narrating voice merely narrates; it only observes; and it observes the purely visual. It is, as I pointed out earlier, the Eye taking over and replacing the I as the poetic center of gravity. Evident also is the cerebral twist of phrase; the clever, cool interpretation of physical reality in a way strongly reminiscent of Abū Tammām's imaginative interpretation in ancient Arabic poetry and of John Donne's or Andrew Marvell's conceits, in what is known to critics as metaphysical poetry, in seventeenth-century English literature.

4.

Just as we witnessed this cerebral, unemotional, subdued and totally non-rhetorical tone (and style) in the poetry of Bayḍūn, we witness the same qualities in the poetry of Bassām Ḥajjār. The latter, however, shows a greater degree of preoccupation with his immediate environment and the world of everyday life. In the two pieces I have selected from his volume, *Li-Arwi Ka-Man Yakhāf An Yarā* (To narrate like someone who fears to see),[34] I shall emphasize the cerebral twist of phrase, the enjambment of the heavy materiality of objects, and the light, ethereal nature of the cerebral game. Listen to this anticlimax caused by the clever shift of focus:

What if they were behind the doors
or behind the curtains
waiting
and after I close my eyes

What do you expect to come next? "They come out and stab me," as in a good detective story. I expected such a phrase. But the text disappointed me. It proved that I still thought in terms of organic growth, logical relationships, development, coherence, predictability, et cetera. What the text actually says is this:

The night begins in my absence.[35]

Imagine! What connection is there between the worried tone of the question "What if they were behind the curtains?" and the night beginning in his absence? Where is he anyway? What logic governs the poem? How does the night begin without him? I have no idea. Do you? But this is precisely my point: the death of logicality and internal coherence; the fragmentation of the world and the self; the severance of connections and relationships; and naturally the fragmentation of the text. Add to this the dominance of cerebral ingenuity. The brain is quickly replacing the heart as the source of poetic flow. The romantic agony is yielding its place to the sharp eye of the observer —an eye controlled by a critical, sardonic, ingenious mind.

5.

Similar qualities are evident in the poetry of younger poets such as Amjad Nāṣir, whose poetry is permeated by that intimate, confessional tone which arises from depicting the details of personal experience in everyday existence, from evoking the past in its vivid curves and shades, and from exploring the intimate aspects of life in exile. Here is a portrait full of sharp visual details:

Squatting

Not because they have deserted the villages
and the winged tents have they lost the yearning for squatting.
Squatting:
Sculptures of bodies dreaming on two legs
with the shape of an obtuse angle,
The eyes are the ladles of words,
as tobacco moves round on the hands which shake
the air.
Deals and anecdotes wrapped in the wax of an
extensive evening.

Disputes over the original ancestors of the
neighboring tribe
and the third grandfather of the white-spotted horse.
Cinnamon tea terminates the argument

. . . .
And all of a sudden the smell of a woman wafts
and the bones crackle.

Squatting,

You can do that at the doors of theaters
police stations
in the foggy distance
in transit lounges
and in front of the anti-terrorists' men
with your face which is gathered from a barley field.

You can squat wherever you wish.
But then,

is all squatting
really squatting?[36]

The tragedy of this younger generation—if it is a tragedy at all—is that they see the heritage they have inherited as being hollow and meaningless. Amjad Nāṣir has depicted this well when he wrote in a poem entitled "Wilderness"

How do I write my poem, when the only thing
I possess is the wreckage of description?

He goes on to say:

I went to the river, and found nothing but
pebbles and the commandments of dryness . . .
I went to wisdom, and found only the crumbs of
sermons.
I went to poetry,
and found only
the wreckage of description.[37]

6.

The emergence of a personal, intimate tone in Arabic poetry can best be illuminated by examining the work of a devoted poet like Maḥmūd Darwīsh, devoted, that is, to big issues: ideology, political struggle, national liberation, et cetera. As I have shown in a recent study,[38] Darwīsh's text gets split into two layers or sides or tones or voices. One is rhetorical, strong, high, political, collective, confident; the other is intimate, broken, sorrowful, individual, low-keyed. A lucid example is his poem "Another Year . . . Only," in which he screams at his beloved friends who have been dying for the national cause:

"My friends, my martyrs,
don't die as you used to die
. . . .
. . . .

another year only is enough,
it is enough for me to love thirty women
and thirty cities."
"Oh, don't die my friends, you traitors."[39]

In this moving elegy, and in similar elegies to friends, as well as in his other recent poetry, the burning, desperate questions which Darwīsh fires at the very heart of existence burst with an intolerable sense of the tragedy of loss, of time passing by, destroying in its crushing motion the passion for life blazing in the heart of an ordinary human being who yearns to live in a manner which both gives meaning to his everyday life and widens the scope and horizons of his experience as a sensitive, contemplative being. Limitations of space do not permit me to quote at length from this agonizing poetry (which gives Darwīsh's work a unique and vital position in the changing trajectory of Arabic poetry today). Suffice it to point out that this lust for fire as a simple, ordinary presence, breaks open like a wound as this longed-for way of life eludes the poet. The rose he plants in an attempt to taste the flavor of ordinary living blossoms into a corpse of a fighter killed on the path of martyrdom. In the absence of the possibility of a real, ordinary life, all life appears meaningless. Thus, the poet begins to dissociate himself from the big issues. What is my business with all this, he asks:

Let this city be the grandmother of the world
and whatever it wants, whatever it wants.
What business of mine is it all?
Any morning which doesn't visit me first
isn't my morning.
No . . .
What business of mine?
Any winds
which do not break me as an open space
are not my winds.
What business of mine?
Any wounds which do not create
a fresh god within me are not my wounds.
No . . .
What business of mine?
Any weapon

which does not return bread to its grains
is not my weapon.[40]

The place he loves, the place which stirs his soul, is

The place is the smell,
the coffee which opens a window,
the obscurity of the first woman,
a father who hanged a sea on a wall.
The place is the cutting desires,
my first footstep to the first legs to light up
my body, to make me recognize it
and recognize the narcissus in me.
The place is the first illness . . . a mother
squeezing the clouds in order to wash a dress . . .
The place is what there was that now prevents me
from being playful.
The place is the Fātiḥa.
The place is the first year,
the noise of the first tear,
the turning of the water towards the girls,
the pains of sex at its beginning,
and the bitter honey . . .[41]

7.

It might be purely accidental and totally insignificant (but it might not) that just as friendship in the tragic context of death has become the sphere of human existence to which Darwīsh turns to embody his tensions, frustrations, and yearning for a purely personal life, friendship has also become the focus of poems by other poets who had previously devoted much of their poetry to the collective self, to national and social issues, as they face the ultimate, tragic reality of the present state of fragmentation and collapse of the "National Project," as it is commonly called. It is as if the Other, as a self to identify with, has shrunk and been reduced from the Group, the Nation, et cetera, to the Other as one, singular, a personally defined entity. The poet's pains and sufferings are now projected onto this individual otherness as opposed to that distant, vanishing otherness of the group (no longer an easily identifiable entity with which one can feel at one).

8.

A poet in whose work friendship occupies a central domain, as a stage for the tragic and fragmentary, comes from the very southern terminus of the Arab world: Yemen. 'Abdal-'Azīz al-Maqāliḥ, quite significantly, opens his latest book of poems, *Awrāq al-Jasad al-'Ā'id min al-Mawt* (The papers of the body returning from death),[42] with a social, national elegy. The poems which follow are highly political, ideological, collective pieces. Then, quite suddenly, the book closes with two elegies for a former friend. Purely personal, intimate, confessional in tone, vaguely contemplative, these pieces contrast sharply with Maqāliḥ's poetry not only in this anthology but that of the previous fifteen years of poetic production. It is as if the I-You (singular) becomes, suddenly, the only surviving core of the I-You (plural) or "I Am You" formula (which had dominated poetry in its "organic," ideological, collective phase), but has itself now crumbled, fragmented, and been torn apart by the tempest of the new era.

On a different level, the stab in the back, in the particular context of Maqāliḥ's poetry, might symbolize the "stab in the back" performed by the homeland as a whole, by the nation, by the leaders (cf. his poem on Sādāt) upon the poet who has devoted his energies and writings to bringing about the miracle of the resurrection of the buried corpse of the nation. Here is the voice lamenting friendship, but facing betrayal with the old passion and love:

> Before you pull out the dagger
> which has sunk deep into the back,
> let me behold you
> for my blood scented as it embraced it,
> a syllable from you in its blade,
> recognized a gesture towards the old embrace
> and recognized the traces of a smell of friendship.[43]

And here is the first movement of another poem:

> To the friend who has sold me,
> I bow,
> full of pity, reverent of heart, reading in his face

our yesterday, the greenness of the childhood of our
days. Oh, dearest of comrades,
why does the dew become bitter,
the lips turn into wounds?
Why do the pearls turn into oyster shells?[44]

In fact, Maqāliḥ's entire volume is imbued with this tone and crowded with images of fragmentation and crumbling. Things appear to break, wounds to open wide. An entire life has been stormed by tragedy. The political struggle, the national dream, has collapsed—so have love, friendship, relationship with place and time. And the volume opens with a tragic poem of an earthquake. It is a real earthquake. No metaphors involved. It struck the Yemen in 1982. Every other poem following it represents the experience of facing an earthquake of one sort or another. Shaking, crumbling, splitting, destroying weave the very texture of poetic language and its imagery. But as these earthquakes progress, we move from the national, public, political, and social to the individual, private, personal and intimate. Thus, the last poems in the volume, directly preceding the two pieces on the severance of friendship, are five highly personal ones which embody the transformation affecting Arabic poetry in its entirety. In the midst of these personal tragedies, only poetry remains as a source of consolation. And it does so not by virtue of any particular quality of its own, not because of any metaphysical, life-giving or faith-inspiring power that is inherent in it—as it might be for a romantic or symbolist believer in the magical power of language and the creative process—but by its very being, by its being the activity uppermost in the poet's interaction with the world or his very presence in it.

Only one street continued to submerge me
in colorful light,
reading me, washing the fire
off my forehead and the ashes,
and carrying me along.
It is the street of poetry,
this galloping horse racing the wind and
sometimes beating it;
its hooves have had no rest
from the boulders of Time,
nor have I had a rest from the time of
boulders.[45]

Of these five poems, "Moods" embodies a state of being which I reckon to be the rising tone of Arabic poetry today. It is contemplative, tender, low-keyed, and totally personal. It is also what I call "the poetry of momentary being," as opposed to the total poem of time and space which dominated the previous two decades—the poem as a complete universe: coherent, integral, unifying past, present, and future in one sweeping vision of reality and history, the poem as organic space encompassing man's life both as an individual and as society. It is as if the new poem of momentary being has lost the sense of possibilities inherent in time as a historical process of development, change, and evolution (or revolution), and fallen victim to a self interacting with reality only in its most immediately perceived aspects. Here is one of the finest of Maqāliḥ's "moods":

The cloud is white
and the Ma'ribite peaks are washed.
What treasure of light is this
that the skies and earth are draped in?
The grass has its taste,
the earth its smell,
the soil is mirrors.
    Come near, O horizon,
    come near.
My fingers lust for you.[46]

III.

1.

Just as it is in life, so it is in poetry: nothing is born out of nothing. The personal, intimate tone I have been describing does not emerge out of nowhere; it is not a completely sudden event. It has its roots in the poetry of the previous decades; but it has now come to occupy center stage as opposed to the marginal regions within which it had blossomed and found itself restricted, even excluded, previously.

Its roots extend to the poetry of individual experience, daily life and personal search for meaning practiced by poets like Muḥammad Māghūṭ, Unsī al-Ḥājj, Sa'dī Yūsuf, and Adūnīs, especially in some of his early work.

Of these origins, I would like to consider briefly some aspects of the poetry of Sa'dī Yūsuf.

2.

While the poetry of Adūnīs, Tawfīq Ṣāyigh, and Yūsuf al-Khāl partakes of that deeply rooted preoccupation with time as an infinite metaphysical region, the poetry of Sa'dī Yūsuf reveals a tendency to negate time, not, for instance, by adopting a philosophical attitude of the variety which asserts the timelessness of the world, experience, or feeling but by focusing completely on presence as an instantaneous, momentary experience which appears luminous and forceful precisely because it exists outside the oceanic domain and tyranny of time. His is the poetry of the fleeting moment, of the spark emanating from the lightning intrusion of man into the universe of things or *vice versa,* of a still-life in which the flow of time (and awareness of it) are reduced to an absolute minimum—to mere presence as the eye of the camera opens and shuts in a flashing instant. Precisely at this flashing point, existence in a minute manifestation of its essence is captured and illuminated.

All this, as well as other characteristics, makes Sa'dī Yūsuf perhaps the poet with the finest sensibility for the poeticality of everyday life: an eye which perceives the delicate vibrations emanating from objects as they radiate warmth and humanity in the sphere of human experience. Objects for him are not primarily occasions for contemplating "hidden" affinities and meanings; they are not mere "signs" or "symbols." On the contrary, they possess a powerful material presence both in themselves and as points of interaction with the richness of man's daily exercise of his existence. But their physical power is made less forceful and sharp by virtue of the luminous language of Yūsuf's poetry. Language reduces the heaviness of objects and cuts out their sharp edges. And very often in his poetry, just as the material presence of an object begins to feel heavy, he snatches us away, with an often startling shift of focus, to an aspect of reality almost totally unrelated to the "scene" he has been depicting and, usually, of little material weight. Here are some of these shifts and juxtapositions:

1. Silence

In the silence comes the other rain,
in the silence comes the cycle of grass,

in the silence comes the first honey,
in the silence I listen to poignant wine,
exuding quietly from my skin . . . slowly,
filling the veins of the woman.[47]

Where, one asks, has the woman suddenly and mysteriously come from? Has she been lying next to him in the silence? Why didn't she make an appearance before the last word? Why was there no hint or focusing previously on her presence?

2. A Raid

The room trembles because of distant shells.
The curtains tremble
and once the heart trembles . . .
Why are you in the trembling?[48]

3. A Room

In it
there is nothing but a bookcase
and a bed
and a poster.
The jet fighter came
hurled into the air the bed
and the last book
and with its rockets it sketched
some poster.[49]

4. Allocations

What do we buy with these allocations?
We are contented with one shirt
an old pair of jeans
half a loaf and cheese
and the flowers
we gather from behind the fence.

What do we buy with the allocations?
Perhaps the moment of unification . . .[50]

5. Iraqi Martyrs

They were four in the Stairs Quarter.
Tank snipers
narrators of poems,
They had been lovers of Palestine
friends in Baghdad.
And they have become trees
in the Stairs Quarter.
Four they were in the Stairs Quarter.[51]

Altogether, the effect of Sa'dī Yūsuf's treatment of material being, as embodied in the objects and details of everyday life, is to create a feeling of transparency and lightness which shrouds the details of everyday existence (both material and experiential) in what I have called elsewhere "The Language of Absence,"[52] no matter how vivid the realities he is depicting are. Very often, the feel of Yūsuf's objects is comparable to the curving, smooth lines of Henry Moore's sculptures. Despite their powerful presence and their great mass, they are light and mellow. Yet Yūsuf is totally unsentimental and clearly unromantic. Here is one of his presentations of an ordinary scene:

Who broke this mirror,
scattered it
fragment by fragment
among the branches?
And now . . .
do we invite al-Akhḍar to look?
The colors tremble.
The image gets confused with the object
and the eyes get burnt; but al-Akhḍar
has to collect that mirror on his palm
and harmonize the pieces as he pleases.

He has to preserve the memory of the branches.[53]

It is difficult to classify this kind of poetry. It is, of course, strongly reminiscent of that great poet on the other shore of the Mediterranean, Yannis Ritsos, who has left his mark on many an Arab poet in the last fifteen years. Significantly, among those who have translated his poetry into Arabic is Saʻdī Yūsuf (as well as Adūnīs and myself). Even more significant, perhaps, is that all these translations were made after the turning point reached in Arabic poetry and the collapse of the organic world, the world of great ideas, ideologies, visions, dreams, prophecies, and mythic grandeur.

3.

To conclude then: Arabic poetry witnessed a period of organic existence and growth in which major achievements were realized. The collapse of the political-social project has been both anticipated and embodied by the poetry of the last twenty-five years. (One recalls such tragic prophecies as Ḥāwī's "Lazarus 1962," Al-Sayyāb's "The City of Sindbad," and Adūnīs's later but no less tragic "An Introduction to the History of the Party Kings.") The linguistic characteristics of the poetic text have embodied in themselves what I have called elsewhere "the epistemological structure" (in order to avoid Goldmann's term "world vision," which seems to me rather "wishy-washy") dominant in the period concerned. With the crumbling of the sociopolitical, nationalist, revivalist, secularist project, a process of fragmentation began and is still going on. Poetry itself fragmented structurally. "Structureless" structures developed; new realms of experience began to be explored. The language of poetry has acquired the properties of fragmentation and nonorganicity pertaining to the nonlinguistic world, the world of actual experience, of presence in reality. Things are thus in a state of flux: the shape of things to come is very difficult to predict. But my own feeling is that exciting things will crystallize at the end of what appears to be a period of free exploration. The twenty-first century—if we all survive to witness it—carries, I think, great promise and possibilities. Let us all hope that we will be there to see the realization of these promises. Meanwhile, let us try to maintain our own wholesomeness and resist the winds of fragmentation blowing against our chests. We might succeed. We might not. At least we should be fully aware of the probabilities facing us. I hope this paper has helped in some minute way to sharpen, if not to create, such an awareness.

1988–1989

Notes

1. The phrase is the actual title of his book *The Struggle of the Modern* (London: Hamish Hamilton, 1963).

2. See Jürgen Habermas, "Modernity—An Incomplete Project," in *Postmodern Culture,* ed. Hal Foster (London and Sydney: Pluto Press, 1985), 3–15.

3. See "Cultural Creation in a Fragmented Society," in *The Next Arab Decade: Alternative Futures,* ed. Hisham Sharabi (Boulder, Colorado: Westview Press, and London: Mansell Publishing, 1988), 160–81. An Arabic translation of this book had been published in 1987 by Markaz Dirāsāt al-Waḥda al-'Arabiyya, Beirut.

4. In a paper presented in 1984 at a conference in Lunds, Sweden, sections of which were later published in a three-part study, "Al-Laḥẓa al-Rāhina li-al-Shi'r," *Al-Shāhid* 38 (October 1988), 76–81; 41 (January 1989): 106–10; and 44 (April 1989): 48–90.

5. Adūnīs ('Alī Aḥmad Sa'īd), *Iḥtifā'an bi-al-Ashyā' al-Ghāmiḍa al-Wāḍiḥa* (Beirut: Dār al-Ādāb, 1988).

6. Adūnīs, *Iḥtifā'an,* 15–18.

7. Adūnīs, *Al-Ḥayā(t)* (London) 15 March 1989.

8. Adūnīs, *Al-Ḥayā(t).*

9. Adūnīs, *Iḥtifā'an,* 75.

10. Adūnīs, *Iḥtifā'an,* 27,31.

11. Adūnīs, *Iḥtifā'an,* 45, 27, and 30, respectively.

12. Adūnīs, *Iḥtifā'an,* 65 and 67.

13. See Maḥmūd Darwīsh, *Dīwān Maḥmūd Darwīsh,* 10th ed. (Beirut: Dār al-'Awda, 1983), 595 ff.

14. Maḥmūd Darwīsh, *Ḥiṣār li-Madā'iḥ al-Baḥr,* 2nd. ed. (Beirut: Dār al-'Awda, 1985), 90. The first edition was published in 1984 in Tunis.

15. Darwīsh, *Ḥiṣār,* 135–6.

16. Darwīsh, *Ḥiṣār,* 149.

17. Darwīsh, *Ḥiṣār,* 38–39, 94, 95, respectively.

18. Richard Milḥem, "Mashā Ṭawīlan Ṣawba 'Aynayhi wa-lam Yaṣil," *Mawāqif* (Beirut), 17–18 (December 1971): 95.

19. Kamāl Abū Dīb, "Taqammuṣāt Kamāl Abū-Dīb fī 'Uṣūrih al-Akhīra," *Mawāqif* (Beirut), 30–31 (winter-spring 1975).

20. Adūnīs, *Iḥtifā'an,* 71, 70 and 57, respectively.

21. Adūnīs, *Kitāb Ḥiṣār: al-Ḥazīrān 82-Ḥazīrān 85,* (Beirut:Dār al-Ādāb, 1985),13.

22. Darwīsh, *Dīwān,* 73.

23. Paul Shāwūl, *Wajhan Yasquṭ wa-Lā Yasīl* (Beirut: Dār al-Nahār, 1981), 19.

24. Shāwūl, *Wajhan,* 28, 30.

25. Shāwūl, *Wajhan,* 31.

26. Shāwūl, *Wajhan,* 34.

27. Kamāl Abū Dīb, "Thumma Ba'da al-Ṣamt," *Al-Quds al-'Arabī* (London) 22, no. 2 (1996). The poem was written in 1984.

28. These are the axis of selection and the axis of combination. See, for instance, his study of aphasia in Roman Jakobson and Morris Halle, *Fundamentals of Language,* 2nd ed. (The Hague: Mouton, 1971).

29. See Adūnīs, *Fātiḥa li-Nihāyāt al-Qarn* (Beirut: Dār al-'Awda, 1980), especially pages 270–80 and the chapter entitled "Bayān al-Ḥadātha" (313–40), which had originally appeared as "Awhām al-Ḥadātha." He has since repeated these views on a number of occasions, expressing them in even stronger terms; see, for instance, *Al-Shi'riyya al-'Arabiyya* (Beirut: Dār al-Ādāb, 1985), 110–12.

30. The phrase is the actual title of his book, *Naqd al-'Alam* (Criticizing pain) (Beirut: Dār al-Maṭbū'āt al-Sharqiyya, 1978).

31. Bayḍūn, *Naqd al-'Alam,* 9.

32. Bayḍūn, *Naqd al-'Alam,* 10.

33. Bayḍūn, *Naqd al-'Alam,* 11.

34. Bassām Ḥajjār, *Li-Arwi Ka-Man Yakhāf An Yarā* (Beirut: Dār al-Maṭbū'āt al-Sharqiyya, 1985).

35. Ḥajjār, *Li-Arwi,* 88.

36. See Bassām Ḥajjār, *Ru'āt al-'Uzla* (Amman: Manārāt, 1986), 155–58.

37. Ḥajjār, *Ru'āt al-'Uzla,* 43.

38. Kamāl Abū Dīb, "Al-Laḥẓa al-Rāhina li-al-Shi'r," pt. 2, *Al-Shāhid* 41 (January 1989): 106–10.

39. In Darwīsh, *Ḥiṣār, 85.*

40. Darwīsh, *Ḥiṣār,* 126–7.

41. Darwīsh, *Ḥiṣār,* 128–9.

42. 'Abd al-'Azīz al-Maqāliḥ, *Awrāq al-Jasad al-'Ā'id min al-Mawt* (Beirut: Dār al-Ādāb, 1986).

43. Maqāliḥ, *Awrāq,* 91.

44. Maqāliḥ, *Awrāq,* 93.

45. Maqāliḥ, *Awrāq,* 82.

46. Maqāliḥ, *Awrāq,* 84.

47. Sa'dī Yūsuf, *Dīwān Sa'dī Yūsuf,* vol. 2 (Beirut: Dār al-'Awda, 1988), 290.

48. Yūsuf, *Dīwān,* 286.

49. Yūsuf, *Dīwān,* 274.

50. Yūsuf, *Dīwān,* 279.

51. Yūsuf, *Dīwān,* 283.

52. In Kamāl Abū Dīb, "Lughat al-Ghiyāb fī Qaṣīdat al-Ḥadātha," *Fuṣūl* 8, nos. 3–4 (December 1989): 77–105.

53. Yūsuf,*Dīwān,* 78. Yūsuf's texts quoted here were all written between 1980 and 1982. The characteristics they display were, however, evident in his poetry from the seventies.

Contesting Languages: Tawfīq Yūsuf 'Awwād's *Ṭawāḥīn Bayrūt*

Sabah Ghandour

Tawfīq Yūsuf 'Awwād's *Ṭawāḥīn Bayrūt*[1] is a *Bildungsroman,*[2] a narrative of developing awareness. The novel tells a story of an individual performance, that of Tamīma Naṣṣūr, who fits into the category of "problematic heroine" as defined by Goldmann: "a character whose existence and values confront [her] with insoluble problems of which [she] cannot be clearly and rigorously conscious."[3] Tamīma arrives at Beirut from her village in southern Lebanon, Mahdiyya, to fulfill her dreams of education and freedom. In Beirut she experiences a series of sexual, romantic, and political adventures that contribute to her construction as a bourgeois autonomous subject who is willing to take the world into her own hands.

At the level of narrative as discourse, *Ṭawāḥīn Bayrūt* presents the developments and disappointments in Tamīma's life and the various social and political changes in Lebanese society in a very structured manner. The novel is divided into four parts, each of which is headed by an epigraph conveying the mood and movement of that particular section. Each part is divided in turn into many chapters, each focusing on a specific character or event. It is important to note that 'Awwād calls each of the novel's divisions a *ḥalqa* (circle), a term in Arabic that denotes an intellectual or a spiritual gathering or meeting. The literal translation of the term means a "link" which usually connects the different parts of a chain. *Ḥalqa* is also used to mean one of the consecutive episodes of a soap opera series. This term, however, is rarely used to designate divisions of a book as 'Awwād uses it in this novel. Thus, when each of the *ḥalaqāt* (pl. of *ḥalqa*) presents an "episode" in Tamīma's life and leads to another, it actually shows the linear development of Tamīma's consciousness about herself and the world she is experiencing. *Ḥalqa* also suggests the idea of a closed narrative. Moreover, the epigraph heading each of the four parts is a discourse projecting its contents, which unfold Tamīma's educational development.[4]

Ṭawāḥīn Bayrūt is presented through a disembodied narrative voice lying outside the parameters of history and is quite removed from the stories it is telling. This voice,[5] which orchestrates the different discourses employed in the novel, tells the story of Tamīma's search for identity and place in a society clouded with political and sectarian divisions. The disembodied voice telling a story from which it is absent also presents a specific vision of the development of Tamīma and other characters in the novel. This voice, however, is not a neutral one that recounts incidents objectively. On the contrary, it interferes in the narrative, comments on the characters' actions, and expresses their inner thoughts and feelings. Put differently, it actively engages with the characters' voices. From the beginning of the novel to the end, it orients the events in order to produce certain effects.[6]

Ṭawāḥīn Bayrūt utilizes various discourses to present Tamīma's development. These discourses, which constitute Tamīma as a free subject, problematize the narrative by not allowing it to be reduced merely to its sexual, romantic, sociopolitical components. In other words, these discourses, while presenting the diversified nature of Lebanese society, call into question its very nature and composition. The diversified nature of this society—as a center of commerce where economy is based mainly on services and as an intellectual milieu where free speech dominates and revolutionary voices challenge the dominant ideology—is conveyed in *Ṭawāḥīn Bayrūt* through *heteroglossia,* the internal stratification of language into different discourses. However, the historical conditions, whether they are related to socioeconomic, political, or ideological issues, are necessary for the production of meaning. For, the stratification of language, as Bakhtin puts it, serves "the specific sociopolitical purposes of the day."[7] The different discourses, "whatever the principle underlying them and making each unique, are specific points of view on the world, [they are] forms for conceptualizing the world in words, . . . each characterized by its own objects, meanings and values."[8] Whether they are related to politics, religion, or social issues, the diversified world views of the speaking subjects are brought together in the form of contesting languages that can be examined from different angles. Moreover, the inclusion of different genres (diary, letter, news-clips, and poetry) is another form of *heteroglossia,* of organizing narrative to produce certain effects or meanings. While enriching the narrative artistically, these various genres help to bring to the fore the individualized speeches and concerns of the characters in both a direct and indirect manner. For, the different genres help to "stratify. . . and further intensify [the novel's] speech diversity in fresh ways."[9]

Ṭawāḥīn Bayrūt can be characterized as representing a "diversity of speech types and diversity of individual voices, artistically organized."[10] Bakhtin's elaboration on the multiform of style and specifically of speech is mainly a discussion of the different ideological positions of the speaking subjects. The discourses of these subjects can be analyzed as contesting languages of various characters—specifically of Hānī and Ramzī—whom Tamīma meets in Beirut. By "contesting" I mean that these discourses are not only different from each other, projecting different world views, but they are also orchestrated in such a way as to serve as a counterpoint to each other in their effect on Tamīma as an object of contestation and desire. Most of the men in this novel try to win Tamīma over, whether intellectually, romantically, economically, or through violence.[11] The common denominator among these men is their endeavor to possess her sexually. As we shall see, the discourses of Ramzī and Hānī project different world views related to socioeconomic and political realities, but they also represent specific subjectivities, each of which contributes to the general picture of Lebanese society that the novel conveys. Each of the voices is invested with an agency which not only marks that character's subjectivity but also calls for the constitution of an autonomous subject.

Each of the discourses, however, points to a kind of subjectivity the Lebanese state would like to create, mainly bourgeois. The construction of various subjects with their autonomous discourses projects a war that is waged at the level of ideology. The discourse of Ramzī Ra'd, for example, is diametrically dialogized,[12] set in conflict, with the discourse of Hānī Rā'ī; Ramzī's point of view, his evaluation of social issues, and his emphasis on changing the social structure is opposed to Hānī's understanding of these issues.

Both Ramzī Ra'd and Hānī Rā'ī, Tamīma's lovers, contribute to her consciousness of herself as a woman and as a politically conscious subject. In other words, each interacts with Tamīma as an "ideologue," with his own words serving as "ideologemes." For "[i]t is precisely as ideologemes that discourse becomes the object of representation in the novel."[13] On the one hand, Ramzī Ra'd, a journalist and poet, utilizes the discourse of a revolutionary leftist ideologue; on the other, Hānī Rā'ī represents the discourse of a right-wing idealist. However, these men's discourses, while shaping Tamīma intellectually, emotionally, and ideologically, contribute first and foremost to her consciousness of herself as an autonomous sexual subject. Put differently, the political issues in this novel are inextricably intertwined with sexual awareness.

We can break down Ramzī Ra'd's discourse into many other languages. For the internal stratification of language is not necessarily found only in contesting languages of different characters but also within a single character's discourse.[14] Ramzī's inflammatory discourse, delivered while addressing students at meetings, differs from both his critical articles against the Yaghmūrīs, the feudal lords in the Biqā' valley, and the poetic, honeyed words he addresses to Tamīma. Ramzī uses "poetic" language[15] as a tool to lure and seduce women generally, and Tamīma specifically.

Another language that Ramzī employs is that of a revolutionary who agitates students for action against the prevalent authorities:

> You, the student [*sic*] who demonstrated, the rulers saw you as you filled the streets and squares. They heard your voice as you shouted in their faces: "No! I do not believe you! I have no faith in you! I reject you!" From the universities voices will rise cursing! And hands will be lifted to the skies like bayonets![16]

The inflammatory language of Ramzī ("do not believe," "have no faith," "reject") instigates the students to oppose the government's policies and to reject its rules and regulations. Ramzī's discourse, epitomized by the title of his article, "No," cannot be understood fully without situating it in the sociohistorical context of the 1967 Arab-Israeli war. As a consequence of that conflict, Arab peoples seriously questioned the legitimacy of their governments. Lebanon, an intellectuals center and a bastion of free speech during that period, witnessed an intense debate that included the questioning of dominant ideologies and calls for change. As Tabitha Petran notes, "the 1967 war deepened the basic cleavages in Lebanese society."[17] These cleavages between the right wing and the progressive camps; between internationalizing Lebanon and making it "another Switzerland"; and between revising "outdated institutions to eliminate sectarian privileges and [allowing] Lebanon to assume its national responsibilities in the Arab world"[18] were best exemplified among the student body in Lebanon. The "No" of Ramzī implies his "rejection" of the idea of westernizing Lebanon and his disbelief in the mechanism of the Lebanese state's ability to defend itself against Israeli raids in the south and in Beirut. 'Awwād's novel presents several incidents related to these issues.

Ramzī Ra'd's discourse is socially oriented towards the makers of the future. He believes that what is needed is a revolution led by the students, one that involves a social and class conflict of "masters and slaves," as the title of his book of that name indicates. It is a revolution which should start with university students and spread throughout the country: "It would be the first of historical revolutions against oppression and coercion, against ignorance and poverty. A revolt of slaves against masters."[19]

However, the "No" of Ramzī Ra'd is echoed by the "No" of Tamīma when he rapes her:

> 'No! No! No!' She screamed only when she felt his hardness against her most secret softness. Up to then it was as if she were watching a film or walking in her sleep. . . . She tried to hold him off with both hands, and closed her eyes, falling back on the broad low bed. The only thing she remembered was that she screamed like someone being murdered. 'No! No! No!'[20]

The revolutionary/public "No" echoes the personal / private "No," but on a very different level. On a deeper level of signification, Ramzī who instigates the students to employ "No" in their discourses and actions does not heed Tamīma's negatives in resisting his sexual assault. Ramzī's act shows a total discrepancy between his words and actions. In fact, Ramzī is quite aware of this divergence. He tells Madame Rose:

> Me? I too hire out my soul. I hire it out to words. Words! Words! Words! Between me and some words there are contractual relationships like those registered with the notary. But most of them come and go, just like that, with no previous agreement between us. . . . The main thing is that I cannot bear to live without them. . . . Every word, like every woman, has its mystery. What is she hiding in the folds of her dress? Yes, words are girls. . . . And I prefer the virgins among them, even when I'm writing about whores.[21]

The comparison of words and women is very significant. Ramzī's fascination with the novelty of words rivals his fascination with new "virgin" women, something reflected in his rape of Tamīma. The poet and journalist is always searching for new words with which to lure his women/readers.[22] He is well aware that words taken at their value are means of deception and betrayal. For, even when words signify their referential meanings, they do not necessarily imply the speaker's intentions. Their function is similar to those used in a contractual agreement; their meanings do not exist outside the contract. Ramzī realizes that Tamīma "loved [his] words. She loved [him] by mistake. She mistook [his] words for [him]. [His] words are not [him]self."[23] In fact, Ramzī admits that his construction of himself as a revolutionary is an illusory and fake image.

It is significant to note how Ramzī perceives language as a tool to be used and abused at the same time. He is quite aware of language's function as medium for controlling minds and spirits. While his poetic words are used to seduce women, his political discourse is employed to seduce students into perceiving him as a leader. His articles against the Yaghmūrīs show his masterfulness and utter deception in using language. At the death bed of Madame Rose, Ramzī delivers a speech that completely contradicts his published speeches, showing that he is capable of using language for the sake of fun and not for any particular vested interest.

Power in this novel does not necessarily mean the exertion of force and coercion over certain entities or individuals. Power can work more insidiously by permeating discourses and consequently affecting the behavior of individuals and groups. While, on the surface, Ramzī's discourse calls for the liberation of women, for a new revolutionary individual, and for the elimination of the feudal lords, Hānī Rā'ī, Tamīma's other lover, wages a war against Ramzī Ra'd on an ideological level. Hānī's discourse, while calling for an autonomous individual, also tries to build bridges across communal life in Lebanese society.

Hānī Rā'ī, an engineering student at St. Joseph University, is a major factor in the development of Tamīma's political awareness. Hānī's discourse is set in opposition to that of Ramzī, though without actual confrontation. Compared to Ramzī, Hānī is a pacifist. Although he participates in the peaceful student demonstrations, he vehemently criticizes Ramzī's call for revolution. He considers Ramzī an anarchist, "spreading doubts about everything, lighting fires, turning liberty into license."[24] While Hānī supports the students' demands for better educational institutions, he abhors the chaotic and unorganized demonstrations. According to Hānī, revolution would be madness:

> "Of course it is! Most of it is madness, but behind all the madness lies a great transformation. The rejection of all the values people have believed in and held sacred up to now. A revolt against all authority and a rejection of every principle. The destruction of everything. And what for? No one knows?"[25]

Hānī's ambivalence about the students' revolt is very telling. While he endorses reforms, he also believes that it should come from within the system, preserving authority's sacred and legal rights. He believes in maintaining family and societal values that endorse the patriarchal system. Although Hānī feels uncomfortable with the students' strikes, he feels very strongly that "Israel is the Number One nightmare and the greatest challenge. She is the latest of the plagues of the Old Testament."[26] Thus Hānī's discourse takes on important political issues: that of Arab reality, the Palestinian debacle, and Israel. For Hānī, the Fedayeen, while attacking the Zionists in Israel, are in fact "striking at the very heart of the Arabs. They are pricking our consciences awake with their bullets."[27] Hāni's perspective on all Arab countries is intended as a criticism of Arab disunity, of outdated regimes, and of ineffectiveness in responding to the Zionist challenge.

Hānī also evokes the sectarian issue by means of the letter form. The first letter that Tamīma receives from Hānī includes an inquiry whether she knows of Ḥasīb, a Shi'ī man from her district who has been appointed as a teacher in Hānī's village. The subsequent discussions between them and the various political and social gatherings they attend explore the sectarian issue, mainly with reference to its historical roots. Sectarianism, Hānī explains to Tamīma, is

> a throw-back to the days of Hikmat Bey and the Ottomans. Back to 1860. Are they asking the students to revolt? I'll tell you what revolt Lebanon expects from us. We've had the period of conflict between Christians and Muslims that carried on even under the shadow of French Mandate. After that we had the spell of peaceful co-existence, the tightrope walk that followed independence. Now the time's come for the two communities to merge. Blood ties—that's the question for Lebanon. That's the question the *Outlook* magazine article has forced on us.[28]

Hānī's discourse points to three major issues related to sectarianism: it grounds the sectarian conflict in its historical context of the 1860 peasant revolt; it refers to sectarianism's enforcement by the colonizing power, France; and it refers to its perpetuation since Lebanon's independence in 1943. Hānī reiterates bluntly that "peaceful co-existence" between the different communities in Lebanon is a "spell"; it is a façade behind which more poignant issues are buried. This façade springs out as a power struggle, manifesting itself in the debate between the supporters and the adversaries of the Muslim teacher in Hānī's village. Father André, whom Hānī supports, holds documents implicating the *mukhtār*'s (village headman's) office in "eating away the church's lands by falsifying the books."[29] The power struggle is not only between the different communities but also within one's own sect. Furthermore, Hānī's discourse raises the question of the future of Lebanon; it invokes the survey taken by the magazine *Outlook* that presents statistics about students favoring the abolition of the sectarian system from all institutions and approving of marriages among the various sects.

In another scene, Hānī's discourse dwells on a more fundamental issue, that of the "confessional God" who is not "a big problem." For He is "the God of . . . politics and the sharing out of official jobs."[30] Hānī believes that the Lebanese could find a solution to the question of the confessional God. Hānī's interpretation of the crisis is of a metaphysical nature, based on

> the flight from heaven to earth . . . on doubt in God, Tamīma. In the final analysis, isn't God just a symbol of values? No, I mean the sum total of the values that make man a creature that deserves the name.[31]

Hānī's analysis of the Lebanese crisis avoids a very fundamental issue: that of economic base and class structure. While the "confessional God" could be dealt with by abolishing the confessional system, by admitting the students to the university on the basis of merit rather than the sectarian system, by providing health care for all Lebanese by advocating civil and intercommunity marriages, Hānī omits the socioeconomic base from his argument. Ḥasīb, the Muslim teacher, is ridiculed by his adversaries for helping his father, the "pot-cleaner,"[32] while a youngster. The villagers' argument goes beyond the fact that Ḥasīb is a Muslim; it is a class argument about a "potcleaner" educating their children. Moreover, the *mukhtār*'s words themselves point to the class division in which Hānī Rā'ī himself is included:

> I'll break his skull for him, that scoundrel of a boy, Hani, son of Tannus, the son of a shepherd. I'll pull his beard out and make the other fellow, follow his father, that potcleaner, to the grave.[33]

It is important to note that Hānī's Arabic surname, "Rā'ī," means "shepherd." The village headman employs a pun intending to put Hānī down by placing him in a lower class than his middle class upbringing. Moreover, the *mukhtār* evokes a generational distinction between those who possess the traditional wisdom like himself and the new generation, represented by Hānī, who lack the knowledge and experience of the older generation.

With all their ramifications and stratifications, the discourses of Ramzī and Hānī are not to be considered only as mere contesting views of the world, but also as discourse affecting the shaping of Tamīma's "ideological becoming."[34] Tamīma has assimilated the revolutionary potential embodied by her lovers' discourses. On the one hand, she has appropriated the libertine views of Ramzī Ra'd on love and freedom of women and, for the most part, his revolutionary discourse as well. On the other hand, she has assimilated Hānī's political outlook on Arab unity and the struggle against Zionism. The process whereby Tamīma assimilates her two lovers' discourses can be broken down further into what Bakhtin calls "authoritative discourse" and "internally persuasive discourse." Authoritative discourse is indivisible; it has to be either totally accepted or rejected. Moreover, it is a discourse connected to a past that is regarded as hierarchical such as that of a father, a respected rhetorician, or a religious man. Internally persuasive discourse is the appropriation and transmission of another's discourse, which shapes the individual's ideological becoming through assimilation.[35] Tamīma regards Ramzī as an authority figure. He is the celebrated poet and journalist whom she has known and cherished previously only through his printed words. So, it is not surprising that, when she meets him for the first time, she feels embarrassed when her landlady calls him by his first name, accusing her of "breaching the sanctuary of famous names."[36] In addition, Ramzī's discourse on the freedom of women and love has become Tamīma's own conviction and belief. His words, "the only sacred thing about love is—Liberty" have become hers, and she acts upon them in the belief that she is the mistress of her destiny, able to dispose with her body as she pleases. Put differently, while for Ramzī his words are merely a discourse, for Tamīma, they represent a whole value system.

Likewise, Tamīma assimilates Hānī's political views on the Palestinian-Israeli problem and acts upon them. In both situations—with Ramzī and Hānī—we rarely see Tamīma engaged in extensive dialogues; she rarely asks questions. However, in both situations we see her act, indicating her assimilation of the two men's discourses. For "another's discourse performs here no longer as information, directions, rules, models and so forth—but strives rather to determine the very basis of our ideological interrelations with the world, the very basis of our behavior."[37] Tamīma's final act of joining the commando forces precisely exemplifies the process of assimilation. She has been constructed throughout the novel as an independent woman who "will live [her] life as [she] wants" and who wants her "place in life before [her] place in society." So her final act, to "live" her life outside society, is an extension of her defiant and autonomous subjectivity.

By joining the commandos at the end of the novel, Tamīma is almost fulfilling her "destiny." As I mentioned above, her educational development can be followed throughout the narrative. Her coming to consciousness of herself as an autonomous subject unfolds in the narrative as she approaches her "destiny." It is important to note that the Arabic term used for "destiny" is *maṣīr,* connoting a state of becoming, and not the term *qadar,* which implies a fatalistic and metaphysical condition. While the four epigraphs heading the different sections unfold Tamīma's "destiny" in chronological order, they also present her coming to consciousness of herself.[38] The first epigraph depicts Tamīma's passivity in that section and equates her to "candles" and "morning." The second epigraph projects traditional self-expression where both the waltz and the wailing of Karbalā' are extremely structured manners of self-expression. The third epigraph shows Tamīma moving away from a belief that things happen to her through a metaphysical power, to finally creating her own *maṣīr* as the fourth epigraph presents. Throughout her search for identity, Tamīma assumed that agency has come from the individuals around her. She assumes that her brother, Jābir, his deputy, Ḥusayn, and even her emigrant father have the power to direct and control the events in her life. At the end, she places the agency in the hands of destiny, "It's my fate—irresistible fate—that has willed this."[39] "This" in Tamīma's discourse refers to her act of abandoning society, "to fight under any sky against all legal codes and traditions sanctioned by society."[40] It is important to note that during Tamīma's search a major issue is her desire for a "place in life before a place in society," as she had previously told Hānī.

Her pressing question about the difference between a "Phoenician" and an "Arab" seems to be answered by her final act, as she constructs herself as an Arab whose destiny is linked to other Arab subjects. Put differently, Tamīma becomes aware of her own oppression and develops a sense of solidarity with other oppressed groups.

Tamīma, then, assumes Ramzī's revolutionary role not only in words but also in action. She realizes that by joining the Fedayeen she will be going away to face a series of unpredictable possibilities which may engender change. The last entry which Tamīma writes to Hānī in her diary suggests that she is assuming Ramzī's role in "naming." In this entry, the word "name" recurs four times, and Ramzī, who has all along been naming, insinuating, directing, and ordering, disappears from the novel. Tamīma takes over his function in "naming" a new social order. In fact, Ramzī disappears with Madame Rose as she dies, and Tamīma refers to him in her last entry as "the bearer of that name,"[41] suggesting Ramzī's effacement with respect to her. Moreover, the last sentence in Tamīma's entry, "no more will be heard of the name of Tamīma Naṣṣūr,"[42] also suggests that, while the name itself, "Tamīma Naṣṣūr," will vanish, its agency or instrumentality will continue to play a role in changing the "legal codes and traditions."

On a different level of signification, Tamīma, by joining the Fedayeen, becomes the voice of revolutionary change. In fact, this revolutionary role has been assumed by Tamīma even before her final act of transcending society. Hānī has trusted Tamīma with summarizing the "enquiry carried out by one of the papers" about whether Lebanon needs a "white or red" revolution. It is significant that, while Tamīma is reading the summaries, we are also reading her mind about the letter Hānī has received from Ḥusayn.[43] Here public revolutionary issues are juxtaposed with private ones. In fact, all the guests at the Friends Party agree that what is needed first and foremost is a revolution "of the self." This diffusion between the public and private is further enhanced at another Friends' meeting during which Tamīma plans to tell Hānī "who she is." In this scene issues related to individual and communal principles and responsibilities—dignity, hypocrisy, honesty, and treachery—are discussed on a public/political level. Tamīma, however, interprets them on a purely private level, "our marriage shall not be a marriage of hypocrisy."[44]

We gain insight into Tamīma's development and maturation not only through her interaction and involvement with other characters but also through her own self-inscription. Tamīma is frequently involved in receiving or writing letters. Although the only letters she writes are directed to Hānī, she receives letters from Hānī, Ramzī, her father in Africa, and her best friend, Mary. The first letter she writes brings up the general topic of Arab women. Tamīma has received a postcard from Hānī while he is in Libya visiting his father, showing a veiled Arab woman. Tamīma's reaction to this card is very telling; the veil which conceals the physical beauty of a woman, she says, has in reality not as large an effect on the woman as the thicker one placed on her soul.[45] Tamīma writes this letter to Hānī after seeing Ramzī for several weeks and receiving a love letter from him. Tamīma, who has come to Beirut with dreams of freedom and realizing her individuality, represents herself as entangled in a relationship with Ramzī as if she were watching a television soap opera where the incidents were happening to someone else. This portrayal of Tamīma is in fact related to the overall structure of the novel in which the divisions are labeled as "episodes" (as noted earlier).

Moreover, the diary form reveals the hypnotic nature of Tamīma's relationship with Ramzī. It is only through Tamīma's diary that we know what she thinks of her relationship with Ramzī. Her infatuation with the poet's verses is that of a naive woman who mistakes the words of the poet for the person himself. As noted above, Tamīma regards Ramzī as an authority figure, which may explain why, when she meets him accidentally in the street, she obeys his order to follow him without even questioning their destination. However, the only insight we get about Tamīma's relationship with Ramzī is through her diary entries:

> Today for the first time I felt the chill of death. I saw love stretched out on the bed with no soul. Love is ugly after it dies. It is like all corpses, and it stinks the way they do.[46]

This is the most telling entry about the way Tamīma views her relationship with Ramzī. One could argue that Tamīma doesn't know what she wants, since she keeps meeting Ramzī in spite of her own admission in another entry that she loves Hānī and dreams of marrying him. A stronger argument would emphasize that Tamīma knows quite well the difference between love and sex. Her relationship with Ramzī fills her with pride that she has conquered the poet even on a very primordial level. "If only people could see the ears of the great writer, Ramzī Ra'd, between the legs of Tamīma Naṣṣūr."[47]

In the tradition of *Bildungsroman, Ṭawāḥīn Bayrūt* presents Tamīma undergoing a series of developments and changes. Tamīma has developed from being a passive recipient of events to being a fully active and conscious subject participating in their making. The moment of change in Tamīma's life comes when she becomes an agent, initiating action and assuming control over her "destiny." Tamīma, however, constructs herself, not only through action but also through discourse. She manages to find subjectivity by using different discourses. She maneuvers her way by using the contesting languages of Ramzī and Hānī in order to create a discourse of herself. At the end of the novel, it is not only the voices of Ramzī and Hānī that disappear but also that of the "disembodied narrative voice." The last voice that we hear in the novel is that of Tamīma writing her last letter and diary entry to Hānī. The diary, as a literary form, is usually addressed to oneself, and the letter, as another literary form, is usually addressed to others. Both forms collapse into one, indicating the maturity of Tamīma as a private/public individual who is now taking responsibility for her own actions.

Notes

1. Tawfīq Yūsuf 'Awwād, *Ṭawāḥīn Bayrūt,* 4th ed. (1972; rpt. Beirut: Maktabat Lubnān, 1985); published in English as *Death in Beirut,* trans. Leslie McLoughlin, (1976; rpt. Washington, D.C.: Three Continents Press, 1984). All references to this novel are from these editions; the first Arabic numeral refers to the Arabic text and the second (in parentheses), to the English translation.

2. Muḥsin Jāsim al-Mūsawī, "Ḥawl Mafhūmay al-Shakhṣiyya wa-al-Buṭūla fī al-Riwāya al-'Arabiyya," *Al-Mawqif al-Adabī* 104–5 (December 1979 and January 1980), 182.

3. Lucien Goldmann, *Towards a Sociology of the Novel* (London: Tavistock Publications, 1975), 130, n. 31.

4. These discourses, while engaging with the contents of the novel, function as "prolepsis," which Gérard Genette defines as "any narrative maneuver that consists of narrating or evoking in advance an event that will take place later." See *Narrative Discourse: An Essay in Method,* trans. by Jane Lewin (Ithaca: Cornell University Press, 1980), 40.

5. Gérard Genette employs the paradigm "extradiegetic-heterodiegetic" in order to designate the narrator's status to the level of the story and his or her relationship to it. See G. Genette, *Narrative Discourse.*

6. See *Ṭawāḥīn Bayrūt,* especially pages 8–9 (2); 30 (18); 29 (17); 162 (110).

7. M. M. Bakhtin, "Discourse in the Novel," in *The Dialogic Imagination,* ed. Michael Holquist, trans. Caryl Emerson and Michael Holquist (Austin: University of Texas Press, 1981), 263.

8. Bakhtin, "Discourse," 291–92.

9. Bakhtin, "Discourse," 321.

10. Bakhtin, "Discourse," 263.

11. Ramzī Ra'd is the one who rapes Tamīma and with whom she develops a sexual relationship entirely void of emotional commitment; Hānī Rā'ī is involved romantically with Tamīma. Both men try to win her both intellectually and romantically in their different ways. Akram Jurdī, a lawyer, tries to win her over by bribing her and securing a job for her. Ḥusayn Qammū'ī, her brother's friend, assaults her sexually and later slashes her face because of her relationship with Ramzī.

12. On a very preliminary level, "dialogism" can be equated with dialogue. On a higher level of signification, Bakhtin observes that "the relationships of agreement/disagreement, affirmation/supplementation, question/answer . . .

are . . . dialogic relationships," in *Problems of Dostoevesky's Poetics,* trans. by Caryl Emerson (Minneapolis: University of Minnesota Press, 1987), 188.

13. Bakhtin, "Discourse," 333.

14. Bakhtin, "Discourse," 272.

15. The poem that Ramzī writes to Tamīma after their first meeting exemplifies poetry as seduction, "To one who escaped from her self, and left her shadow with me and her fragrance in my soul. Shall I say to you, "Come back! . . . I shall be waiting for you, I who found myself in you, and whose shadow is with you wherever you may be": *Ṭawāḥīn Bayrūt,* 35–36 (21–22).

16. *Ṭawāḥīn Bayrūt,* 30 (17).

17. Tabitha Petran, *The Struggle over Lebanon* (New York: Monthly Review Press, 1987), 95.

18. Petran, *Struggle,* 95–96.

19. *Ṭawāḥīn Bayrūt,* 29 (17).

20. *Ṭawāḥīn Bayrūt,* 41–46 (25–29).

21. *Ṭawāḥīn Bayrūt,* 247 (170).

22. During their meeting in Ramzī's room, Tamīma wants to discuss his latest poem and to know whether it is really written for her. Ramzī deliberately avoids answering her.

23. *Ṭawāḥīn Bayrūt,* 247 (170).

24. *Ṭawāḥīn Bayrūt,* 72 (47).

25. *Ṭawāḥīn Bayrūt,* 72 (47).

26. *Ṭawāḥīn Bayrūt,* 72 (47).

27. *Ṭawāḥīn Bayrūt,* 99 (66–67).

28. *Ṭawāḥīn Bayrūt,* 114 (77).

29. *Ṭawāḥīn Bayrūt,* 66 (43).

30. *Ṭawāḥīn Bayrūt,* 187 (128).

31. *Ṭawāḥīn Bayrūt,* 186 (127).

32. Ḥasīb's father was a "potcleaner," a man who wanders around asking to polish people's pots, especially those made of copper.

33. *Ṭawāḥīn Bayrūt,* 65 (42).

34. In "Discourse in the Novel," Bakhtin notes that "the ideological becoming of a human being . . . is the process of selectively assimilating the words of others," 341.

35. Bakhtin, "Discourse," 342–6.

36. *Ṭawāḥīn Bayrūt,* 29 (16).

37. Bakhtin, "Discourse," 342.

38. The first epigraph reads, "Why does the morning die? Why do the candles immolate themselves?"; the second, "In my blood there is a waltz and in my bones is the lamentation of Karbala"; the third, "But why, oh! Lord, do I call upon you? Are you anything but yet another stranger to me?"; the fourth, "Imagine, just imagine, that there is nothing ahead of you but your destiny."

39. *Ṭawāḥīn Bayrūt,* 268 (184).

40. *Ṭawāḥīn Bayrūt,* 269 (184).

41. Tamīma writes to Hānī after he has slapped her on the face, "If your blow was directed through me at that name, then you were beating someone already dead," 267 (183).

42. *Ṭawāḥīn Bayrūt,* 269 (185).

43. Hānī receives a threat letter from Qammū'ī ordering him to sever the relationship between Dayr al-Mtul and Mahdiyya, that is, between Hānī and Tamīma.

44. *Ṭawāḥīn Bayrūt,* 258 (177).

45. *Ṭawāḥīn Bayrūt,* 57 (36).

46. *Ṭawāḥīn Bayrūt,* 107 (72).

47. *Ṭawāḥīn Bayrūt,* 42 (26).

A Different Voice: The Novels of Ibrāhīm al-Kawnī

ROGER ALLEN

Introduction

In using *Don Quixote* to subvert the generic purpose of the romance, Cervantes opened the way for the emergence of a literary genre that would turn away from the idealized life of the castle and its feudal adjuncts and focus instead on the ever proliferating institution of the city and those who lived in it. As the novel genre developed, the "bourgeois" (city dwellers) and their aspirations and problems became the primary topic of the great writers of the nineteenth century; the novel became, in Hegel's well-known phrase, "the burghers' epic." In its transfer to an Arab world context, the same set of prerequisites can be seen: every novel penned by Najīb Maḥfūẓ, Egypt's Nobel Prize winner, has been set in a city and mostly among the middle-class folk whom he knows and portrays so well.

The novel is a revolutionary genre, one that is by definition intolerant of the status quo; whence perhaps the frequent claim that as a genre it has died. Roland Barthes can even characterize it as death itself.[1] Since its primary topic is the process of change, it should hardly come as a surprise that it is continually transforming itself in order to deal with new topics, to confront new cultural situations, and to respond to new readerships and publication modes (in the contemporary context of the computer, for example, the hypernovel). A younger generation of novelists writing in Arabic has begun to explore ways in which this quintessentially modern genre can be adapted to reflect the issues confronting the Arab world and its littérateurs, perhaps no more so than in a reconsideration of the linkages with the past and its cultural heritage. This exploration has taken a pleasing variety of forms, but the one on which I would like to focus here is that of venue. For, while the Middle Eastern region boasts a number of cities, some of them—Damascus, for example—of considerable antiquity, in many regions they constitute a relatively recent phenomenon.

The predominant geographical feature of the region is desert, perhaps the most unpromising of novelistic venues. And yet, a number of novelists have made most effective use of the desert as the backdrop to their fiction. We might start by mentioning Ghassān Kanafānī (1936–1972) who in several of his works of fiction uses the desert as a living, pulsating organism. At the beginning of *Rijāl fī al-Shams* (1963; trans. as *Men in the Sun,* 1978), for example, Abū Qays lies on the desert floor feeling its heartbeat, while in the later *Mā Tabaqqā la-Kum* (1969; *All That's Left to You,* 1990) Ḥāmid also throws himself to the sandy ground

> and felt it like a virgin trembling beneath him, as a beam of light silently and softly swept across the folds of sand. Just at that moment he riveted himself to the ground and felt it soft and warm.[2]

In the latter novel the desert becomes one of the characters, creating a feeling of compactness that, in the author's own words, "includes time and place to such a degree that there can be no precise dividing line between places that are far apart." However, while the characters in Kanafānī's works develop a feeling of empathy with the physical environment of the desert, they are primarily city dwellers for whom the desert wastes are a place of transit; in the particular case of the Palestinians who are Kanafānī's overriding concern, the act of transit is usually taking them from one exile to another. And, as *Rijāl fī al-Shams* shows with tremendous symbolic force, the shelter of the cool desert night is transformed in the heat of the day into a burning inferno that represents in physical form all the torture and rejection of the displaced.

'Abd al-Raḥmān Munīf's depictions of the desert in his novels show all the familiarity of one who is intimately acquainted with the environment. Indeed, the very naturalness that he is able to bring to the process gives to his works an almost mythic quality that links them directly with the values of the desert tribes in the earliest period in Arabic literature—solidarity, generosity, and endurance in the face of adversity—and with the spectacular descriptions of desert life that the early poetry contains. In *Al-Nihāyāt* (1977), Munīf introduces his readers to the village of al-Ṭība. The novel concerns the life of a community and, in particular, its uneasy links with the faraway city through the members of its younger generation who have fled the rigors of village life. But, as the narrator carefully informs us, the desert proper starts at the very edge of the village and its meager area of cultivation. If the village is a symbol for the struggle to survive in the face of tremendous odds, then the function of the desert is to provide the ultimate test of survival. As human beings enter the desert in this novel, the discourse assumes a present tense that becomes truly gnomic:

> There exist places where nature can be seen in all its unbridled power; in seas and oceans, at the summits of mountains, in the depths of valleys, in the frozen ice-floes, in the darkness of jungles. In all these locales nature gives all sorts of warnings of changes to come. There is an internal charge present which cannot remain the same for long and will inevitably change at any moment. The desert, on the other hand, the mysterious, cruel, savage desert with all its surprises, transcends the normal laws of nature simply in order to corroborate them.[3]

The personal experiences of a hunting party that is marooned by a violent sandstorm become interweaved with the eternal verities of survival in the face of desert realities:

> In the desert waiting for death to arrive is one thousand times worse than death itself. . . . In the desert even time assumes its own special meaning. It turns into tiny atoms: the second, the minute, these represent the whole of time.[4]

When Munīf turns in the 1980s to his greatest novelistic project, the five-volume *Mudun al-Milḥ,* the first volume in the series, *Al-Tīh* (The wilderness), 1984 (published in English as *Cities of Salt,* 1987), creates the same atmosphere of the desert and its power over humanity as a means of showing how the discovery of oil and the rampant exploitation and corruption that it brings with it destroy an environment and a traditional way of life; the "disappearance" of Mut'ib al-Hadhdhāl on his camel and occasional reports of sightings of him mark the transformation of the tribal past in the region from the merely idealized into the genuinely mythic.

For Munīf, the desert is an environment to protect and to respect for its awesome power; to learn how to survive in it is to preserve the traditions of a people in the face of the overwhelming and mostly destructive impact of the modern world. Even so, Munīf's narrators, for all their appreciation of the desert, remain respectful visitors to the environment rather than residents in it. And here is where the extra spatial dimension of Ibrāhīm al-Kawnī comes in.[5]

Al-Kawnī was born in 1948 in Libya and worked as a journalist there before going to Moscow to study at the Gorky Institute. Since his return to Libya he has devoted himself full-time to creative writing. In this he seems to share a quality with Munīf: after a relatively late start to a career as a creative writer, he has now published a truly astonishing amount of fiction in a short period that suggests that, while his inspiration is clearly a major motivating force at this juncture, some of the works at least may have been composed well before their date of initial publication. Details about his published works are somewhat difficult to obtain, but a partial list (along with known dates of publication) includes eight collections of short stories: *Al-Ṣalāt Khārij Niṭāq al-Awqāt al-Khamsa* (Prayer outside the bounds of the five prayer-times) 1974; *Jur'a min Dam* (Mouthful of blood) 1983; *Shajarat al-Ratam* (The retem tree) 1986; *Al-Qafaṣ* (The cage) 1990; *Dīwān al-Nathr al-Barrī* (The collection of terrestrial prose) 1991; *Al-Khurūj al-Awwal ilā Waṭan al-Ru'ā al-Samāwiyya* (First exit to the haven of heavenly visions) 1992; *Kharīf al-Darwīsh* (The dervish's autumn) 1994; and *Al-Waqā'i' al-Mafqūda min Sīrat al-Majūs* (Lost events in the Magi's life-history) 1992 and several novels: *Al-Khusūf* (The eclipse) 4 parts, 1991; *Al-Tibr* (Gold-ore) 1990; *Nazīf al-Ḥajar* (Bleeding rock) 1990, *Al-Majūs* (The magians) 1991, and *Al-Saḥara* (The magicians) 2 parts, 1994. In 1970 he published *Thawrat al-Ṣaḥrā' al-Kubrā* (The revolution of the Great Sahara), a work of history on the geography and politics of the Libyan desert region. While al-Kawnī clearly has the education and world experience of an highly educated contemporary Arab intellectual, he also appears to want to live the life and culture of his region by spending some time each year living in the desert itself.

Al-Kawnī sets his works far in the desert. This is not the semidesert conveniently close to major conurbations that most western visitors to the region get to see but the desolate wastes of the Sahara in the southwestern region of Libya from where caravans move in all directions: to the west to the fabulous city of Timbuktu, for example, and to the south to Kano in northern Nigeria. Here are two descriptive passages to provide some idea of the way in which al-Kawnī is able to evoke the environment he knows so well:

> The first time he heard him sing was as a boy while he was tending goats in the valleys of Matkhandush. At midday the desert's eternal flayer in the sky would whip him with its burning lash. Wearing a thick green pelt he would seek shade under a tall acacia tree. The goats would flock around him. The south wind would blow in his face and sear him with the fires of the southern wastes. He would take a sip from the water-bottle and sprinkle a couple of drops on his face, but still the south wind would blow.[6]

> Of all desert creatures gazelles are the most sensitive and alert. They can smell the scent of a human being at a considerable distance. The only time they can be spotted is at dawn or on days when the wind drops to nothing and the air is completely still. . . . Gazelles can show enormous endurance in adversity. Their mode of running is different from that of all other animals. Unlike the mouflon, for example, which takes to the rocky hillsides when chased, the gazelle doesn't zigzag but moves over the desert wastes in a straight line. It believes that any infringement of the rules of the chase constitutes an offense against decency, something that invites censure. Rather than using crafty stratagems the gazelle opts for sheer heroism. Tricks and deceit are eschewed as it chooses to adhere to the rules of chivalry.[7]

The life he depicts in these passages and many others is one found among endless sand dunes but also among the massive escarpments from which character can look down on the caravans below with a sense of almost godlike power. It is hardly surprising that in such surroundings mountains and animals assume the qualities of deities. Indeed, a part of the region in question is known as Tassili, and the valleys of the region are the site of some ancient frescoes that depict the life of the peoples who inhabited the region in prehistoric times. These frescoes have been the subject of archeological research, most especially that conducted by the French scholar, Henri Lhote, whose work is quoted by al-Kawnī in *Nazīf al-Ḥajar.*[8] A prominent feature of these frescoes is a mountain sheep with extremely long horns; al-Kawnī calls it by the Berber word *"waddān,"* only to be found in Dozy's invaluable *Supplément aux dictionnaires arabes;* the English language seems to have adopted the French term "mouflon" for the animal. In several of al-Kawnī's works, this animal that clearly held a central importance for the ancestral inhabitants of the region comes to assume a truly mythical function as a preserver of desert chivalry (a trait in animals that is illustrated in the second of the above quotations) and helper of those humans who, in their struggle to survive in such inimical surroundings, often need to be rescued from dire straits.

In al-Kawnī's novels then, heat, wind, hunger, and thirst are constants. The power of nature is a given, as is the company of animals—goats, sheep, and camels—as a symbol of the possibilities of continuity in the face of a perpetually changing landscape. Routines are slow and painstaking; conversations are deliberate and punctuated by long silences. Those readers of novels who are accustomed to expecting a plethora of action and the bustle of communal life, whether of city or village, as well as the potential afforded by the dramatic qualities of dialogue, will find their expectations unmet in al-Kawnī's works. Al-Kawnī takes his readers away from the quotidian into the realm of fantasy and uses the myths contained in the lore of the Tuareg tribes of the region and in the frescoes of their ancestors as a framework for a confrontation between the values of past and present. This feature can be illustrated with a novel such as *Nazīf al-Ḥajar*.

Asūf, a recluse dweller in the desert hills and valleys, a skilled hunter of animals and the son of a hunter, has been appointed guardian of the valley where a particularly famous and gigantic fresco has been drawn on the rock depicting a man and his companion mouflon. He receives tourists when they come but otherwise subsists off the meager food resources of the region. The novel opens with the scene that establishes the framework for this tragic allegory of confrontation; its juxtaposition of the timeless elements of the desert, the conjunction of man and animals, and the disruption caused by the noise of a modern vehicle are typical of al-Kawnī's gift for description:

> It is only when he starts praying that the billy-goats feel like butting each other in front of him. As evening falls and the blazing disk high up in the sky begins its daily farewell, threatening all the while to return the next day and complete the task of burning to a cinder everything it hasn't managed to burn today, Asūf digs his hands into the valley's sands and starts to do the sunset prayer.
>
> He heard the sound of the engine in the distance and decided to give God his due quickly so that he'd be finished before the Christians arrived. In recent years, he got used to welcoming them to the valley to look at the frescoes.

Particularly noticeable here is the tense shift from the generic present of the eternal desert verities that Asūf's existence tries to represent and respect (similar to the passage from Munīf's *Al-Nihāyāt* quoted above) to the specific past of the second paragraph that introduces the disruptive element into the story. The new arrivals are not, in fact, Christians but two men of the region, one of whom lends a further symbolic element by being named Qābīl Ādam (Cain Adam). This latter character has been ill-starred from birth and has developed an insatiable need for meat. The goal of his visit is not to look at the fresco on the valley wall but to persuade Asūf, the famed hunter of animals, to satisfy his cravings by hunting the fabled mouflon. The novel proceeds to explore the childhood backgrounds of both Asūf and Qābīl as a background to the inevitable confrontation. Asūf initially refuses to help in the hunt then is constrained to do so. When Qābīl's madness reaches its acme in the face of Asūf's recalcitrance, the former crucifies the desert dweller on a rock and, imagining him to be the animal whose flesh he so craves, slits his throat. Thus are the rocks made to bleed, as the title suggests.

The brutality implicit in this ending also makes its way into other novels of al-Kawnī, but it is also worth remembering that the environment itself is a bringer of sudden death—a prominent theme of the earliest Arabic poetry. In *Nazīf al-Ḥajar,* for example, Asūf finally has to live alone when his mother is swept away by a flash flood that overwhelms their encampment in a valley; it is his gruesome task to scour the trees and rocks of the valley in search of her remains. Another novel, *Al-Tibr,* is concerned with the relationship of a man with a prized camel that he owns and races and then is forced to sell to the leader of a tribe from the south in exchange for marriage to one of the leader's female relatives. The deal, the novel's hero soon realizes, is a mistake from every point of view. The exchange of gold and the sedentary life to which he has agreed prey upon his sense of honor. The camel returns to him and becomes the cause of much friction both between him and his wife and between him and the tribal leader. He finds himself forced to kill his wife's relative; whereupon he is hunted down by the other men of the tribe. He takes refuge in a cave high in the mountains (which also contains wall-paintings), but the men track him down. In yet another gruesome scene, the novel ends with his beloved camel being tortured to death, while he meets his end being torn apart between two camels.

Al-Kawnī's novels clearly function as a fictional re-creation of the desert culture of Saharan Africa that he knows so well. This is a part of the world where, needless to say, the incursions of twentieth-century culture and values have had, thus far at least, a reasonably minimal effect; indeed *Nazīf al-Ḥajar* is, at least in part, a most effective allegory dealing with the catastrophic effects of such occasional disruptions. The Tuareg tribesmen with their veiled faces, the caravan trails between Timbuktu, Kano, Marzaq, and Ghadames, and the high escarpments of Tassili, Messak Mellet, and Tamanghasset, these serve as the backdrop for a novelistic landscape that is virtually timeless. In his lengthy novel, *Al-Majūs,* al-Kawnī does make use of that specific knowledge of the region's history that is evidenced by his 1970 book on the topic. I translated "al-Majūs" above as "the Magians," which is its literal dictionary meaning, but in this geographic context it refers to the non-Islamic tribes to the south with whom the Qādiriyya and Rifā'iyya Ṣūfī brotherhoods initiated an interesting series of discussions regarding the use and efficacy of ritualistic and animalistic worship practices; this is in fact one of the topics debated by characters within the novel itself, often centered around the changing historical fortunes of the fabled city of Timbuktu. The values of Islam as propounded by the *darwīsh* are juxtaposed with the traditional rites of the *'arrāfa* (fortune-teller) with her amulets and charms. Al-Kawnī's instincts as a historian combine with his desire to provide a different novelistic vision in contemporary Arabic literature when he includes in his texts complete Tuareg inscriptions, transcribed into Arabic characters and translated into Arabic.[9] *Al-Majūs* is illustrated with pictures of the Tassili frescoes, and the novels in general are packed full of Tuareg names for people and places.

Al-Kawnī's novelistic voice is clearly an original one, and at the same time fascinating not only because it introduces Arabic readers to a region with whose history and culture most people will be entirely unfamiliar but also because it evokes sets of values that will inevitably stir in the minds of those readers memories of the earliest periods in our awareness of the Arabic literary heritage. His output thus far has been impressive, and the thematic focus that he has chosen thus far is one that clearly provides him with much inspiration. It is these features that I have chosen to focus on in this short study that pays tribute to a great teacher and scholar in the study of Arabic literature and culture. With so much talent at his disposal, we may hope that al-Kawnī may at some point turn his undoubted talents to other themes and venues, thus further enriching the tradition of Arabic fiction.

Notes

1. Roland Barthes, *Writing Degree Zero* (Boston: Beacon Press, 1970), 39.

2. Ghassān Kanafānī, *Al-Āthār al-Kāmila,* vol. 1, *Al-Riwāyāt* (Beirut: Dār al-Ṭalī'a, 1972), 169. The English translation is my own.

3. 'Abd al-Raḥmān Munīf, *Al-Nihāyāt,* 6th ed. (Beirut: Al-Mu'assasa al-'Arabiyya li-al-Dirāsāt wa-al-Nashr, 1988), 71; I am quoting my own translation: *Endings* (London: Quartet Books, 1988), 62.

4. Munīf, *Al-Nihāyāt,* 72–73; *Endings,* 64–65.

5. Al-Kawnī's names may be a source of some confusion. I have transliterated it "al-Kawnī" for the purpose of this study in order to convey accurately the graphemes of the name. My Libyan colleague, Hussein al-Khafaifi, informs me that the closest dialectal pronunciation of the name would be transliterated as "al-Koni." I have also seen it printed as "al-Kouni."

6. Ibrāhīm al-Kawnī, *Al-Majūs,* vol. 1 (Tripoli: Al-Dār al-Jamāhīriyya li-al-Nashr wa-al-Tawzī' wa-al-I'lān, 1991), 74.

7. Ibrāhīm al-Kawnī, *Nazīf al-Ḥajar* (London: Riad Rayyes Books, 1991), 103–4.

8. The work is available in an English translation: Henri Lhote, *The Search for the Tassili Frescoes,* trans. Alan Houghton Brodrick (London: Hutchinson and Co., 1959).

9. See *Al-Majūs,* vol. 1, 289, and most notably, the poem in "Ṣafḥa min Kitāb al-Ṣaḥrā'" in *Al-Waqā'i' al-Mafqūda min Sīrat al-Majūs* (Limasol, Cyprus: Dār al-Tanwīr li-al-Ṭibā'a wa-al-Nashr, 1992), 22–23.

Instead of the Song of the Nightingale

CORNELIS NIJLAND

Introduction

The novel *Du'ā' al-Karawān* (Cairo, 1941), translated as *The Call of the Curlew* (Leiden, 1980), was written by Ṭāhā Ḥusayn in 1934, as stated at the end of the text. The novel is dedicated to 'Abbās Maḥmūd al-'Aqqād whose sixth *dīwān, Hadiyyat al-Karawān* (The present of the curlew) (Cairo, 1933), is completely devoted to this bird indigenous to the Egyptian countryside. Al-'Aqqād defended his choice saying that the *karawān* is heard in Egypt from spring until autumn, whereas the favorite of the poets, the nightingale, is rare there. The cry of the *karawān* became a leitmotiv in the story by Ṭāhā Ḥusayn.

The novel has been quite successful, as one may conclude from the fact that the *Dalīl al-Kātib al-Miṣrī* (a list of Egyptian books published) for 1976 mentions a fourteenth impression. This success as well as the fame of the author meant that anybody writing a history or a study of the Arabic novel had to analyze this novel and discuss its value. Not everybody was as pleased with the novel as the sales figures would suggest. Most of the criticism was directed against the linguistic side of the novel, or against its style, whereas the story as such and its message received much less attention. In this article we shall, with due regard for earlier studies and discussions of the novel, discuss the novel in the following order:

1. The story
2. The plot
3. Criticism of the novel
4. Stylistic aspects
5. Poetic aspects of the novel
6. The message
7. Conclusion

The Story

Du'ā' al-Karawān is the story of a mother, named Zahra, and her two daughters, Hanādī and Āmina, and the mother's brother, Nāṣir. The latter compels the mother and her daughters to leave their village for some time because her husband has been killed during one of his amorous exploits and has brought them into disgrace. The three women are led across the river in an easterly direction. They reach a town where they find household jobs. Once a week the mother and her daughters meet in a room that she has rented for that purpose. No further information is given about the house where the mother found work, whereas the working conditions of the girls are neatly described. Hanādī's job is in the house of an unmarried irrigation engineer. Āmina is employed by the subprefect *(ma'mūr)* to look after his daughter, Khadīja, who is of the same age as Āmina. Before long they become playmates and study the same lessons.

The three women lead a quiet life until, after a year or so, the mother decides to leave the town immediately. Āmina discovers that something awkward has happened to Hanādī in the house of her employer. The three women stay at the mayor's guest house in a distant village until the mother's brother arrives. He rides with them into the desert. They halt in the middle of the night and the brother kills and buries Hanādī. The women are told to say that Hanādī has died a victim of the plague. Then they continue their journey home.

Āmina is terribly shocked by what has happened, and she cannot understand why her mother did not prevent her uncle Nāṣir from killing Hanādī. Āmina decides not to stay, and, taking advantage of her uncle's absence for a few days, she leaves for the town where she, her mother, and her sister had lived together. She finds employment again with the same family, resuming the thread of her interrupted lessons, et cetera. At the same time, she wants the irrigation engineer to pay for his crime, and therefore she devotes much of her attention to the house next door, where Hanādī had worked.

Āmina is dealt a new blow when she hears that Khadīja and the irrigation engineer, Hanādī's seducer, will marry and that the family expects her to remain the servant of Khadīja after the marriage. Āmina informs the family of what had happened to her sister. The marriage is canceled. Āmina leaves the family because she does not want Khadīja to know what has happened. Soon after, Khadīja and her parents move to a distant town.

Āmina finds a new job in the house where her mother worked. It is the house of a rich and traditional family. The boys are sent to Cairo to study but the girls do not receive any formal education. Āmina discovers that the boys read the *One Thousand and One Nights* rather than their study books. She obtains a copy the book and starts reading, but then she is discovered and kicked out of the house.

Finally Āmina, calling herself Su'ād, is employed by the irrigation engineer, who tries to seduce her. Āmina, however, succeeds in keeping him at a distance without losing her job. They slowly grow to like each other. The engineer asks her to marry him, but Āmina tells him what happened to Hanādī. While showing his regret, he asks her again to marry him.

The Plot

The novel opens with the nightly homecoming of the irrigation engineer where the female first-person narrator, as his servant, is waiting upon him. The engineer tries to touch her but she steps back, evading him. He then commands her to follow him in order to assist him while he is preparing to go to bed. This scene is broken off and followed by a soliloquy in which the girl addresses the *karawān,* saying that for twenty years she has been accustomed to await its call before going to sleep. She tells it that its call reminds her of the spirit of her sister whose tragic end she and the bird witnessed. She ends the scene by saying, "Do you allow me to tell some ends of my story so that people may find in it a warning protecting pure souls from being destroyed and innocent blood from being shed?"[1] The call of the *karawān* dies away, and the first-person narrator looks around in her luxurious room, saying that there are lessons and warnings in the events and mishaps of life and that she will tell herself the story of Āmina, who is now called Su'ād. The story then unfolds itself in a straight line, the opening scene being repeated in the twenty-second chapter followed by the first-person narrator's assertion that she had met the enemy on his own ground and that she had emerged victorious. The narrative ends after the irrigation engineer's proposal, his being told what had happened to his servant Hanādī and to her sister Āmina, and his assertion of his love for Su'ād.

The call of the *karawān* becomes a leitmotiv in the novel. Āmina had first heard this call when they left the city and were waiting for the mother's brother to arrive, and she heard it again when Hanādī was killed, and after that every night at midnight. She confided in the bird during the ensuing period every time she heard the call. The irrigation engineer notices the call of the bird, saying: "Do you think that its song echoed like that when Hanādī fell into infinite solitude?"[2]

Criticism of the Novel

Ṣalāḥ 'Abd al-Ṣabūr concludes a brief assessment of the novel saying that the ideas in the story are French and that its style shows the influence of al-Azhar.[3] However imprecise this remark may be, it leads one to ask how French or rather how un-Arabic the story is. In my opinion this "Frenchness" lies mainly in the motif of a girl addressing a bird, and in the social success of the poor Bedouin girl, who indeed goes from rags to riches. The un-Arabic element would be the chasing away of the mother and her two daughters after her husband had been killed in one of his scandalous exploits, as Aḥmad Haykal rightly asserts.[4] It is difficult to see what other elements of the story would qualify for being called French or un-Arabic.

Stylistic Aspects

The style of the story is described as "Azharite" by Ṣalāḥ 'Abd al-Ṣabūr,[5] as "fossilized" by Muḥammad Mandūr,[6] whereas 'Alī al-Rā'ī[7] considers it as a work of art, as an opera. A. B. as-Safi writes in the preface to his translation that "In fact, it is on its style that this novel has established its literary fame."[8] Regarding the adequacy of the style of the novel, Muḥammad Mandūr,[9] Aḥmad Haykal,[10] Ḥamdī Sakkūt,[11] and Marsden Jones[12] share the opinion that there is a discrepancy between the educational level of the characters of the story and the language they use. This is especially the case with Āmina, according to Muḥammad Mandūr[13] and Aḥmad Haykal.[14]

One has to remark that the critics, though insisting on a more natural language for the characters, did not mean that Ṭāhā Ḥusayn should have used the colloquial. The use of the colloquial had been defended and tried by authors like Mīkhā'īl Nu'ayma in *Al-Ābā' wa-al-Banūn* (Parents and children),[15] and Maḥmūd Taymūr in his early stories, but both authors did not repeat this experiment and Maḥmūd Taymūr, who rewrote many of his stories, even went so far as to change originally colloquial passages into the *fuṣḥā* (the modernized version of the classical language). The consensus among authors and critics was that only the *fuṣḥā* could be used in a literary text, and so the characters were required to speak a language which they barely knew or did not know at all. Ṭāhā Ḥusayn solved this problem by relying on one narrator who at the time of the narration had reached a rather high level of literacy.

A second remark is that not one of the critics tried to compare Ṭāhā Ḥusayn's concept of language as he wanted it to be with the language he actually used. He is quite precise about language in his *Mustaqbal al-Thaqāfa fī Miṣr* (The future of culture in Egypt). The current vernacular, in his view, cannot be called a language. It can be absorbed into the *fuṣḥā* when we give it the necessary attention and when we elevate the people through education and culturalization and when we lower it (i.e., the *fuṣḥā*) through simplification and reform to a level where both (i.e., the language and the people) meet without trouble, toil or distortion.[16] He concludes by saying that the options are to do as he proposes; otherwise, the *fuṣḥā* will become merely a religious language, a language like Latin in the Catholic Church.

After these words one would expect an easy vocabulary and an easy grammar, and that is exactly what Ṭāhā Ḥusayn offers in this novel. The author does not display the slightest tendency to use "difficult" words or intricate constructions.

One would like to explore the issue of whether Ṭāhā Ḥusayn's style is "Azharite" or whether it reflects a wider education in Egypt and abroad. One may assume that Ṣalāḥ 'Abd al-Ṣabūr did not have anything in mind but an elevated style that is admirable in theological works but that he did not think adequate for the rendering of narration by a simple person. It is true that Ṭāhā Ḥusayn discovered literature and literary style at al-Azhar through Muḥammad 'Abduh and al-Marṣafī, and their followers,[17] and this may have had a lasting influence on him. However, he continued his education at the Egyptian University, later called the King Fu'ād University, and finally Cairo University, and then went abroad to continue his studies.

◆ ◆ ◆

In France, Ṭāhā Ḥusayn took literary courses taught by G. Lanson at the Sorbonne, between 1915 and 1917.[18] Lanson's writings on stylistics were very popular at that time in France and his *L'Art de la prose* was printed ten times between 1907 and 1911. Lanson insists that there is a so-called prose art and that the author has to treat words in prose in the same way as one treats words in poetry. It should be remarked that Lanson has a style of his own which can be characterized as cumulative. Describing the prose of an author, he writes: "c'était une prose sensuelle, molle, voluptueuse, touchante, décorative, un ruissellement de descriptions et d'images. . . ." (It was a sensual, soft, voluptuous, touching, decorative prose, an effluence of descriptions and images.)[19] One could add to this numerous instances where Lanson accumulates subjects followed by one single verb or objects following one single verb or adjectives qualifying one and the same noun, and clusters of sentences which describe one and the same thing in each cluster.

Pierre Cachia writes that the most marked of Ṭāhā Ḥusayn's stylistic characteristics, and the one most often commented on by admirers and detractors, is his repetition of words,[20] adding, "it is in emphatic or consciously artistic writing that Ṭāhā Ḥusayn most commonly displays this mannerism."[21]

Indeed, Ṭāhā Ḥusayn's style in this novel is marked by repetition, by the accumulation of adjectives, nouns, and phrases, of which I will present some random examples. Sometimes the accumulated adjectives rhyme, such as: *"al-mahībati r-rahība"* on page 10, *"rā'i'atan bāri'atan"* on p. 12, along with other instances on pages 13, 19, 20 and 21, to name just a few. An accumulation of four adjectives can be found in the sentences: *"wa-mā bayna tilka l-aydī r-raqīqati r-rafī'ati n-nā'imati l-mutrafa"* (in those delicate, fine, smooth, luxury-softened hands)[22] and "qaḍaytu laylatan sāhiratan ḥā'iratan mufakkiratan maḥzūna" (I spent a sleepless night, worried, thoughtful, sad),[23] but that is as far as Ṭāhā Ḥusayn goes. He rather restricts the number of adjectives in comparison to the number of nouns and verbs. Clusters of sentences occur already in the first chapter, where Āmina says: "Mā ziltu sāhiratan arqubu maqdamaka wa-antaẓiru nida'aka, wa-mā kāna yanbaghī lī an anāma ḥattā aḥussa qurbaka wa-asma'a ṣawtaka wa-astajība li-du'a'ika." (I am still awake, watching for your arrival and waiting for you to sing. I forbid myself to sleep until I have felt your presence, heard your voice and responded to your call.) Other clusters worth mentioning occur in chapter nine, where Āmina, counting her negative feelings about her native village, says in a *monologue intérieur*: "Mā kuntu aḥfilu bi-l-ḥuqūli l-munbaththa, wa-lā ajidu shawqan ilā hādhā l-khaṭṭ mina l-mā', wa-lā ajidu kalafan bi-hādhā s-sahli l-jamīli n-naḍir, wa-lā ajidu raghbatan fī t-taṣ'īdi l-hayyin ilā hādhihi l-haḍbati l-mahība, wa-lā ajidu ḥanīnan ilā hādhihi l-qaryati l-wādi'a. . . ." (I had no desire to see the fields, no longing for the line of water nor for the green plain, and I had not the least desire to climb slowly the imposing plain; I had no sense of nostalgia for the quiet village. . . .)[24] Four of the five clauses begin with *wa-lā ajidu* (I had no) followed by the object. In the following four sentences, each beginning with *innā hunāka* (there), Āmina lists for herself her positive feelings with regard to the city where she stayed with her mother and her sister. Then she thinks again about her home village, the sordidness of which is emphasized in three clauses, each beginning with *kulluhā* (entirely). These negative thoughts are, exactly as the negative clauses, balanced by positive thoughts comparing herself favorably with her mother and sister in six clauses: "Akhadhtu ash'uru bi-annī aḥsanu minhumā fahman li-l-ḥayāti wa-aṣdaqu minhumā ḥukman 'alā l-ashyā', wa-ashaddu minhumā ṣabran 'alā l-khuṭūb wa-amharu minhumā fī t-takhalluṣ mina sh-shadā'id wa-l-kārithāt. A-lastu adnā minhumā ilā ṭ-ṭufūlati wa-ajdaru minhumā an akūna gharratan ghāfila." (I began to think that I understood life better than they did and that I had a better judgment of things than they had, and that I had a better self-control than they in the face of calamities and that I was more skillful than they in getting away from adversities and disasters. Am I not nearer to childhood than they and more proper to be negligent and thoughtless?)[25] One wonders how far Lanson is away from Ṭāhā Ḥusayn repeating *"lā ajidu,"* when one reads three sentences by Lanson beginning with *"Ce n'était pas"* followed by a sentence beginning with *"C'était. . . ."*[26]

The most frequent enumeration I noticed was the repetition of *fīhā* ten times, followed by words like *ḥubb, bughḍ, amal, ya's,* and so on (love, hate, hope, despair).[27]

Apart from the rhyming adjectives, there are some rhyming lines, such as "Yabqā hādhā r-ra'su l-bā'isu l-maḥzūn (=despondent) mustarīḥan ilā hādhihi l-katifi ṣ-ṣaghīrati l-ḥanūn (=loving)." (This miserable and despondent head is still resting on the small and loving shoulder.)[28] An example of *saj'* is found in the line: "Ufakkiru fī hādhihi l-fatāti l-yā'isa wa-fī hādhihi l-mar'ati l-bā'isa." (I think of this despairing girl and of this unhappy woman.)[29] Lines of *saj'* are spoken by the guests of the *'umda,* thanking him for the food. The *saj'* here is dictated by the situation rather than being an embellishment for its own sake. "Yuwaththiqu llāhu ḥizāmahu, wa-yu'lī maqāmahu, wa-yaṣrifu 'anhu d-dā', wa-yanṣuruhu 'alā l-a'dā'." (May God gird his flank and exalt his rank; may He spare his woes and let him triumph over his foes.)[30]

Poetic Aspects

Ṣalāḥ 'Abd al-Ṣabūr,[31] Pierre Cachia,[32] 'Alī al-Rā'ī,[33] A. B. as-Safi,[34] and 'Abd al-Ḥamīd Yūnus[35] characterize the novel as a work of poetry. Some of them do so without comment, but others do indicate what exactly makes the novel deserve this qualification. Ṣalāḥ 'Abd al-Ṣabūr writes that it comes close to the style of ancient Arabic poetry in its loudness and its rhetoric, in the construction of its sentences, and in the clamor of its music.[36] 'Abd al-Ḥamīd Yūnus goes one step further in asserting that, as a student together with his fellow-students, he would look for musical rhythms in Ṭāhā Ḥusayn's prose and that they were surprised to find that whole paragraphs could be scanned applying the traditional Arabic meters and that one student, who was a singer, would sing portions of *Du'ā' al-Karawān* in the way other singers would sing poetry. A. B. as-Safi, finally, defines it as a piece of poetry, illustrating his assertion with a free-verse rendering of a part of the first chapter.

It is not our purpose to pursue this matter any further, but to be satisfied with what Arab authors have written about it.

The Message

There have been many suggestions concerning the message of the novel, ranging from a struggle between duty and emotion,[37] to a struggle between the urge to take revenge and feelings of love,[38] to a class struggle,[39] to an ethical message making people aware of the crimes committed in the name of honor, to praise for the feeling of love.[40] ʿAlī al-Rāʿī, finally, writes that it is the story of two girls who try to free themselves from the yoke of an inimical society, which robs them of their most basic and vital rights: the right to love and the right to look for a partner.[41] The first girl, he writes, seeks this liberation unconsciously, without a plan and without proper equipment, and she fails. The second girl, armed with enlightening knowledge, succeeds.[42]

◆ ◆ ◆

The novel itself spells out the message very clearly when Āmina asks the *karawān,* "Do you allow me to tell some ends of my story so that people may find in it a warning protecting pure souls from being destroyed and innocent blood from being shed?"[43] But Āmina refers to more undefined warnings and lessons when she begins to tell her story.[44] In view of this it is more appropriate to speak of the messages of the novel instead of one single message. The warning against the killing of girls who have been seduced is certainly one of these messages. The struggle between love and hatred and the victory of love over vengeance may be considered as another message. However, there is another aspect of the novel which might be more important than the other aspects mentioned so far, namely, the education of girls.

Two girls, being full sisters, only differ from each other in that one of them accidentally received an education whereas the other did not. Both of them were confronted by the same temptation which they had to face on their own without outside assistance or recourse. They both were maid-servants of the man who tried to seduce them. The simple, uneducated girl falls victim to the seducer, whereas the educated girl succeeds in holding her own and in winning the love and admiration of the man. Education enables Āmina to stand on her own, in contrast to her mother who says that a woman cannot live in security without a father, a brother, or a husband protecting her.[45] Education for girls is also important in the encounter between Āmina and the uncultured family. The go-between, Zannūba, tells Āmina that the daughters of the family had not been spoiled by attending school or by teachers coming to the house. Their father had been too careful with his daughters to expose them to such "corruption." He is severely shocked when he discovers Āmina reading a book of his sons', who are thus revealed to be reading frivolous books instead of the serious ones he believed to be in their hands. The result is that Āmina is thrown out of the house.[46] Āmina says that this family would nowadays be the laughingstock of some, whereas others would smile.[47] Instead of corrupting the girls, the novel seems to say that education prepares them to face the dangers of life on their own.

Conclusion

Du'ā' al-Karawān is a novel in which Arabic and French literary practice meet. The story has its Arabic elements next to those which betray a European origin, and the same is true for the style. The discrepancy between the style of the novel and the story, which some of the critics point out, is based on the assumption that the speech of the various characters should be in conformity with their social and intellectual status. The novel, however, has been written from a different esthetic point of view, which is based on French literature as well as Arabic rhetorical practice. The simple message of the novel has been wrapped in an exquisite language, turning it into a work of art with a message.

Notes

1. Ṭāhā Ḥusayn, *Du'ā' al-Karawān,* (Cairo: Maṭba'at al-Ma'ārif, 1941), 11.

2. Ṭāhā Ḥusayn, *The Call of the Curlew,* trans. A. B. As-Safi, Arabic Translation Series of the *Journal of Arabic Literature,* Vol. 5 (Leiden: E. J. Brill, 1980), 130. I have followed as-Safi's translation in principle except in cases where his translation does not follow the original closely. The use of as-Safi's translation is indicated in the notes with a citation of his name and the page number, e.g. (as-Safi, 130). The other translations are mine.

3. Ṣalāḥ 'Abd al-Ṣabūr, *Mādhā Yabqā minhum li-al-Tārīkh* (Cairo: Dār al-Kātib al-'Arabī li-al-Ṭibā'a, 1968), 13.

4. Aḥmad Haykal, *Al-Adab al-Qaṣaṣī wa-al-Masraḥī fi Miṣr* (Cairo: Dār al-Ma'ārif bi-Miṣr, 1968), 220f.

5. Ṣalāḥ 'Abd al-Ṣabūr, *Mādhā Yabqā,* 13.

6. Muḥammad Mandūr, *Fī al-Mīzān al-Jadīd,* 3rd ed.(Cairo: Maktabat Nahḍat Miṣr wa-Maṭba'atuhā, n.d.), 53.

7. 'Alī al-Rā'ī, *Dirāsāt fi al-Riwāya al-Miṣriyya* (Cairo: Al-Mu'assasa al-Miṣriyya al'Āmma li-al-Ta'lif wa-al-Tarjama wa-al-Ṭibā'a wa-al-Nashr, 1964), 140–56.

8. As-Safi, preface *The Call of the Curlew.*

9. Muḥammad Mandūr, *Fī al-Mīzān,* 53.

10. Aḥmad Haykal, *Al-Adab al-Qaṣaṣī,* 211–26.

11. Ḥamdī Sakkūt, *The Egyptian Novel and Its Main Trends, 1913–1952* (Cairo: The American University in Cairo Press, 1971), 31–36.

12. Ḥamdī Sakkūt and Marsden Jones, *Ṭāhā Ḥusayn, A'lām al-Adab al-Mu'āṣir fī Miṣr* series, vol. 1 (Cairo: The American University in Cairo Press, 1975), 43–47.

13. Muḥammad Mandūr, *Fī al-Mīzān,* 53 and 58.

14. Aḥmad Haykal, *Al-Adab al-Qaṣaṣī,* 224.

15. See Mīkhā'īl Nu'ayma, *Al-Ābā' wa-al-Banūn* (New York: n.p., 1917) and especially his foreword to the first edition of the play explaining his decision to have illiterate characters use the colloquial, distinguishing them from the literate ones using the *fuṣḥā.* The foreword was republished in *Al-Ghirbāl* (The sieve) (Cairo: Al-Maṭba'a al-'Aṣriyya, 1923).

16. Ṭāhā Ḥusayn, *Mustaqbal al-Thaqāfa fi Miṣr* (Cairo: n.p., 1938), 315.

17. Pierre Cachia, *Ṭāhā Ḥusayn: His Place in the Egyptian Literary Renaissance* (London: Luzac & Company Ltd., 1956), 50ff.

18. Cachia, *Ṭāhā Ḥusayn,* 55.

19. Gustave Lanson, *L'Art de la prose* (Paris: Librairie des annales, 1911), 114. For more information on Lanson, see André François Poncet, Jean Pommier, et Pierre Clarac, *Gustave Lanson 1857–1934* (Paris: Société des amis de l'école normale supérieure, 1958). It is also worth noting that the well-known Egyptian literary critic Muḥammad Mandūr published in 1946 a book entitled *Manhaj al-Baḥth fī al-Adab wa-al-Lugha,* which is a translation of a book by Lanson.

20. Cachia, *Ṭāhā Ḥusayn,* 220.

21. Cachia, *Ṭāhā Ḥusayn,* 221.

22. Ṭāhā Ḥusayn, *Du'ā',* 35 (As-Safi, 25).

23. Ṭāhā Ḥusayn, *Du'ā',* 125 (As-Safi, 99).

24. Ṭāhā Ḥusayn, *Du'ā',* 54 (As-Safi, 42).

25. Ṭāhā Ḥusayn, *Du'ā',* 54 (As-Safi, 42).

26. Lanson, *L'Art,* 114.

27. Ṭāhā Ḥusayn, *Du'ā',* 144.

28. Ṭāhā Ḥusayn, *Du'ā',* 27.

29. Ṭāhā Ḥusayn, *Du'ā',* 29.

30. Ṭāhā Ḥusayn, *Du'ā',* 35 (As-Safi, 25).

31. Ṣalāḥ 'Abd al-Ṣabūr, *Mādhā Yabqā,* 10.

32. Cachia, *Ṭāhā Ḥusayn,* 194–95.

33. 'Alī al-Rā'ī, *Dirāsāt,* 140–56.

34. As-Safi, preface *The Call of the Curlew.*

35. 'Abd al-Ḥamīd Yūnus, "Ṭāhā Ḥusayn bayna al-Ḍamīr al-Ghā'ib wa-al-Ḍamīr al-Mutakallim," in *Ṭāhā Ḥusayn, Ka-mā Ya'rifuhu Kuttāb 'Aṣrihi* (Cairo: Dār al-Hilāl, n.d.), 63–70.

36. Ṣalāḥ 'Abd al-Ṣabūr, *Mādhā Yabqā,* 10.

37. Muḥammad Ḥasan 'Abdallāh, *Al-Wāqi'iyya fī al-Riwāya al-'Arabiyya* (Cairo: Dār al-Ma'ārif, 1971) 176.

38. Ṣalāḥ 'Abd al-Ṣabūr, *Mādhā Yabqā,* 11.

39. Haykal, *Al-Adab al-Qaṣaṣī,* 217

40. Sakkūt and Jones, *Ṭāhā Ḥusayn,* 43f.

41. 'Alī al-Rā'ī, *Dirāsāt,* 15.

42. 'Alī al-Rā'ī, *Dirāsāt,* 151.

43. Ṭāhā Ḥusayn, *Du'ā',* 11.

44. Ṭāhā Ḥusayn, *Du'ā',* 13.

45. Ṭāhā Ḥusayn, *Du'ā',* 33.

46. Ṭāhā Ḥusayn, *Du'ā',* 132f.

47. Ṭāhā Ḥusayn, *Du'ā',* 128.

Modern Arab Theater: The Journey Back

JOSEPH T. ZEIDAN

When the Lebanese Mārūn al-Naqqāsh, the founder of the modern Arab theater, decided to import the European model of theater in 1847, he did not forget to copy the structures of the stage itself. The British traveler David Urquhart, who had the chance to attend a performance of al-Naqqāsh's *Abū Ḥasan al-Mughaffal* in 1850, left us a most interesting document about the nascent theater struggling to take root in an unfamiliar environment. The architects of al-Naqqāsh's theater were somewhat confused: "they had seen in Europe footlights and a prompter's box, and fancied it an essential point of theatricals to stick them on where they introduced chairs for the Caliph and his Visir, and cheval glasses for the ladies."[1] The irony of the matter was that women were totally excluded, not only from the audience, but also from the troupe: boys played women's roles. Interestingly enough, some devices were invented to accommodate the audience, who were used to a coffee house setting where the popular arts of entertainment were performed rather than to such theaters, "ample spaces being allowed for the service of pipes and nargilles."[2] Not only did the design of the theater reflect the old and new striving to coexist, the performance itself indicated the same endeavor. The

Research for this study was supported by a grant from the National Endowment for the Humanities through the American Research Center in Egypt during the 1989–1990 academic years. I would like to thank both organizations for their support.

major event was a play written in an imported, Westernized form, but for the sake of pleasing the audience, familiar indigenous farce was performed in the intermission. Urquhart described how the audience's intimate identification with this popular act was reflected in the active participation of the ex-mufti of Beirut who was in the audience and responded verbally to the events taking place on stage.[3] The insertion of this short farce indicates al-Naqqāsh's awareness of and expectations of his audience. It was a kind of compensation for the limited interaction between his Europeanized plays and the audience, which was used to popular entertainment in which a great deal of improvisation was practiced.

This combination of the two worlds, the imported and indigenous, was a smart move on al-Naqqāsh's part in order not to alienate his audience. The imported component, however, was more forcefully emphasized by al-Naqqāsh in an attempt, I believe, to somehow distance himself from the indigenous popular theatrical forms. This tendency was highlighted in the speech he gave before staging his first play, *Al-Bakhīl,* in 1847. He told his audience at that time that he was introducing them to "a literary theater, European gold cast in an Arab mould."[4] This emphasis on literary theater, *masraḥ adabī,* has a certain significance: this type of theater, it is implied, differs from the primitive types of traditional entertainment void of any literary value. Al-Naqqāsh, we have to keep in mind, was after all a man of *belles lettres* who was certainly aware of the inferior status of popular literature with which he did not wish to be associated. In his autobiography, Jurjī Zaydān provides us with an idea about the status of one genre of popular theater in Beirut in the second half of the nineteenth century, a short period after the establishment of al-Naqqāsh's theater. Zaydān refers to the *karagöz* (or what the Egyptians called "shadow play") indicating that it was much in demand during the 1870s. "Today," Zaydān reflected, "I wonder how people would be prepared to attend this performance, since it was obscure, thoroughly loathsome, and indecent. No wonder, though, since it reflected the mores of the lowest classes of Beirut . . . whose only occupations were pimping, stealing and provoking passers-by."[5]

Without putting myself in the delicate situation of arguing that the shadow play *(khayāl al-ẓill)*, known to the Arabs at least from the year A.D. 1171, is a full-fledged theater even though it does not comply with the Aristotelian model, I would like to suggest a linkage between this tradition and modern Arab theater which emerged toward the middle of the nineteenth century. Plays of the former sort date from the sixties and seventies of the thirteenth century. Their author, Muḥammad ibn Dāniyāl al-Mawṣilī (ca. 1248–1311), wrote three plays in poetry and rhymed prose: *Ṭayf al-Khayāl* (The shadow spirit), *'Ajīb wa-Gharīb* (The amazing preacher and the stranger), and *Al-Mutayyam* (The lovestricken one).[6]

In addition to the shadow play, I would like to point out the existence of other dramatic activities performed by human actors in the Arab world before the importation of a ready-made theater from Europe.[7] Some of these activities were reported by European travelers themselves. The earliest of such descriptions is provided by the Danish traveler, Carsten Niebuhr, who recounts seeing a farce in Egypt in 1761. The lead role was performed by a man dressed in women's attire who had to struggle to hide his long beard. Niebuhr claims to have discovered a troupe which included Muslim, Christian, and Jewish actors who earned their meager living by performing in public places.[8] An account of such crude rustic performances by human actors is also given by the Italian traveler G. Belzoni, who witnessed them in 1815.[9]

Edward William Lane, the British Orientalist who lived in Egypt during the 1820s and 1830s, tells about a farce that he watched in which a *fellah* (peasant) was beaten and jailed because he was unable to pay his taxes. Lane says, "The Egyptians are often amused by players of low and ridiculous farces which are called *al-Muḥabbiẓūn*. They are frequently performed in the festivals prior to weddings and circumcisions, at the houses of the great and sometimes attract auditors and spectators in the public places in Cairo. Their performances are scarcely worthy of description; it is chiefly by vulgar jests and indecent actions that they amuse, and obtain applause."[10] This popular farce, known as *faṣl muḍḥik,* or "comic act," which emerged before the beginning of the contact between the Arab world and the West and before the advent of the Renaissance *(al-nahḍa)* remained alive in some parts of the Arab world and flourished alongside the Europeanized Arab drama despite its being labeled as vulgar and lacking in a "sophisticated" plot and its being performed mainly for uneducated audiences.

In modern Egypt the cart was put before the horse as far as the Arabic theater was concerned. It was the first Arab country to witness the erection of a European theater when General Menon established a French theater in 1799. It was a short-lived theater where the French, as the Egyptian historian 'Abd al-Raḥmān al-Jabartī tells us, used to gather once every ten days to watch plays presented by members of their own community for entertainment and amusement.[11] The establishment of theaters in Cairo in the late 1860s was only one aspect of Khedive Ismāʻīl's obsession with European culture. The Azbakiyya theater was erected in 1868 to serve foreign touring troupes. The other theater, the Opera House, was built in a great hurry so that Verdi's opera *Aïda* could be performed on the occasion of the completion of the Suez Canal in 1869.[12] These two court theaters were entirely Europeanized, state-funded, and built to accommodate visiting foreign companies. Subsequently, a number of theaters were built in both Cairo and Alexandria primarily to serve foreign troupes.

One of these Europeanized theaters, the Opera House, became the stage of Yaʻqūb Ṣannūʻ's pioneering theater in 1870. Again, as we have seen in al-Naqqāsh's case, Ṣannūʻ chose to overemphasize his indebtedness to Western theater; he gave credit to European troupes visiting Egypt and to Molière, Sheridan, and Goldoni for establishing his theater.[13] Without discounting this influence, one is tempted to examine more closely the indig-enous elements borrowed from the shadow play and comic acts which helped to shape Ṣannūʻ's theater. ʻAlī al-Rāʻī, who did extensive research on early Egyptian drama, noted that Ṣannūʻ's characters, such as the quick-witted native, the religious man *(al-faqīh)* who insists on speaking *fuṣḥā* whether he is understood or not, the foreigner who speaks Arabic in a funny way, and the wife who complains of her husband's injustice despite her loyalty are borrowed from the puppet theater.[14] Ṣannūʻ's theater showed some striking similarities to the technique of the commedia dell'arte. He, however, was performing on a traditional stage and since his actors were inexperienced amateurs not fully prepared to act in straightforward improvisation, an alternative device was invented to give the air of improvisation. Acting as a prompter, Ṣannūʻ would instruct the actors on how to respond to the interruptions and input from the audience. This theater, which succeeded, to a great extent, in interacting with some forms of popular theater and in trying to tackle some of the social and cultural problems of the Egyptian people by using the Egyptian colloquial, came to an abrupt end when Khedive Ismāʻīl ordered its closure in 1872, two years after its inception. Ṣannūʻ's theater had a well-defined aesthetic which delicately balanced what Ṣannūʻ conceived of as the dual mission of the theater—both to entertain and to agitate. Consequently, Ṣannūʻ's aesthetic reflected his interest in developing a direct and interactive link between audience and stage. Artistic characteristics such as dramatic content involving the use of themes, characters, and plot sequences drawn from contemporary society, popular culture, and folklore; skeleton scripts suitable for highly improvisatory performances; the use of the Egyptian colloquial Arabic; and the incorporation of music and other comic elements borrowed from the popular shadow play and puppet theater helped encourage the audience's active participation.

The emergence of Levantine troupes on the Egyptian scene in the 1870s signaled the end of one era and the beginning of a new one. The theater became more institutionalized and overwhelmingly commercial. There are some objective reasons for abandoning the tradition of improvisation:

1. The actors as well as the playwrights, adapters, and translators were, especially in the beginning, non-Egyptian, and the Egyptian vernacular was not a natural medium for them.

2. These troupes were inheritors of Mārūn al-Naqqāsh's theatrical heritage. They believed that *fuṣḥā* was the appropriate language for any intellectual activity. The use of *fuṣḥā,* which is not a spontaneous means of communication, would not have allowed the tradition of improvisation to continue.

3. The repertoire of these troupes relied heavily on translations and adaptations from the theater of Europe. Consequently, the subject matter of these productions remained alien to the audience.

The arrival of the first Levantine troupe in Egypt in 1876 is shrouded with some mystery. Salīm Khalīl al-Naqqāsh, Mārūn's nephew and disciple and the director of the troupe, disclosed that after meeting Draneth Bey, the manager of the Opera House, the Khedive issued an order allowing him to perform Arabic plays in this theater.[15] Immediately after that crucial meeting, Salīm went back to Beirut to organize a theatrical troupe and started to prepare his repertoire. Because of the hot summers of Cairo, the troupe was allowed to rehearse in Beirut with the understanding that it would come to Cairo in the autumn. The costumes, however, were sent to Cairo in advance. But the outbreak of cholera in Beirut and the subsequent ban imposed by the Egyptians on passengers coming from Beirut disrupted al-Naqqāsh's plans. To our amazement, we read in *Al-Ahrām,* on December 16, 1876, about the arrival of Salīm's troupe, consisting of twelve actors and four actresses, at Alexandria rather than Cairo. As expected, Salīm brought with him his uncle's three plays in addition to five plays which he had translated or adapted from

Italian and French: *'Ā'ida,* adapted from Verdi's opera *Aïda; Mayy aw Hūrās,* adapted from Corneille's play *Horace; Al-Kadhūb,* adapted from Corneille's *Le Menteur;* and two other works, *Gharā'ib al-Ṣudaf* (Strange coincidences) and *Al-Ẓalūm* (The tyrant), assumed to be based on European plays. But unfortunately, Salīm soon realized that the songs that his uncle used in his plays were not as common in Egypt as they were in Lebanon. So he asked a private tutor, Buṭrus al-Shalfūn, to teach the troupe Egyptian popular music and devoted himself to this for three months.[16] That might explain why Salīm refrained from producing *Al-Bakhīl* (an opera) despite the fact that the troupe had rehearsed it in Beirut. Instead, he chose to produce *Abū al-Ḥasan al-Mughaffal* followed by *Al-Salīṭ al-Ḥasūd,* two operettas, and other plays adapted from French (especially, *Horace* by Corneille). These did not meet with much success. So Salīm sought the help of an old friend from Beirut, Adīb Isḥāq, who had already made an adaptation of Racine's *Andromaque* at the request of the French consul. Isḥāq joined al-Naqqāsh in Alexandria, but despite their serious efforts to succeed, they finally gave up, turned to journalism, and left the fate of the troupe in the hands of one of its gifted actors, Yūsuf al-Khayyāṭ.

The other important Levantine troupe arriving in Egypt was that of Aḥmad Abū Khalīl al-Qabbānī from Damascus. Al-Qabbānī's cultural orientation was completely different from Salīm al-Naqqāsh's. He had received a purely traditional education, which excluded European languages, first in a *kuttāb* and then at the Umayyad mosque in Damascus. From his early youth, he showed a profound interest in singing and music, public popular literature, and the puppet theater. These elements were to determine the direction that al-Qabbānī's theater took and were responsible for his continuous success in Egypt. Al-Qabbānī's theatrical activities flourished around the year 1878 when, thanks to the Turkish governor Midḥat Pasha, he joined hands with Iskandar Faraḥ to form a theatrical group. This troupe soon ran into trouble with the conservative camp in Damascus for a variety of reasons, among which was their inclusion of two Lebanese actresses and their representing the personage of Hārūn al-Rashīd on stage. As a consequence, the Ottoman authorities sealed al-Qabbānī's theater. The troupe, however, did not give up. As a result of the encouragement received from different parties, especially from the famous Egyptian singer 'Abduh al-Ḥamūlī,[17] the troupe moved to Alexandria in 1884, and there resumed its activities. Al-Ḥamūlī's encouragement was especially vital and translated into active participation in the troupe's performances from the very first performance. When the troupe moved to Cairo to perform on the Opera House stage, al-Ḥamūlī took part in ten of its fifteen performances during January of 1885.

This Egyptian element, missing in the case of Salīm al-Naqqāsh's group, proved to be crucial in winning the acceptance of the Egyptian audience. Al-Qabbānī was closer to the taste of the Egyptian audience because of his choice of sources for his plays, namely folk literature, the *Arabian Nights,* and Arab history. Singing was another important factor, together with the introduction of a collective dance called *raqṣat al-samāḥ,* which resembles ballet. In addition, al-Qabbānī did not abandon the popular farces, *al-fuṣūl al-muḍḥika,* and incorporated acts in pantomime which were performed in the intervals or at the end of his formal plays.

Al-Qabbānī's lasting contribution to the Arab theater does not, certainly, lie in his skills as playwright. His flowery *saj'* (rhymed prose) was often combined with verse dealing with historical themes having little or no modern context made him a continuation of the static past and prevented him from creating a lively and flexible style. Al-Qabbānī's greatest impact is in the sphere of musical theater, where he was both master and mentor. Even such a talented singer as Salāma Ḥijāzī used to send him students.

The two troupes, those of Salīm al-Naqqāsh and al-Qabbānī, were the two master troupes from which several splinter troupes emerged. In the year 1891, for instance, all the major active theatrical troupes in Egypt were Levantine:

1. Yūsuf al-Khayyāṭ's troupe (1877)
2. Sulaymān al-Qurdāḥī's troupe (1882)
3. Al-Qabbānī's troupe (1884)
4. Sulaymān al-Ḥaddād's troupe, *Al-Jawq al-Waṭanī al- Miṣrī,* (1887)
5. Iskandar Faraḥ's troupe (1891)

All these troupes struggled hard to attract and retain the Egyptian audience. Al-Khayyāṭ was the first one to accommodate Egyptian actors in his troupe. The real ticket to the hearts and minds of the Egyptian audience, however, was the renowned singer Salāma Ḥijāzī, and most of the Levantine troupes tried to recruit him. Ḥijāzī started his career with al-Khayyāṭ's troupe in 1884 as a singer in the intermissions. In the following year, Sulaymān al-Qurdāḥī succeeded in luring him to sing and act in his troupe. By 1891,

Ḥijāzī had joined the troupe of Iskandar Faraḥ where he continued to work until forming his own troupe in 1905. The fortunes of a certain troupe were determined to a great extent by whether or not Ḥijāzī was in it.

The repertoire for these troupes was supplied by a small cadre of writers most of whom were Levantines such as Salīm Khalīl al-Naqqāsh, Najīb al-Ḥaddād, Amīn al-Ḥaddād, Ṭānyūs ʻAbduh, and Ilyās Fayyāḍ. Most of the plays produced in Egypt in the last quarter of the nineteenth century were translations or adaptations of European originals. Most of the persons involved in this task were graduates of French schools in Lebanon, Syria, or Egypt. This phenomenon, together with the fact that French was the most important European language in Egypt from the time of Muḥammad ʻAlī's reign until the British occupation in 1882, was responsible for the fact that most of the European plays chosen were either originally written in French or had been translated into French from some other European language. Some of Shakespeare's plays, for instance, were translated into Arabic from French, rather than from English. The most remarkable example was Ṭānyūs ʻAbduh's popular adaptation of *Hamlet,* which was produced by the troupe of al-Qurdāḥī, Ḥijāzī and Yūsuf Wahbī.

By resorting to *taʻrīb* (Arabization) rather than straightforward translation, the men of the Arab theater were trying to bring these plays closer to the tastes and environment of the audience. Some facts should be kept in mind in order to keep their activities in proper perspective and to evaluate them more objectively. First of all, the early audience came to this new theater from other forms of entertainment in which music and singing were indispensable ingredients. Therefore, we have seen that the early adapters inserted verses to be sung in the body of the play or incorporated common songs of the period. Some of these, strangely enough, were in the vernacular, whereas *fuṣḥā* was the language of the rest of the text. Secondly, some of the originals underwent drastic changes by virtue of the adapter's freely omitting, condensing or altering the source. Edward al-Yāfī, for instance, was able to identify four hundred instances of alteration of the original text in Najīb al-Ḥaddād's adaptation of *Le Cid* by Corneille.[18] In other extreme cases the whole course of events was twisted around without any intrinsic justification. In Ṭānyūs ʻAbduh's version of Shakespeare's *Hamlet,* for instance, one is certainly bewildered to find out that the play ends with Hamlet alive and victorious after having managed, with the help of his father's ghost, to defeat his enemies and to regain the Danish throne! The reasoning which underlies this tendency must be understood in light of folk literature and its universal desire to achieve happy endings. Some of these adapters did not hesitate to blame their audiences for their need to make such changes.[19]

The final and most striking feature of the Levantine theater was its preoccupation with historical themes, whether Arab or foreign, formal, or popular. This phenomenon should be studied against the problem of the dichotomy in the Arabic language itself. *Fuṣḥā* has been, generally speaking, acclaimed as the appropriate language for the translation of the European classics and for the writing of historical plays. The colloquial language, on the other hand, has generally been considered to be the adequate medium for both comedies and social plays, for the former type because the vernacular itself is rich, due to historical factors, in comic potential and for the latter because colloquial is the actual medium of communication used on a daily basis in society. Therefore, it is held to be more "natural" or "life-like."

Arab playwrights were confronted with this issue from the very beginning, starting with Mārūn al-Naqqāsh, al-Qabbānī and Ṣannū'. Whereas the first two playwrights solved the problem by adhering to *fuṣḥā,* Ṣannū' chose the Egyptian vernacular. Ṣannū''s justification for this choice can be found in Mitrī's phrase in *Molière Miṣr wa-mā Yuqāsīh* (The Molière of Egypt and his sufferings), where he comments that "comedy is about what actually takes place and happens among the people."[20] Let us not forget that these troupes were overwhelmingly controlled by Levantine playwrights, producers, and actors. We cannot, therefore, expect them to stage plays in the Egyptian vernacular, particularly early on. Consequently, Ṣannū''s plays, which had dominated the Egyptian stage only four years before the arrival of the first Levantine troupe, were totally ignored. Furthermore, Muḥammad 'Uthmān Jalāl was forced to initiate a new trend in the history of Arab theater, that of publishing plays before they were staged. He published two separate volumes of translations of plays into metrical Egyptian vernacular: one volume containing four comedies by Molière in 1890 and a second volume in 1894 containing three tragedies by Racine. Not until 1912 was one of these plays, *Al-Shaykh Matlūf (Tartuffe)* by Molière, actually staged.[21] 'Abd Allāh al-Nadīm's plays, since they were written in vernacular, had to be performed by his own students rather than by the Levantine troupes.[22]

From that time until the 1960s, the mainstream theater in the Arab world became more and more Westernized, letting the popular theater fade away, especially in the urban areas. This insistence on ignoring local issues and dwelling on Arab or historical ones led some Egyptian critics, like Louis 'Awaḍ, to argue that this Levantine phase in the history of the Egyptian theater, although it extended well into the 1920s, was a transient one but one that still was able to halt the development of a national Egyptian theater like the one founded by Ṣannū' and Muḥammad 'Uthmān Jalāl. 'Awaḍ believes, and rightly so, that one aspect of the Levantine contribution to the Egyptian theater is reflected in "the choice of benign themes which have no social or political implications."[23]

Starting in the second decade of the twentieth century, the Westernization of the Egyptian theater, the most active in the Arab world, was carried out by actors and/or producers who either studied the art of theater or were profoundly exposed to it in the West. Perhaps the first of this breed was George Abyaḍ,[24] who studied theater in France for six years at the expense of Khedive 'Abbās II. In 1912 he established a company for Arabic performances completely after the European model. He was hailed as the founder of the first real artistic theater in Egypt which could stand on its own without resorting to music or farcical episodes. His repertoire consisted of classics like *Oedipus, Louis XIV,* and *Othello,* and in all of them he himself played the leading part. Yūsuf Wahbī, another actor-manager and playwright, traveled to Italy in 1921 where he attended a school of elocution and acting. Another important figure who tried to solidify the Western orientation of the Egyptian theater was Zakī Ṭulaymāt, who was educated in France. Upon his return from France in 1930 after four years of study, he established a school of drama *(Ma'had Fann al-Tamthīl)* which was overwhelmingly Western oriented. This school led to the foundation of the Academy of Arts, a prestigious institute.

The Westernized form of the drama reached a high degree of maturity and sophistication in the early 1960s. Tawfīq al-Ḥakīm and to a lesser extent Maḥmūd Taymūr played an important role in expanding the scope and range of Egyptian drama. In half a century Arab playwrights had tried their hand at almost every dramatic trend in Europe from vaudeville to the theater of the absurd. Their accomplishments are undoubtedly impressive. A new ambitious generation of playwrights who emerged after the 1952 revolution showed a clear inclination to focus on the social and political malaise in Egypt. They knew how to take advantage of the relative freedom Egypt enjoyed in the first years of the revolution before the regime's grip on the theater was tightened. They were particularly safe because they were dealing mainly with the shortcomings of the previous royal regime. The initial readiness of Nasser's government to find solutions to some of these compelling social problems, symbolized by the so-called Socialist Ordinances of 1961, gave this generation a good dose of optimism. However, signs of conflict between the regime and the intelligentsia began to appear toward the middle of the 1960s.[25] At any rate, it is safe to say that the new regime paid a great deal of attention to long-forgotten classes in Egypt, especially the peasants and workers, who were considered the builders of Arab socialism.

We ought to understand some of Tawfīq al-Ḥakīm's experiments in the field of drama against this background. Already in his play *Al-Ṣafqa* (The deal, 1956) al-Ḥakīm tried to find a solution for, among other things, the lack of theatrical facilities in the countryside. The action takes place entirely in a village square and therefore it needs a minimum of props for staging. Another important aspect of this work lies in the fact that it was the first play to try to utilize features of *al-sāmir,* a peasant theater-in-the-round which employed dance, music, and singing. In his next experiment, *Qālabunā al-Masraḥī* (1968), al-Ḥakīm resorted to yet another traditional dramatic style: the narrator *(al-ḥakawātī)* and impersonator form. The narrator introduces the show, directs it openly, and pauses to explain expressions and thoughts whenever necessary. The second actor plays the part or parts designated for him after mentioning his real name. In an effort to demonstrate the suitability of this theatrical form to a variety of plays throughout history, al-Ḥakīm presented extracts from seven playwrights: Aeschylus, Shakespeare, Molière, Ibsen, Chekhov, Pirandello and Dürrenmatt. Although this type of theater, labeled by 'Alī al-Rā'ī as "a poor man's theater,"[26] does not require a stage, decor, lighting, make-up or costumes, it is, al-Ḥakīm is convinced, a vehicle to popularize the art of high culture. Despite all these experiments attempting to explore new dramatic formulas to suit certain audiences and places, al-Ḥakīm's belief in the Westernized form of drama was never shaken. He envisaged that these formulas could coexist with the mainstream one.

Yūsuf Idrīs's point of departure was totally different from that of al-Ḥakīm. In three articles published by the Cairo monthly *Al-Kātib* (1964) significantly entitled "Towards an Egyptian Theater,"[27] Idrīs raises some essential issues related to the very nature of the theater in Egypt. Perhaps the most important one is his denial of the existence of an Egyptian theater in the true sense. The present form of the theater found there, Idrīs argues, is non-Egyptian; it was brought from Europe (especially from France) by

Levantine immigrants through the adaptation and translation of plays and the total embracing of Western dramaturgy. After 1919, a whole generation of Egyptian playwrights and producers, who were brought up within this alien tradition, helped to solidify and perpetuate the trend. The truly national Egyptian theater, Idrīs believes, is yet to be born. It is a quest for an authentic Egyptian form able to express Egyptian themes. Idrīs states:

> For creating our Egyptian theater it will not be enough to find only an Egyptian theme, but it is necessary for us to create a form which would spring from the theme, would be adequate to it, and could underline and present it in a way loaded with content.[28]

Idrīs follows a path characteristic of Egyptian thought after 1952: that the true Egyptian spirit is to be found in the countryside which remained untainted by foreign elements. He singled out *al-sāmir,* a peasant theater-in-the-round composed of acting, music, and dance, as a relevant dramatic form which could replace the Westernized one. This popular theatrical form contains an important feature in Idrīs's formula; it allows a free interaction between the performers and the audience. This interaction is a prerequisite to that spiritual elevation, *"al-tamasruḥ,"* which can only be achieved by the theater when actor and spectator become one and the same.

If one is fascinated by the idea of comparing theory to practice, Idrīs's case is an interesting one. Idrīs tried to apply his theory to a play, *Al-Farāfīr,* that he wrote during this period (it was staged in 1963–1964). In his prefatory notes to the printed version, Idrīs provides some instructions on the staging of *Al-Farāfīr:*

> 1. The play requires the active participation of the audience during the performance.
>
> 2. The appropriate stage for performing the play should be a theater-in-the-round, in which the audience should form a circle around the actors.
>
> 3. Actors should not get carried away by their parts; they should remain keenly aware of the needs and reactions of the audience.[29]

The first requirement, however, could not be fulfilled primarily owing to political circumstances that Idrīs, I believe, overlooked in his theorizing. Instead of free input by the audience, Idrīs was satisfied in the printed form with feigned improvisation by placing some of his actors in the midst of the audience. In the performed script, these actors were put on stage as a chorus. (First state censorship, then the producer, determined the fate of this essential component of Idrīs's play, i.e., the participation of the audience.) If the first prerequisite is eliminated, I wonder if the issue of the form of the stage (whether it is the Italian box or the theater-in-the-round) is still a valid one. Furthermore, one is tempted to ask why the insistence on the actors keeping an eye on the audience's reaction once this reaction has ceased to be part of the game.

Idrīs's experimentation in *Al-Farāfīr* is neither revolutionary nor original. Most, if not all, of the issues have been raised and dealt with in modern Western theater and there is no reason to believe that Idrīs was not aware of this when he articulated his own theory. One can identify much more easily the areas of Idrīs's indebtedness to Western theater than to *al-sāmir*. Clearly, Idrīs has benefited greatly from the commedia dell'arte, Pirandello, Beckett, and above all Brecht, especially in his technique of alienation. *Al-Farāfīr* was a one-time experiment. It failed to serve as a model for a new theater in Egypt. Even Idrīs himself abandoned this form in his succeeding plays.[30]

The devastating defeat of 1967 forced the Arabs to rethink their social, political and cultural institutions. The theater was not exempt from this soul-searching, particularly since it was state run in most Arab countries. A pressing need was felt by some Arab intellectuals to utilize this tool to bring about the desired changes in society. The "theater of politicization," *masraḥ al-tasyīs,*[31] advocated by the Syrian playwright Sa'd Allāh Wannūs, was one manifestation of this awareness. Prior to 1967 Wannūs, a graduate of the Theater Institute at the Sorbonne, wrote plays within the tradition of the French avant-garde school, dealing rather calmly with a variety of social and metaphysical issues. His message, however, was never urgent and his perception of the ultimate function of the theater was somewhat vague. After 1967 Wannūs, realizing the potential political role of the theater, became preoccupied with the other half of the equation of the shows, the audience. The audience, Wannūs believes, should be actively involved and should become more aggressive. To quote him:

> The spectator is not a pupil in an elementary school who has to listen in total silence and submission to whatever he is ordered to do. The spectator is the essential half of any dramatic performance. He is the target of this show and he is also accountable for it. Therefore, he has to fully practice his rights and completely and positively fulfill his role.

> He has to take part in every theatrical activity; to accept and reject, to exert pressure and interrupt, to say whatever he wants and correct what he is told. . . . The spectator is required to be attentive and forward. In this way only will many trivialities and lies be abolished. Then the theater will become an efficient social and cultural activity forging the stage and audience in a rich and strong dialectical relation.[32]

The theater of politicization, according to Wannūs, should have an agitational function which leads first to awareness, then to positive action. The audience should be charged rather than discharged by the theatrical experience.

Wannūs's free use of Brecht's principles of the epic theater is rather obvious here. Brecht had already stated, "The spectator was no longer in any way allowed to submit to an experience uncritically . . . by means of simple empathy with the characters in a play."[33] Brecht's technique of alienation was borrowed by Wannūs, but he coupled it with an insistence on the active participation of the audience through spontaneous or pretended improvisation.

Wannūs's initial attempt to carry out this version of theater was bound to lead him to a confrontation with the authorities. When he wrote *Ḥaflat Samar min Ajl Khamsa Ḥazīrān* (A party to celebrate the fifth of June) he found himself forced to publish it in a periodical in Beirut (*Mawāqif,* 1968) rather than in Damascus. The play was banned in Syria, and its staging was unthinkable until 1971, when a new regime rose to power. Interestingly enough, the new regime behaved like the revolutionary regime in Egypt after 1952: it allowed the freedom of criticizing the previous regime and *Ḥaflat Samar min Ajl Khamsa Ḥazīrān* was staged in Damascus in 1971. A subtle way to avoid direct confrontation with the political establishment was now much needed. Wannūs turned to Arab history in search of material that would correspond to and illuminate the present.

The official date and place of birth as well as the parentage of the Arab theater (1847, Lebanon, Mārūn al-Naqqāsh) started to be widely challenged in the Arab world in the 1960s. A number of scholars, as well as playwrights, refused to accept the notion that the Greco-Roman model was the only criterion for determining the existence of theater in a culture. Several attempts were made to draw attention to some classical literary genres rich in dramatic elements like *al-maqāma* and *al-risāla.* The Egyptian ʿAlī al-Rāʿī labeled the *maqāma* as a drama in embryo. He analyzed Badīʿ al-Zamān al-Hamadhānī's *maqāma,* "Al-Maḍīriyya," in an attempt to prove that it was very close to a one-act play. Al-Rāʿī concluded, "It was a play which only religious restrictions deprived of the title of play."[34] On the other hand, the Egyptian Bint al-Shāṭi' ('Ā'isha 'Abd al-Raḥmān) rewrote the *risāla* of Abū al-'Alā al-Ma'arrī, *Risālat al-Ghufrān,* in the form of a three-act play, describing it as "a dramatic text from the fifth century A.H."[35] Other scholars highlighted the fact that Arabs knew the shadow play *(khayāl al-ẓill)* at least as early as A.D. 1171 and that three such plays *(bābāt)* of Ibn Dāniyāl have survived.

The rise of political movements with socialist orientations, especially that of Nasser in Egypt, and the gradual secularization of some Arab states were decisive factors in creating an atmosphere of tolerance towards popular literature and folklore. The period when regions of the Arab world achieved national independence from European colonial powers spawned an interest in recapturing and reasserting indigenous aspects of Arab culture in an attempt to confront and remove the more subtle vestiges of the region's century-and-a-half experience of domination by the West. Under the influence of Nasser's ideology of Arab socialism, Arab intellectuals set out to reconstruct, using indigenous elements, an Arab cultural identity that could encompass Arabs from all levels of society, from the uneducated rural peasantry to the highly sophisticated urban elites. This trend paved the way for accepting popular art forms as part of the legacy of the Arab theater. In the field of the shadow play, for example, a line of continuity was suggested between the oldest plays of Ibn Dāniyāl, written in the thirteenth century in *fuṣḥā,* and the Manzala manuscript (unearthed by Paul Kahle in 1909) written in the seventeenth century in Egyptian dialect. A more ambitious theory, although one not without serious flaws, was put forward by 'Alī al-Rā'ī who argued that the *faṣl muḍḥik* (popular farce) which entertained Arabs well into the first quarter of the twentieth century can be traced back to the *maqāmāt* of the tenth century. So "a long and uninterrupted line of drama," al-Rā'ī indicates, "can thus be seen to extend over several centuries." The Arab theater was born long before Mārūn al-Naqqāsh, as al-Rā'ī states, "To say that the Arabs have known the theater since the Middle Ages no longer need seem strange or provocative."[36]

Not only was popular theater widely acknowledged, it became, in Egypt for example, a symbol of authentic art reflecting the true spirit of the people. In Yūsuf Idrīs's case, the popular theater, *al-sāmir,* was elevated to replace the mainstream, Westernized theater which had failed to express the real needs of the Egyptian people because it was the product of a totally different culture.

The endeavor to rediscover an indigenous literary aesthetic, in terms of both form or genre and content, has produced some decidedly nontraditional results. The most striking of these has been the emergence of the Arabic theater, replacing the *qaṣīda,* or oral poetry, as the genre of choice among Arab authors, playwrights, and intellectuals seeking to address the broadest possible audience on issues and problems of concern to them and to stimulate those audiences to active participation in solving them. In the past, poetry had performed this function in Arab society. But modern innovations, largely the result of influence from Western literary circles, had rendered Arabic poetry a far more literate genre, characterized by frequent references to non-Arabic myth and symbol. Modern Arabic poetry as a genre, then, became far more suitable for private reading than public recitation, a transformation which moved poetry out of the reach of mass or popular audiences and placed it in the purview of educated intellectuals. In light of this development in Arabic poetry, the Arabic theater emerged as the most effective and efficient literary tool through which to present contemporary social, political, and economic problems to mass audiences and with which to stimulate their active participation in confronting these problems.

Notes

1. David Urquhart, *The Lebanon: (Mount Syria): A History and Diary,* vol. 2 (London: Thomas Cauttey Newby, 1860), 178.

2. Urquhart, *The Lebanon,* 179.

3. Urquhart, *The Lebanon,* 180.

4. Mārūn al-Naqqāsh, *Arzat Lubnān,* ed. Niqūlā al-Naqqāsh (Beirut: al-Maṭba'a al-'Umūmiyya, 1869), 15.

5. Jurjī Zaydān, *Mudhakkirāt Jurjī Zaydān,* ed. Ṣalāḥ al-Dīn al-Munajjid (Beirut: Dār al-Kitāb al-Jadīd, 1968), 21. Philip Hitti in *Lebanon in History from the Earliest Times to the Present,* 3rd ed. (London: St. Martin's Press, 1967), 426,.gives us the following account regarding the entertaining life in Syria during the Egyptian invasion in the 1830s:

> Shadow plays, story tellers dramatizing the exploits of 'Antar, Ṣalaḥ al-Dīn and Baybars, players on the castanet and tambourine, Egyptian dancing girls with eyes full of fire, faces tattooed and besmeared with kohl (Ar. *kuḥl*), entertained merrymakers sipping coffee and smoking hubble-bubble (Ar. *nārjīlah*). Coffee-house relaxation was a near Eastern version of American Students bullsessions."

6. Ibrāhīm Ḥamāda's publication of these plays suffered greatly from a self-imposed "moral" censorship. See his book, *Khayāl al-Ẓill wa-Tamthīliyyāt Ibn Dāniyāl* (Cairo: Al-Mu'assasa al-Miṣriyya al-'Āmma li-al-Ta'līf wa-al-Tarjama wa-al-Nashr, 1963). Paul Kahle's edition, which was prepared for publication by Derek Hopwood and Mustafa Badawi, does more justice to Ibn Dāniyāl's work. See Paul Kahle, ed., *Three Shadow Plays by Muḥammad Ibn Dāniyāl* (Cambridge: Trustees of the E. J. W. Gibb Memorial Fund, 1992).

7. Shmuel Moreh cogently argues that there was a tradition of Arabic dramatic literature during the Islamic Middle Ages. See his book *Live Theatre and Dramatic Literature in the Medieval Arabic World* (New York: New York University Press, 1992).

8. Carsten Niebuhr, *Travels Through Arabia and Other Countries in the East,* trans. Robert Heron (Edinburgh: R. Morrison, 1792), 145

9. Giovanni B. Belzoni, *Narratives of the Operations and Recent Discoveries in Egypt and Nobia* (London: J. Hurray, 1820), 19.

10. Edward William Lane, *An Account of the Manners and Customs of the Modern Egyptians* (London: New York: Ward & Lock Co., 1890), 384. For more details regarding *al-muḥabbiẓūn,* see Muḥammad Qindīl al-Baqlī, "Al-Muḥabbiẓūn fī al-'Aṣr al-Mamlūkī," *Al-Jadīd* (Cairo), 210 (October 1, 1980): 52-53.

11. Abd al-Raḥmān al-Jabartī, *'Ajā'ib al-Āthār fī al-Tarājim wa-al-Akhbār,* vol. 3 (Cairo: Būlāq, 1879), 142.

12. *Aïda* was not completed in time for the opening of the Suez Canal, and a performance of *Rigoletto* was given instead. *Egyptian Gazette,* 27 July 1933, p. 2. Quoted in Nevill Barbour, "The Arabic Theatre in Egypt," *Bulletin of the School of Oriental Studies,* 8 (1935–37): 173.

13. Quoted in Muḥammad Yūsuf Najm, *Al-Masraḥiyya fī al-Adab al-'Arabī al-Ḥadīth* (Beirut: Dār Bayrūt, 1956), 80.

14. 'Alī al-Rā'ī, *Funūn al-Kūmīdyā min Khayāl al-Ẓill ilā Najīb al-Rīḥānī* (Cairo: Dār al-Hilāl, 1971), 84–92.

15. Salīm Khalīl Naqqāsh, "Fawā'id al-Riwāyāt aw al-Thiyātrāt aw Nisbat al-Riwāyāt ilā Hay'at al-Ijtimā'," *Al-Jinān* 15 (August 1, 1875): 516–23. See also "Al-Riwāyāt al-'Arabiyya al-Miṣriyya," *Al-Jinān* 13 (July 1, 1875): 443.

16. Buṭrus Shalfūn, "Al-Tamthīl al-'Arabī," *Al-Hilāl* 15, no. 2 (November 1906): 117.

17. Some sources mention that al-Qabbānī was encouraged to move to Egypt by Sa'd Allāh Ḥallāba, a wealthy Syrian merchant who was residing in Alexandria. See Muḥammad Yūsuf Najm, introduction to *Al-Shaykh Aḥmad Abū Khalīl al-Qabbānī,* by Aḥmad Abū Khalīl al-Qabbānī (Beirut: Dār al-Thaqāfa, 1963), 1; Muḥammad Kamāl al-Dīn, *Ruwwād al-Masraḥ al-Miṣrī* (Cairo: Al-Hay'a al-Miṣriyya li-al-Kitāb, 1970), 40–41.

18. Edward S. al-Yāfī, *Najīb al-Ḥaddād al-Mutarjim al-Masraḥī* (Cairo: Ma'had al-Buḥūth wa-al-Dirāsāt al-'Arabiyya, 1976), 8.

19. See, for example, the confession of the playwright George Ṭannūs who took the liberty of making alterations in one of Voltaire's plays which he adapted, as quoted in Maḥmūd Ḥāmid Shawkat, *Al-Fann al-Masraḥī fī al-Adab al-'Arabī al-Ḥadīth,* 2nd ed. (Cairo: Dār al-Fikr al-'Arabī, 1970), 37. Adīb Isḥāq found it appropriate to alter the end of Racine's *Andromaque* to a happy one in his adapted version to please his audience. See Sa'd al-Dīn Daghmān Ḥ., *Al-Uṣūl al-Tārikhiyya li-Nash'at al-Drāmā fī al-Adab al-'Arabī* (Beirut: Jāmi'at Bayrūt al-'Arabiyya, 1973), 213.

20. Ya'qūb Ṣannū', *Ya'qūb Ṣannū' (Abū Naḍḍāra),* ed. Muḥammad Yūsuf Najm (Beirut: Dār al-Thaqāfa, 1963), 200.

21. Najm, *Ya'qūb Ṣannū',* 200.

22. Naffūsa Zakariyyā Sa'īd, *'Abd Allāh al-Nadīm bayna al-Fuṣḥā wa-al-'Āmmiyya* (Alexandria: Al-Dār al-Qawmiyya li-al-Ṭibā'a wa-al-Nashr, 1966), 9.

23. Louis 'Awaḍ, "Problems of the Egyptian Theater," in *Studies in Modern Arabic Literature,* ed. R. C. Ostle (London: Aris and Phillips, 1975), 181.

24. For more details about George Abyaḍ, see Su'ād Abyaḍ, *George Abyaḍ: Ayyām lan Yusdal 'alayhā al-Sitār* (Cairo: Dār al-Ma'ārif, 1970).

25. For a discussion of the conflict between the theater and the regime in Egypt during Nasser's rule, see Nissim Rejwan, *Nasserist Ideology: Its Exponents and Critics* (Jerusalem: Israel Universities Press, 1974), 143–61. See also Fāṭima Yūsuf Muḥammad, *Al-Masraḥ wa-al-Sulṭa fī Miṣr min 1952–1970* (Cairo: Al-Hay'a al-Miṣriyya al-'Āmma li-al-Kitāb, 1994).

26. 'Alī al-Rā'ī, "Some Aspects of Modern Arabic Drama," in *Studies in Modern Arabic Literature,* ed. R. C. Ostle (London: Aris and Phillips, 1975), 169.

27. Idrīs used these three articles as an introduction for his play *Al-Farāfīr* (Cairo: Dār Miṣr li-al-Ṭibā'a, n.d.).

28. Idrīs, 51.

29. Idrīs, 64–65.

30. For more discussion of *Al-Farāfīr,* see Rajā' al-Naqqāsh, *Fī Aḍwā' al-Masraḥ* (Cairo: Dār al-Ma'ārif, 1965), 106–35; Julius Gella, "*Al-Farāfīr:* A Problematic Experience in the Search for the Egyptian National Dramatic Form," *Graecolatina et Orientalia* 9–10 (1977–1978): 225–40. For the political implication of this play, see Fatḥī Ibrāhīm, *Kūmīdyā al-Ḥukm al-Shumūlī* (Cairo: Al-Hay'a al-Miṣriyya al-'Āmma li-al-Kitāb, 1991), 39–64.

31. See Wannūs's definition of *masraḥ al-tasyīs* in Sa'd Allāh Wannūs, *Bayānāt li-Masraḥ 'Arabī Jadīd* (Beirut: Dār al-Fikr al-Jadīd, 1988), 88–113. For a comprehensive study of Wannūs's dramatic works and theory, see Roger Allen, "Arabic Drama in Theory and Practice: the Writings of Sa'dallāh Wannūs," *Journal of Arabic Literature* 15 (1984): 94–113.

32. Sa'd Allāh Wannūs, "Bayānāt li-Masraḥ 'Arabī Jadīd," *Al-Ma'rifa* 104 (October 1970): 31.

33. Bertolt Brecht, *Brecht on Theatre,* ed. and trans. John Wille (New York: Hill and Wang, 1966), 71.

34. 'Alī al-Rā'ī, "Some Aspects of Modern Arabic Drama," 173. See also 'Alī al-Rā'ī, *Funūn al-Kūmīdyā,* 47.

35. Bint al-Shāṭi' ('Ā'isha 'Abd al-Raḥmān), *Jadīd fī Risālat al-Ghufrān: Naṣṣ Masraḥī min al-Qarn al-Khāmis al-Hijrī* (Beirut: n.p., 1972).

36. 'Alī al-Rā'ī, "Some Aspects of Modern Arabic Drama," 173.

Film and Pharaonism: Shādī 'Abd al-Salām's *Eloquent Peasant*

Allen Douglas and Fedwa Malti-Douglas

In 1986, cancer robbed Egypt of Shādī 'Abd al-Salām, arguably its finest filmmaker, and without question its most sophisticated artistic interpreter of the Pharaonic tradition. His 1970 film, *Al-Fallāḥ al-Faṣīḥ (The Eloquent Peasant),* is at once a little-known masterpiece of Egyptian cinema and the most faithful and sophisticated retelling of an authentic ancient Egyptian text in a modern medium.

Shādī 'Abd al-Salām was born in 1930 into an upper-middle class Muslim family in Alexandria. Like that other great Alexandrine director, Yūsuf Shāhīn, Shādī 'Abd al-Salām studied in that city's prestigious Victoria College. Visits to family in Upper Egypt awakened in the young Shādī a profound fascination with the Pharaonic past and admiration for the traditional popular culture of the Nile Valley.

From his adolescence, Shādī combined his attraction to the remote past with a passionate love for the most modern of art forms, the cinema. On the insistence of his parents that he prepare himself for a "serious" career, the young Alexandrine took a degree in architecture, though he never abandoned his love for the seventh art.

Shādī began his professional film career as an art director for films set in ancient Egypt. He assisted in both Mankiewicz's infamous *Cleopatra* and Kawalerowicz's *Pharaoh*. But the Egyptian filmmaker's most important artistic collaboration was with Roberto Rosselini for whom he also served as art director. Though Rosselini came closer than anyone else to being Shādī's artistic godfather and it was he who gave the young Egyptian the crucial encouragement to jump into feature filmmaking, Shādī's cinematic style is not in any important way derivative from that of the pioneer of Italian neorealism. (There are, however, some important similarities between the historical, almost documentary, focus of some of Rosselini's late films and Shādī's film corpus.)

Shādī 'Abd al-Salām's filmography, though tragically short, is diverse, consisting of documentaries, educational films, and fictional features. The documentaries are widely different in focus and character. *Horizons* (1972) surveys the contemporary Egyptian creative arts, while *The Armies of the Sun* (1975) celebrates the October War. The educational trilogy, *The Golden Chair of Tutankhamon* (1982), *Before the Pyramids* (1986), and *Ramses* (1986) use superficially simple stories to introduce aspects of ancient Egyptian culture. Shādī also produced two feature films. *The Mummy* (1969), released in the West to critical acclaim as *The Night of Counting the Years,* was Shādī's only full-length feature film. It is based on the story of the recovery of a cache of royal mummies in the Deir al-Bahri in 1881. The Egyptian filmmaker's shorter feature, *The Eloquent Peasant,* appeared the following year.

Death caught Shādī 'Abd al-Salām as he worked on his second major project, an ambitious historical drama on the life of the heretic Pharaoh, Akhnaton. He had completed a detailed scenario and had just received the backing of French and British promoters for the projected film.[1]

Though all but one of these projects deal, explicitly or implicitly, with Egypt's relation to its Pharaonic past, only *The Eloquent Peasant* makes a direct link to ancient Egypt. It is a larger part of what made Shādī 'Abd al-Salām Egypt's leading modern artistic Pharaonist.

Since the last century, Pharaonic (or, more properly speaking, ancient Egyptian) themes, motifs, or mere topoi have played a continual, if highly uneven, role in the culture of modern Egypt.[2] In the domain of literature, the influence of Pharaonic models, while considerable, has been minor when compared with the virtual hegemony of the Arabic literary tradition, itself seriously challenged only by the cultural imperialism of the West. Only one

Pharaonic text has excited sufficient interest among modern Egyptian writers to jump the cultural gulf of Islamic Egypt and be taken up fully into the modern Egyptian literary-cultural reserve. The Middle Kingdom narrative usually called *The Eloquent Peasant*[3] has taken its place alongside the ubiquitous Arabic tradition as potential literary model and referent. More than any other, this ancient narrative speaks directly to two of the most important concerns of contemporary Egyptian letters: justice and artistic creation. Briefly, *The Eloquent Peasant* tells the story of a man of modest means, robbed by a lower official and denied justice so that the judge, acting for the Pharaoh, can collect all the plaintiff's eloquence. As such, the narrative serves as frame for a series of speeches in favor of justice and against iniquity. Essential to the story, therefore, is a dialectical relation between the idea of justice and the process of textual creation.[4]

The concern with textual creation, the conscious treatment of the process of writing within the text itself (that is writing about writing), is one of the most distinctive elements of the contemporary cultural movement known as postmodernism and specifically of the literary type of metafiction.[5] The overwhelming concern (an outsider might even say obsession) with social justice is a dominant of contemporary Arabic literature. In fact, it is the integration of this concern with the universal/Western focus on the process of writing itself that most distinguishes contemporary Arabic postmodernism.[6] All of this makes *The Eloquent Peasant* a strikingly contemporary piece of literature.

The modernity of this Middle Kingdom text is not, however, completely coincidental. It forms part of a larger process through which most modern cultural movements have been reappropriating ancient, or culturally foreign, artistic forms. Much of modern Western art, for example, has drawn its inspiration from the rejection of post-Renaissance canons and their replacement with artistic visions taken from Japan, Sub-Saharan Africa, and even Pharaonic Egypt. In literature, the process has been much slower, but there has been a similar attempt to break out of the dominant Western narrative tradition. European writers have not, however, by and large, found a literary equivalent to non-Western or pre-Renaissance visual languages. It is here that contemporary Arabic culture (part of world culture much of whose artistic agenda has been set by the West) has exceptional opportunities. Not only is the traditional Arabic literary discourse (so different from that of the modern West) available as an ancient/postmodern model but, in the case of Egypt, the Pharaonic heritage, both visual and literary, provides an additional reservoir of native alterity. Some of these possibilities for the postmodern application of traditional Arabic discourse have already been explored somewhat tentatively by Imīl Ḥabībī and more extensively and consistently by Jamāl al-Ghīṭānī.[7]

It is in this cultural context of Pharaonic reappropriation amid a modern consciousness that one must see the contemporary revival of *The Eloquent Peasant,* and especially the short subject of that title by Shādī ʻAbd al-Salām, a film which is at the same time the most artistically modern and the most faithfully Pharaonic of the modern Egyptian versions of this tale.

The Middle Kingdom *Eloquent Peasant* is not essentially a work devoted to social justice. Indeed, this concern, though certainly present, is effectively subordinated to the process of text creation. Rather than producing justice, the peasant's eloquence delays it. The initial response of Grand Steward Rensi, after hearing the peasant's complaint and his courtiers' defense of the criminal official, is to say nothing, effectively reserving judgment. When the peasant responds with his first rhetorical flights, Rensi, instead of rendering justice, informs the Pharaoh of his subject's eloquence. The royal response, of course, is to tell Rensi not to heed the peasant's pleas but to carefully record them instead. Not only can justice delayed be called justice denied (despite the fact that the peasant and his family are maintained during this period) but we are also told that the unfortunate speech maker is whipped after repeatedly exhorting Rensi to grant him his due.[8] The creation of the text about justice takes precedence over the rendering of justice, whose non-delivery is the condition for the production of art.

In this process, a third thematic element acts as the essential linking principle between the two interacting problems of justice and text creation. In *The Eloquent Peasant,* the plaintiff's eloquence is provoked neither by the moral deafness of Rensi nor by the latter's desire to create a text (either of which could have made adequate literary frames for the nine supplications). Instead, it is the Pharaoh who instructs Rensi in how to draw the eloquence from his subject. The concern of the ruler transcends mere justice to englobe the creation of culture. The resulting display of Pharaonic wisdom supports a monarchist-Pharaonic ideology. It can even be used to suggest that the appearance of injustice (the case for some time in *The Eloquent Peasant*) can hide more profound Pharaonic purposes. And in the ancient Egyptian text the Pharaoh is clearly linked to art, not justice. He carefully instructs his minister in the cultivation of the text but never renders justice himself, leaving this lesser task to the discretion of his grand steward. When Rensi covers the peasant with gifts we do not know if he is rendering justice or rewarding the speaker for his eloquence. Indeed, the two actions have become indistinguishable.

Non-Egyptologists cannot argue with Breasted's conclusion that *The Eloquent Peasant* signals, in the ancient Egyptian context, the development of a greater concern with justice, and especially with the role of middle level officials in its administration.[9] There is, of course, no contradiction between this argument and the proposition that, in a basically monarchist society, such currents become subordinated to the defense of the political order. More fundamentally, once it leaves its immediate audience, a text by its nature takes on a kind of projectability, the ability to be read in an infinite variety of new contexts.[10]

The relationships between justice, text creation, and monarchist ideology have presented choices to the modern Egyptians who retell *The Eloquent Peasant*. Among the three playwrights who have recast the Pharaonic story, only Fatḥī Sa'īd has maintained the basic structural elements of the tale and its dialectic of justice and text, simply adding a more dialogical relationship between the peasant and the court officials. 'Alī Aḥmad Bākathīr effectively burlesques the entire Middle Kingdom by condensing it into the introduction to a standard comedy of court life. Justice appears through the idea that the peasant's speeches have helped to stir up a popular revolt that he himself must quell through further eloquence. Only Muḥammad Mahrān al-Sayyid has directly taken on the official, monarchist implications of the tale by making his version of the story one of political oppression. The peasant starts and ends in jail and produces his eloquence despite the attempts of the rulers to silence him.[11]

The Eloquent Peasant is present as verbal referent and subtext in two other modern works, both of which also break with the optimistic implications of the Pharaonic original. Jamāl al-Ghīṭānī's "Shakāwā al-Jundī al-Faṣīḥ" (The complaints of the eloquent soldier) tells the story of a modern civil servant who, dismissed from his position after his military service, writes a long letter of complaint. Not only does the letter frame most of the narrative (instead of the other way around) but we never hear that justice has been given. In some ways, the most striking reformulation of the basic structure of *The Eloquent Peasant* is Yūsuf al-Qa'īd's trilogy *Shakāwā al-Miṣrī al-Faṣīḥ (The Complaints of the Eloquent Egyptian)*. Al-Qa'īd reverses the relationship between justice and textual creation. An author eventually writes a book about social problems, but it never becomes well known and his own fate remains ambiguous. None of the possible endings, however, suggest that justice has in any sense requited the modern Egyptian's eloquence.[12]

Curiously, but not really coincidentally, the contemporary version closest narratively and in spirit to the ancient Egyptian classic is a comic-strip rendition written by Jamāl Salīm and drawn by Aḥmad Ḥijāzī, which appeared in the very popular children's magazine from Abu Dhabi, *Mājid.*[13] There are two reasons for that. The first is that Salīm's text is aimed at children. In all societies, children's literature is more self-consciously normative. The moral ambiguities or radical political messages inherent in so many of the modern Arabic literary retellings, while not completely absent from children's comics in the Middle East, are certainly not typical of that production. If the first reason, thus, seems specifically tied to the genre of children's literature, the second relates to the problem of word and image and, hence, is relevant to Shādī's cinematic version as well. Since part of the artistic process of both comic strip and film consists of translating the Middle Kingdom classic from purely verbal text to a new form which combines verbal and visual language, neither Salīm and Ḥijāzī on the one hand nor Shādī 'Abd al-Salām on the other were obliged to change the words or plot of the story in order to constitute the originality of their texts.

Yet the "faithfulness" of Shādī's film belies the transformations involved in the transfer from word to image. Shādī employed, as always, a unique visual language which possesses its own ideological implications.

Even the story represented a selection, since Shādī has presented an extremely compact rendition of the ancient Egyptian tale. He appears to have done so principally by following the summary version given in Breasted's *Dawn of Conscience,* rather than, for example, the more complete translation available in French by Lefebvre (Shādī read French). For example, Breasted, summarizing and not quoting, eliminates most of the dialogue between the peasant and the thieving official. Shādī goes further and eliminates all of it (in contrast with Salīm's comic-strip version, which includes the dialogue). The lines Shādī puts into the mouth of the peasant after he has been robbed and beaten by the servants of the official are part of the original dialogue between the peasant and his attacker. This is close but not identical to Breasted's condensed version. Similarly, Shādī eliminated the dialogue between the peasant and Rensi at the end of the tale when the latter explains why he has denied him justice for so long.[14]

The effect of these choices is a general elimination of dialogue from the film. Other than the speeches of the peasant, there are few words. The priest instructs Rensi and invites him into the royal presence, and Rensi answers with only one sentence. The grand steward is heard again only at the end of the film when he reads the now-written words of his eloquent petitioner. The peasant, the manifestation of the word, is almost completely surrounded with silence.

Reducing the verbal component, especially that part which directly relates to the narrative (as is the case with the dialogue), puts increasing demands on the visual language of the film. Of course, nothing would be more normal for a master of visual storytelling like Shādī 'Abd al-Salām. But, in the case of *The Eloquent Peasant,* as with so many of his other works, Shādī deliberately sets himself an artistic challenge.

The story behind *The Eloquent Peasant* is by its nature difficult to translate into film. A narrative consisting of a set of actions, including the psychological reactions of characters, is relatively easy to express in visual terms. All that is necessary is the representation of the actions (or reactions) themselves. The Middle Kingdom tale, however, is distinguished by a relatively brief set of actions (in narrative time, if not in real time) framing a long set of spoken discourses. The challenge of filming these is considerably greater than that of putting them on the stage, though even the playwrights have generally broken up the peasant's monologues through a variety of narrative and dramatic devices. Ḥijāzī and Salīm's version for children simply abandoned any attempt to transmit the content of the majority of the peasant's supplications, referring instead only to the existence of complaints on various subjects. Shādī, however, neither eliminated the peasant's speeches nor broke them (though he did collapse them into two and shorten them) nor increased the emphasis on the active and dialogic elements in the story. The Egyptian filmmaker's elimination of dialogue and the summary treatment of the actions in the tale preserve the relative weight of action and oration in the original.

Three basic choices are open for transforming the peasant's speeches into cinema: (1) film the peasant actually delivering his supplications; (2) film figuratively by representing concretely the images of the discourse, in this case, balance scales, floods, et cetera; (3) use visual imagery which is a representation of neither the actions taking place nor those suggested by the rhetorical figures. Shādī has restricted himself to a combination of the first and third solutions.

Since both these approaches are effectively nonnarrative, that is, they do not really tell a story, they throw the filmmaker back on a kind of montage that can be called musical. Shādī himself once explained that cinema was like music in that it existed in time and depended on its own internal sense of rhythm and variation[15]—that is, of course, if one sets aside the representational aspects of the film medium. Shādī exploits "musical" montage to maintain an accelerating visual intensity throughout the long discourse of the peasant. Shots of the peasant speaking are balanced with scenes of his listeners and other shots in which, though one sees the peasant, he does not speak directly to the camera. Often his words seem like a voice-over, juxtaposed to a visual text. The characteristically Shādīan long shots are ideally suited to the "musical" transposition of the hero's eloquence. The finest example is the very long shot which begins with the figure of the peasant on the ground (where he was thrown by Rensi's guards) and then travels slowly across the grass-filled sand to again find the peasant now kneeling, only to then tilt slowly upwards across barren sand dunes to the listening group of Rensi and his attendants. The slow visual rhythm of such long shots perfectly matches the long rhetorical periods of the orations.

The absence of direct representation does not mean the absence of signification. First of all, as with several other of Shādī's films, notably *The Mummy,* the classicism of the frames allied with that of the language (both films are completely in literary Arabic) reinforces that of the text. But the visual language of *The Eloquent Peasant* also includes elements whose significations interact with the more general themes of the film.

The first image of the film, between the opening titles and the credits is of an ancient Egyptian bas-relief showing a peasant leading a group of donkeys. The peasant and his beasts are in profile, all facing screen right. In essence, this immobile image frames the rest of the work. After the credits the film proper begins with the image of the peasant hero, with his loaded donkeys and his wife, also in profile. Clearly the image evokes the wall relief except that it is reversed. Hero and donkeys face screen left. At the end of the film, we again see the peasant hero and his beasts in stark profile. Now, however, they are facing screen right, the opposite direction from the beginning, the same direction as the peasant in the bas-relief. Finally, in the last sequence, a second major visual element has been added, the solar disk, against which the peasant and his train evolve rightwards.

It is obvious that these profile shots frame the film and echo each other. It is equally normal that the final shot, by reversing that of the beginning (and echoing the wall carving) ends a cycle and signifies closure. It is the relationship between the shots of the peasant at the beginning and end of the film and the stone image from the film's introduction which is problematic. The most obvious signifier of the relief (as of most any antiquity) is Pharaonic authenticity. It suggests that the peasant whom we will soon see (and whom we know to be a modern recreation) faithfully reflects an original ancient peasant pictured in the relief. But the wall carving really reflects, not so much the opening profile of the peasant, as, because of its direction, the closing one. Further, since the closing profile is that of justice and order restored, the opening "authentically Pharaonic" one becomes so as well. The real Pharaonic Egypt was a society of justice and of a true order, one that includes art.

The Pharaonic, monarchist implications of *The Eloquent Peasant* are further reinforced by other elements of visual coding. One of the most striking episodes in the film, because it breaks with both the general tendencies and the standard versions of the tale, is the one in which the priest, backing through the golden door, invites Rensi into the Pharaonic presence solemnly reciting the ruler's titles. This scene is followed by a close-up of the door itself, in the center of which is the winged solar disk of Ra. This image forms the occasion for a striking visual juxtaposition, unique in the film, for the very next shot shows the sun near the horizon so that it appears as a solar disk. Trees spreading out on both sides reproduce the form of the winged sun seen on the golden door. Still in the same shot, the camera tilts downward across the Nile (which has turned red from the reflection of the sun) and eventually to the peasant.

It is evident that the two linked shots, of the door and then of the sun and river, have no immediate narrative necessity. They do not "tell" the story of *The Eloquent Peasant*. For this reason, they interpret it. Associating the sun on the horizon with the sun on the door (itself defined through the litany of Pharaonic titles) makes the heavenly body a signifier of Pharaonic civilization in general and of the royal principle in particular. This is the same sun on the horizon, however, which accompanies the peasant in the final profile and closes the film. The resolution combines the restoration of the form on the original relief with the intervention of the Pharaonic sun.

The two linked shots of door and sun also serve as the visual markers of an important division in Shādī's film. In effect, *The Eloquent Peasant* can be divided into three sections, marked by visual breaks. The first runs from the setting of the peasant on his journey to the attack. The new state of disequilibrium thus created is symbolized by the peasant's being thrown into the river. This episode is shot with a rapidity and violence reminiscent of the murder of the brother in *The Mummy* and in sharp contrast with the deliberate rhythm of most of *The Eloquent Peasant*. The peasant is, in a sense, reborn from the river into his new state. The second phase, which could be called the search for order and justice, lasts, effectively, from the robbery until the Pharaonic intervention, itself visually terminated by the closing of the golden door. The last section extends from that event to the end of the film, when the text is recorded, the evil-doer punished, and the rewarded peasant sent back on his way. This third period of the narrative is essentially different from the second, a difference clearly marked out in the visual language of the film.

It is possible to consider the various speeches of the peasant, in all of which he demands justice and in all of which he displays his eloquence, as part of the same process. But this would miss the quasi-sacred phenomenon which Shādī underlined through a subtle use of visual language. Before the intervention of the Pharaoh, the peasant is *merely* pleading for justice. His words may impress Rensi but they are not recorded. After Rensi receives the royal instructions, however, the peasant is engaged in the higher task of textual creation. If the first speech is for a cause, the second is for eternity. In the process, the oral word is transformed into the written, another sacralization of ancient Egyptian high culture.[16]

This difference is visually marked in several ways. It should be remembered that the third phase, the phase of textual creation, was inaugurated with the linked sun shots. In fact, the peasant's speech at this time starts while he is off screen. It begins as a voice-off during the long shot with the sun on the horizon and the tilt down across the river. This majestic imagery of eternal Egypt sets the tone for the oratorical text creation. It is at this point, also, that, for the first time in the film, the musical background consists of a singing voice. The effect (when compared, for example, with the plucked *'ūd* which accompanied the first phase of the film) is like an auditory balm, appropriate to the calming imagery. A therapeutic process has begun. This point is ideologically significant as well. The healing of the wound created by the initial robbery is accomplished as much by art as by justice. The river in this opening shot sequence forms an effective pendant to the only other use of the river in the film, when the peasant is knocked into it during the robbery. The first association is violent and disruptive, the second healing.

Even the vegetation testifies to the sacred, fundamentally ordering process that commences when Rensi records the peasant's speech. The luxuriant vegetation of the first descent into the Nile valley and the twisted, threatening trunks and branches of the robbery episode are replaced by the stately, carefully spaced verticals of the palm trees surrounding Rensi's palace. Even the long traveling shot along the ground ending with the kneeling peasant shows a clear and careful spacing of grass and sand.

It is evident that something more profound than the administration of justice is transpiring. The eloquence results from a special relationship between the peasant and Rensi. Each is the alter ego of the other: opposite yet complementary. Rensi's silence is the condition of the peasant's eloquence. It is only when, in the opening episode, Rensi refuses to speak that the peasant begins his oration. He continues it after the Pharaonic intervention as Rensi maintains his silence. Rensi resumes speech at the end of the film to read the peasant's words back to him. Now, of course, it is the petitioner who is silent, never to speak again once his speech has been turned into written text. And it is Rensi's off-screen voice that speaks the key phrases from the peasant's now-written oration, as its author climbs out of the valley. The peasant's words have now become Rensi's. The only time that Rensi speaks on his own account is to define the peasant: "He is truly an eloquent man" *(innahu ḥaqqan rajulun faṣīḥ)*. In this central episode of the interview between priest and grand steward, Rensi completes the peasant's identity by putting it into words. Above the two young men, like the sun, is the unseen Pharaoh, who transforms the encounter between Rensi and the peasant. Under his influence, the quest for justice is transmuted into the creation of art.

Thus, as in the last scene of *Horizons* which shows the film crew packing up and driving away and the final shot of *The Golden Chair of Tutankhamon* with the child-hero in the photograph, Shādī has exploited the very modern notion of the self-conscious creation of art in his works of art themselves. In so doing, he has brought out what is most modern in the Middle Kingdom classic of *The Eloquent Peasant*.

Notes

1. Details of Shādī 'Abd al-Salām's biography and career are based on numerous conversations with the artist himself, with members of his family, and with artistic collaborators like Ṣalāḥ Mar'ī and on access to Mr. 'Abd al-Salām's professional papers and library. We would like to take this opportunity to thank Ṣalāḥ Mar'ī and members of the 'Abd al-Salām family for their friendship and generosity. See, also, Claude Michel Cluny, *Dictionnaire des nouveaux cinémas arabes* (Paris: Editions Sindbad, 1978), 91–94.

2. See, for example, Israel Gershoni and James P. Jankowski, *Egypt, Islam and the Arabs: The Search for Egyptian Nationhood, 1900–1930* (New York and Oxford: Oxford University Press, 1986), 164–90. For a discussion of some recent examples in the context of Egyptian identity, see Allen Douglas and Fedwa Malti-Douglas, *Arab Comic Strips: Politics of an Emerging Mass Culture* (Bloomington: Indiana University Press, 1994), 9–26.

3. Lefebvre, for example, argues that the hero is an oasis dweller and probably not a peasant. See Gustave Lefebvre, *Romans et contes égyptiens de l'époque pharaonique* (Paris: Adrien-Maisonneuve, 1949), 41. Nevertheless, the title "Eloquent Peasant" has become well established and is the one adopted by all modern Egyptians when referring to this text.

4. For translations, see Lefebvre, *Romans,* 47–69; Miriam Lichteim, *Ancient Egyptian Literature,* vol. 1, *The Old and Middle Kingdoms* (Berkeley: University of California Press, 1975), 170–82.

5. See, for example, Patricia Waugh, *Metafiction* (London: Methuen, 1983).

6. This is clear, in different ways, in the works of Yūsuf al-Qa'īd, Imīl Ḥabībī, and Jamāl al-Ghīṭānī. See, for example, Fedwa Malti-Douglas, "Yūsuf al-Qa'īd wa-al-Riwāya al-Jadīda," *Fuṣūl* 4, no. 3 (1984): 190-202. See also the introduction of Marie-Thérèse F. Abdel-Messih to her English translation of Yūsuf al-Qa'īd, *Akhbār 'Izbat al-Manīsī* (Cairo: Al-Hay'a al-Miṣriyya al-'Āmma li-al-Kitāb, 1987), 16–21.

7. This is true of virtually all of al-Ghīṭānī's novels. See, for example, Jamāl al-Ghīṭānī, *Al-Zaynī Barakāt* (Cairo: Maktabat Madbūlī, 1975), and *Khiṭaṭ al-Ghīṭānī* (Beirut: Dār al-Masīra, 1981). Imīl Ḥabībī exploits classical materials, for example, in *Ikhṭayyi.* See Imīl Ḥabībī, *Ikhṭayyi* (Cyprus: Kitāb al-Karmil, 1985). See, also, Fedwa Malti-Douglas, "Mahfouz's Dreams," in eds. Michael Beard and Adnan Haydar, *Naguib Mahfouz: From Regional Fame to Global Recognition* (Syracuse: Syracuse University Press, 1993), 126–43 (text), 183–5 (notes).

8. This fact is noted even in Breasted's very summary version. See James H. Breasted, *The Dawn of Conscience* (New York: Charles Scribner's Sons, 1933), 189.

9. James Henry Breasted, *Development of Religion and Thought in Ancient Egypt* (New York: Harper & Row, 1949?), 199–226; Breasted, *Dawn,* 193–94, 207–12.

10. Paul Ricoeur, *Hermeneutics and the Human Sciences,* ed. and trans. John B. Thompson (Cambridge: Cambridge University Press, 1981). This issue is discussed in Allen Douglas, "Al-Mu'arrikh, al-Naṣṣ, wa-al-Nāqid al-Adabī," trans. F. Kāmil, *Fuṣūl* 4, no. 1 (1983): 95–105.

11. Fatḥī Sa'īd, *Al-Fallāḥ al-Faṣīḥ* (Cairo: Al-Hay'a al-Miṣriyya al-'Āmma li-al-Kitāb, 1982); Muḥammad Mahrān al-Sayyid, *Ḥikāya . . . Min Wādī al-Milḥ* (Cairo: Mu'assasat 'Inān li-al-Ṭibā'a, 1984); 'Alī Aḥmad Bākathīr, *Al-Fallāḥ al-Faṣīḥ* (Cairo: Maktabat Miṣr, 1985).

12. Jamāl al-Ghīṭānī, "Shakāwā al-Jundī al-Faṣīḥ," in Jamāl al-Ghīṭānī, *Arḍ-Arḍ* (Beirut: Dār al-Masīra, 1980), 123–43; Yūsuf al-Qa'īd *Shakāwā al-Miṣrī al-Faṣīḥ,* vol. 1 (Beirut: Dār al-Masīra, 1981), vol. 2 (Cairo: Dār al-Mustaqbal al-'Arabī, 1983); vol. 3 (Cairo: Dār al-Mustaqbal al-'Arabī, 1985).

13. Jamāl Salīm and Aḥmad Ḥijāzī, "Al-Fallāḥ al-Faṣīḥ," *Mājid,* 182 (August 14, 1982): 5–10. On *Mājid* and its politics, see Douglas and Malti-Douglas, *Arab Comic Strips,* 150–73.

14. See Breasted, *Dawn,* 183–93 and the translations of Lichteim and Lefebvre cited above. Shādī's choices can be partially seen in the pencil markings of his copy of Breasted's *Dawn,* which we were able to consult in his personal library.

15. Shādī 'Abd al-Salām expressed this to us in the days before his final hospitalization in the summer of 1986.

16. This process of transformation of oral to written under monarchic auspices is, of course, similar to that in the frame of *The Thousand and One Nights.* On the comparison, see Fedwa Malti-Douglas, *Woman's Body, Woman's Word: Gender and Discourse in Arabo-Islamic Writing* (Princeton: Princeton University Press, 1991), 22–28.

The Last Days of Imru' al-Qays: Anatolia

IRFĀN SHAHĪD

The tempestuous life of Imru' al-Qays came to an end in Anatolia, where he died far away from his people and country, and in a manner not altogether inappropriate for one who was aptly described as the Vagabond King, *al-Malik al-Ḍillīl.* Accounts of these last days are a curious melange of fact and fiction, with the latter receiving the lion's share in these narratives. But it is important to disentangle the one from the other, since the stories involve the foremost poet of pre-Islamic Arabia, with some important implications for the history of Arabic poetry before the rise of Islam.[1]

Before some positive conclusions are drawn, it is important to dispose of the tissue of fabulous accounts that have been woven around the last days of the poet. He may have reached Constantinople, but all the following have to be dismissed as purely fictitious: that he had close relationship with the emperor Justinian, who is called Qayṣar in the sources; that he saw him in the bathroom; that Justinian's daughter (the emperor in reality was childless) fell in love with him; that the emperor set him at the head of a Byzantine army; that he sent him a poisoned embroidered robe, which reached him when he was in Ancyra; that he died as a result of putting on that robe; and that the emperor had a statue made for him.[2]

What survives from this sifting is that Imru' al-Qays, after traversing Bilād al-Shām, reached the region that separated al-Shām from Anatolia at a place that he calls al-Darb and that he died somewhere in Anatolia, most probably in Ancyra (Arabic Anqira, modern Ankara) in A.D. 542, either before or after reaching Constantinople. This bare outline of his journey in Anatolia may now be set against his own poems,[3] which are replete with details on his short journey from al-Darb to Ancyra; they are, as well, the only sources on this journey, since the poet is not mentioned in the Greek sources[4] or at least those that are extant. These poems provide information on the places where he was, such as al-Darb and Ancyra; on his possible contacts with Qayṣar, the emperor Justinian in Constantinople; on ʿAsīb, the mountain he refers to in a verse he composed before his death; on his two companions Jābir and ʿAmr; and on the disease that finally caused his death.

Al-Darb

Al-Darb, referred to in the *rā'iyya* as the place whence the poet crossed from Bilād al-Shām into Anatolia, is the most easily identified spot in his *Dīwān* for his Anatolian journey. It was here that his companion, ʿAmr ibn Qamī'a, wept when he saw it before him:[5]

Bakā ṣāḥibī lammā ra'ā d-darba dūnahu
    wa-ayqana annā lāḥiqāni bi-qayṣarā
Fa-qultu lahu lā tabki ʿaynuka innamā
    nuḥāwilu mulkan aw namūta fa-nuʿdharā

This toponym raises the following questions, the first of which concerns the location of al-Darb. As a common noun in Arabic, the term means "the path, the way"; and many were the paths and ways which led from Bilād al-Shām and Mesopotamia into Anatolia.[6] So which one of these did al-Darb in the verse indicate?

Most probably,[7] it was the famous Cilician Gates, called in the language of the period *Pylai Kilikias,* the narrow pass that leads through the Taurus Mountains from the plain of Cilicia into central Anatolia.[8] The term applies not only to the narrow pass but also to the whole road through the mountains. The province in Anatolia to which it belonged, Cilicia, was on the highway that connected northern Bilād al-Shām with Constantinople, Imru' al-Qays's destination. This is confirmed by Yāqūt, who identifies this Darb without the qualifications he includes in the other entries of that name in his *Dictionary* and says that al-Darb, *the* Darb, is the one near Tarsos[9] (which was the capital of Cilicia Prima).

The reference to the Cilician Gates as al-Darb without any qualification suggests that the term, al-Darb, had by the sixth century become a well-known toponym, a proper noun, well known among the Arabs, so well known that no further qualification was needed presumably because it was in the Byzantine period the gateway through which many Arab princes and kings passed on their way to meet with the emperor in Constantinople, as Imru' al-Qays's own cousin[10] had done around A.D. 530. And it is just possible that Imru' al-Qays's calling the Cilician Gates al-Darb came from his cousin, with whom he most probably conferred before he made his journey to Anatolia. From this toponym, the denominative verb *adraba* was formed, indicating in Islamic times the crossing of the Cilician Gates by the Muslim Arab armies in campaigns against the Byzantines, the Rūm, in Anatolia. The verse in which Imru' al-Qays mentions al-Darb suggests that the Arabs or the Semitic peoples of Bilād al-Shām considered passing through the Cilician Gates as crossing into a foreign country (presumably because those across these Gates spoke languages other than Arabic or Aramaic):[11] witness the reference to the tears of the poet's companion 'Amr, when he suddenly saw the Cilician Gates before him.

Constantinople

Imru' al-Qays's destination was Constantinople, where he planned to see the emperor and enlist his aid. And it was about his encounters with Justinian that most of the embroideries of the legend of Imru' al-Qays have been woven. While these have been collected by Louis Cheikho,[12] the most complete edition of the poet's *Dīwān*[13] adds details not to be found in Cheikho's account, all of which must be dismissed as unhistorical. The question, however, must be asked whether the poet ever reached Constantinople or died in Ancyra before he reached in the capital. Arguments may be advanced for either position.

Against the view that he reached Constantinople and had an audience with the emperor, the following may be said: The poet is not mentioned in the Greek sources, which in this period are quite specific on Kinda. These sources speak of the poet's cousin, Qays ibn-Salama, who was quite different from the poet in almost everything: he is the one who reached Constantinople and dealt with the authorities.[14] Imru' al-Qays's journey to Constantinople may thus have been confused with his cousin's or with the journey of another Arab chief also called Imru' al-Qays, who did reach Constantinople during the reign of the emperor Leo in the fifth century and whose name is spelled correctly as Amorkesos.[15]

Another version of his stay in Constantinople and his encounter with Justinian may also be dismissed, namely, that after the poet's departure from Constantinople the emperor sent him a poisoned robe, which reached him while he was in Ancyra, and it caused his death.[16] This can be dismissed as a topos: it is the story of Nessos's robe from Greek mythology, fastened on to Justinian and Imru' al-Qays. That the emperor plotted the poet's death after he left Constantinople may also have been confused with a perfectly historical account involving another Arab prince, who after leaving Constantinople was arrested in Anatolia. This was the Ghassānid al-Nu'mān (the son of al-Mundhir) who during the reign of the emperor Maurice (A.D. 582–602) tried to negotiate the release of his father, who had been treacherously arrested by the Byzantine authorities in Ḥuwwārīn in Syria. After the failure of the negotiations with the authorities, who tried to convert al-Nu'mān from the Monophysite to the Chalcedonian position, the prince departed from Constantinople, and while he was on his way back to Bilād al-Shām, the emperor ordered his arrest and brought him back to Constantinople.[17]

On the other hand, a case can be made that the poet did reach Constantinople, since it can be argued that the Greek sources that refer to his cousin, Qays, date to around A.D. 530, a decade before the poet's journey to Constantinople and that Greek sources that may have recorded the poet's journey have not survived.[18] This is possible. The Greek sources for the history of the Arab allies of Byzantium, such as Kinda, are sparse and sporadic for this period, and it is possible that the journey may not have been recorded, or that, if it was, the account has not survived. That the poet may have reached Constantinople and died in Ancyra on his way back from the capital may be supported by two verses that are preserved and that have been attributed to this poet, in which he speaks of his having met the emperor, who entertained him at his imperial table, treated him well, and sent him back to Bilād al-Shām on the *veredi,* Arabic *barīd,* the state post.[19] The two verses contain three terms that suggest an historical Byzantine scene: Qayṣar, *veredi (barīd),* and *furāniq.*[20] The second verse, in which he speaks of his outstripping the *furāniq* on the journey, sounds very much like the impetuous and impulsive poet, who, as the "Vagabond King," spent much of his life on horseback and who excelled in describing his mount. The two verses read as follows:[21]

Wa-nādamtu Qayṣara fī mulkihi
    fa-awjahanī wa-rakibtu l-barīdā
Idhā mā zdaḥamnā 'alā sikkatin
    sabaqtu l-furāniqa sabqan shadīdā.

On the other hand, the two verses may have been forged later and attributed to Imru' al-Qays as part of the fantastic accounts that were woven around his journey to Constantinople.

Ancyra/Ankara

All the accounts agree that he died and was buried in Ancyra. This rests on a single reference in one of his *rajaz* verses and the statement in the later Islamic accounts that the caliph al-Ma'mūn saw his statue in that city. What matters is the reference to Ancyra in Imru' al-Qays's verse and whether he did indeed die and was buried there. The chances are that Imru' al-Qays's presence in Ancyra has to be accepted as true.

The toponym is such a rare one that it is mentioned only once in pre-Islamic poetry,[22] and it is difficult to believe that it was chosen by a forger as part of the yarn he spun in order to embellish the legend. Besides, the association of Imru' al-Qays with Ancyra persisted in later Islamic times, to the time of the Abbasid caliph al-Ma'mūn. That this caliph saw a statue of the poet is certainly a legend, but that he *thought* he saw the poet's statue suggests that the association of the poet with Ancyra was taken seriously in early Islamic times and thus could go back to a sound early tradition.[23]

More important is the fact that Imru' al-Qays did indeed cross one of the "Gates" (most probably the Cilician) on his way to see the emperor Justinian in Constantinople. He had to pass through Ancyra on his way. In the words of a specialist on the city,

> Ankara owed its growth and prominence to its location on a highway which in Late Antiquity became one of the most heavily trafficked in

> the Empire. It occupied, in addition, a strategic junction from which roads radiated in all directions. The main highway led from Europe to the eastern frontier: from Thrace and Constantinople through Nicomedia and Nicaea to Ankara, thence to the Cilician Gates and Syria. . . . In Late Antiquity the factors which had been responsible for the growth of Ankara gave it continued and even increased importance and prosperity. When the capital was moved to Constantinople, the highway through Ankara became the main route between the capital and the East.[24]

So a traveler who started his Anatolian journey from the Cilician Gates on his way to Constantinople would have had to pass through Ancyra either on his way out to the capital or on his way back therefrom.

Nothing is known about the reception accorded to the poet in Ancyra; but Ancyra, according to Arabic sources, was the place in which the Arab tribe of Iyād settled in pre-Islamic times, either in it or in its vicinity.[25] So there was an Arab group known to Imru' al-Qays, while he as a prince of Kinda must have been known to them. Thus they might have been the poet's hosts when he reached Ancyra. The city was known for its hospitality; in the words of Libanius in the fourth century, "the only reproach usually made against the people of Ankara by strangers was that they were reluctant to let them leave."[26] So if the remains of Imru' al-Qays were taken care of ceremoniously after his death, and if his memory remained green till the time of al-Ma'mūn, it must have been due to the solicitousness of an Arab community in Ancyra or its vicinity, such as Iyād. The poet's swan song, transmitted in various versions, consisted of four *rajaz* verses, not in the usual trimeter but in dimeters, and their *rajaz* is *mashṭūr*. The last word in the verses, presumably the last word he uttered before he died, was "Ancyra." One version of this *rajaz* reads as follows:[27]

> Rubba ṭa'natin muth'anjira
> Wa-jafnatin mutaḥayyira
> Wa-qaṣīdatin mutakhayyara
> Tabqā ghadan fī anqira.

Closely related to the poet's death in Ancyra is the problem of the erection of a statue for him by the Byzantines, or even by Qayṣar himself, the Roman emperor, which al-Ma'mūn is said to have seen.[28] Bakrī[29] transmits an account to the effect that the Rūm (Byzantines) erected for him a *ṣūra,* as they used to do for eminent personages. And he adds, on the authority of al-Tawwazī,[30] that the latter was told by al-Ma'mūn that he had seen the statue and that the poet's face was round *(mukaltham)*.

What is involved in the account is of course not a picture but a statue, which *ṣūra* can also mean, most probably a sculptured likeness, an effigy such as those set up on sepulchral monuments. The Romans or the Byzantines, let alone the emperor Justinian, setting up a statue on the tomb of Imru' al-Qays must be adjudged pure fiction. If Imru' al-Qays was accorded the honor of a tomb, it must have been made by some Arab group such as Iyād which, as has been argued, is said to have settled in Ancyra. But al-Ma'mūn's involvement deserves to be examined carefully. Noteworthy in Bakrī's account is the fact that the author transmits the story and mentions his source, the caliph himself, who was a highly cultured man and a connoisseur of Arabic poetry and, thus, would have been interested in a statue said to have been that of the foremost poet of pre-Islamic Arabia. Furthermore, the transmitter was a reputable philologist who was a younger contemporary of al-Ma'mūn and who derived the account from the horse's mouth, so to speak. In spite of all this, it is doubtful that what the caliph saw in the ninth century was a statue of Imru' al-Qays. The city had been ravaged by the Persians[31] in A.D. 622; al-Ma'mūn must have been shown a statue that was only described to him as that of the poet,[32] given the caliph's interest in poetry. What, thus, can be salvaged from this account is that the poet's association with Ancyra must have been genuine since it survived until the ninth century, three centuries after his death, albeit distorted by a legend that ascribed the erection of a statue for him by the emperor Justinian.

'Asīb

Before his death in Ancyra, Imru' al-Qays is said to have been made aware of the tomb of a Byzantine princess buried in a nearby mountain, called 'Asīb; whereupon the poet composed two or three verses:[33]

Ajāratanā inna l-khuṭūba tanūbu
    wa-innī muqīmun mā aqāma 'asību
Ajāratanā innā gharībāni hāhunā
    wa-kullu gharībin li-l-gharībi nasību.

The verses may have been composed as part of the legend that grew posthumously around the figure of Imru' al-Qays, but they could have been genuine. If so, the question arises as to where 'Asīb is to be located.

The legendary account suggests that it was in or near Ancyra in the province of Galatia, but al-Harawī, the traveler of the twelfth and thirteenth centuries, says it was not far from Qiṣāria (Caesarea),[34] which is far from Ancyra, in the province of Cappadocia. This is out of Imru' al-Qays's way, as he, traveling to Constantinople from the Cilician Gates, would proceed to Ancyra and thence to Constantinople; Caesarea is not quite on his direct route. Besides, the account associates 'Asīb with Ancyra, not Caesarea.

The truth is that neither place has any mountain bearing that name,[35] and the 'Asīb in the verse has to be explained otherwise. The geographers, Yāqūt and Bakrī,[36] locate it in Arabia in the country of the tribe of Hudhayl and add that saying *lā af'alu dhālika mā aqāma 'asīb* is an idiom indicating a long duration. Bakrī cites a verse by Ṣakhr (the brother of the poetess al-Khansā') who says:

Ajāratanā lastu l-ghadāta bi-ẓā'inin
wa-lākin muqīmun mā aqāma 'asību.

Hence, 'Asīb must be rejected as the name of a mountain near Ancyra or Caesarea, and must be accepted as a mountain in Arabia. The toponym forms part of a common saying, indicating long tarrying or residence in a place. Imru' al-Qays was, of course, familiar with it and, appropriately for one who was about to die, employs it in his verse for obvious reasons.[37]

The Plague

His own immiment death is precisely described by Imru' al-Qays, and in such a manner that it gave him his other sobriquet, Dhū al-Qurūḥ, "the man of the ulcers." He mentions more than once the *qurḥ* or *qurūḥ* which infected his body, the debilitating influence of these ulcers, how he languished, and how his body started to decay and slough away so that he had to be carried on a litter.[38] These are valuable data for diagnosing his disease. It certainly was none other than that induced by the famous plague, the bubonic plague, that ravaged the entire Near East during the reign of Justinian. Luckily, a detailed description has survived in the pages of the historian Procopius, a contemporary; descriptions have also been preserved in Evagrius and John of Ephesus, and in even later Arabic sources.[39] These writers speak of buboes, black pustules, and carbuncles. Two passages in Procopius may be cited, which are instructive on how this pestilence affected the human body:

> Now some of the physicians who were at a loss because the symptoms were not understood, supposing that the disease centered in the bubonic swellings, decided to investigate the bodies of the dead. And upon opening some of the swellings, they found a strange sort of carbuncle that had grown inside them.
>
> Death came in some cases immediately, in others after many days; and with some the body broke out with black pustules about as large as a lentil and these did not survive even one day, but all succumbed immediately. With many also a vomiting of blood ensued without visible cause and straightway brought death.[40]

This famous plague ran its course for a triennium (A.D. 541–544) and hit Constantinople and Anatolia, and with it Ancyra,[41] in A.D. 542. There were other outbreaks of the plague later in the sixth century, the closest to this famous one coming in the 550s,[42] too late to have affected Imru' al-Qays. The death of the poet thus must have taken place in A.D. 542, and in Ancyra, which was hit by the plague in that year.

One of the poems in the *Dīwān* that refers to his malady presents a problem. The *sīniyya* is a longish poem that speaks of bloody ulcers and the sloughing of his skin, but it also speaks of his "old malady," which the poet fears is recurring.[43] The verse in which this phrase occurs is not crystal clear and raises the question whether the malady, the *dā',* mentioned in it is used literally or metaphorically; he uses the same term when he speaks of that mysterious figure al-Ṭammāḥ,[44] said to be an Asadī tribesman who plotted against the poet in Constantinople. In Ṭammāḥ's case, there is no question of *dā',* "malady" in the literal sense. The commentators speak of the poisoned robe first worn by Ṭammāḥ, then by Imru' al-Qays; but the whole story of the robe is utterly fictitious. Besides, the verse may be a later interpolation in the poem, inserted because of congruence with the story of al-Ṭammāḥ. If the verse that speaks of his old malady proves to be authentic, it might be interpreted as referring to the possibility that Imru' al-Qays had been hit by the plague before, that he had recovered, and that the disorder recurred while he was in Anatolia; or, more probably, that he had been taken ill, smitten by some disorder similar to the plague, perhaps a skin disease, at some place and time while he was still a wandering, errant king, *"malik ḍillīl."* He was known to have been a notorious philanderer, and it is just possible that he might have contracted some disease while celebrating the rites of Venus in Arabia.

Two Companions

In addition to the *rā'iyya,* there are two other poems[45] that refer to three personages, related to the poet's journey in Anatolia: the *nūniyya* and the *sīniyya.* Both are longish poems, and have the accent, style, and breath *(nafas)* of Imru' al-Qays, although they may have undergone some interpolation. Before discussing his two companions, Jābir and 'Amr, reference should be made to the already discussed Ṭammāḥ, who appears in the *sīniyya.* He is said to have belonged to Asad, the very tribe that had killed Imru' al-Qays's father, the homicide that triggered the poet's adventures and career of revenge. It is possible that some such figure did appear in Constantinople, pleading the case and cause of Asad against Imru' al-Qays. But it is more likely that he was invented later in order to embellish the theme of revenge[46] by providing a counterpoise to Imru' al-Qays; hence, *inter alia,* the poisoned robe. As has been argued, the poet died in Ancyra, hit by the bubonic plague in A.D. 542, in circumstances that are historically attestable and that relegate both the story of the poisoned robe to the realm of mythopoesis. The episode of al-Ṭammāḥ is nonsignificant, even if al-Ṭammāḥ should turn out to be an historical figure.

What is significant is the reference to the two others who accompanied Imru' al-Qays on his journey: they were poets, namely Jābir ibn Ḥunayy of the Taghlib tribe and 'Amr ibn Qamī'a from the sister tribe Bakr. The first is referred to in the *nūniyya,* where Imru' al-Qays says that after he was taken ill he was carried by Jābir ibn Ḥunayy:[47]

Fa-immā taraynī fī riḥālati jābirin
'alā ḥarajin ka-l-qarri takhfiqu akfānī

Jābir is the less important of the two companions,[48] and presumably he is the one who survived, returned to Arabia, and transmitted the poems composed by Imru' al-Qays during his Anatolian journey.

More important is the other, 'Amr ibn Qamī'a, of the Bakr tribe, whom Imru' al-Qays is said to have picked as his companion to accompany him on his journey to Constantinople. He was a major pre-Islamic poet,[49] and the older contemporary of Imru' al-Qays. He has been credited with the composition of the earliest extant *qaṣīda,* and A.D. 480 has been suggested as the year of his birth.[50] The accounts of 'Amr as found in the sources may now be compared with the conclusions drawn on Imru' al-Qays in this article.

'Amr is called *al-Ḍā'i',* "the Lost One," and is said to have perished with Imru' al-Qays, and he may have died from the same plague. The literary tradition states that he lived to the ripe old age of ninety, but this is impossible to accept. A nonagenarian could hardly have undertaken the journey to Constantinople. While the figure ninety, *tis'ūn,* was picked up from a poem of his,[51] this could have been seventy, *sab'ūn,* or sixty, *sittūn.* This is more consonant with the fact that he accompanied Imru' al-Qays on his long and arduous journey. His suggested birth date, A.D. 480, seems right, as he would have been around sixty when he died during his journey with Imru' al-Qays in Anatolia. The year of his birth is not as important as that of his death, and now this can be established with tolerable certainty as approximately the same year in which Imru' al-Qays died.

Chronology

More important for the history of Arabic pre-Islamic poetry is the year of Imru' al-Qays's death, on which critical opinion has been divided.[52] But it can be pinpointed to A.D. 542, now that the manner of his death has been established, related to the great plague of the reign of Justinian. If the Greek sources are silent on the death of the poet in Ancyra, they are not so on the fact that the plague hit this city where Imru' al-Qays is said to have died. It did so in the year A.D. 542, giving corroborative evidence that the reference to Ancyra by the poet as the place where he was about to die was not fabricated later by a clever storyteller.

This is a permanent gain for the history of Arabic poetry before the rise of Islam, plagued, as is well known, by the lack of a precise chronology for its poets. The year A.D. 542, thus emerges as perhaps the one precise and certain date for the death of a pre-Islamic poet. Since Imru' al-Qays happens to be the foremost poet of pre-Islamic Arabia, the date is of considerable importance. The historian of this poetry can now go forward and backward from the date to establish the approximate dates of many of the poets of pre-Islamic Arabia.

As the poet was the great master of the pre-Islamic *qaṣīda,* and as his *mu'allaqa* is adjudged the best of the Seven Suspended Odes, this date becomes also important for the history of the development of the forms of pre-Islamic Arabic poetry. By A.D. 542, the *qaṣīda* had reached the peak of its development (or one of them) in the hands of Arabia's foremost poet, and thus his *mu'allaqa* should be considered the earliest of the *mu'allaqāt,* since all the other six or nine are posterior to it, with the possible exception of that of 'Abīd, his contemporary.[53] The presumption is that before Imru' al-Qays the *qaṣīdas* had not been as well developed as his was; otherwise, the anthologist who collected the *mu'allaqāt* might have chosen one from a poet who flourished before him. And so the view that Imru' al-Qays was the one who perfected the *qaṣīda* seems to be well established.

Notes

1. For Imru' al-Qays with bibliography on him, see F. Sezgin *Geschichte des arabischen Schrifttums,* vol. 2 (Leiden: E. J. Brill, 1967), 122–26.

2. For all this, see Louis Cheikho, *Shu'arā' al-Naṣrāniyya qabl al-Islām,* 2nd ed. (Beirut: Dār al-Mashriq, 1967), 32-35.

3. For the best collection of his poems, see *Dīwān Imru' al-Qays,* ed. M. Ibrāhīm, *Dakhā'ir al-'Arab* 24 (Cairo: Dār al-Ma'ārif, 1958), hereafter *Dīwān.* The poems most relevant for his journey in Anatolia are three longish ones; the *rā'iyya,* poem rhyming in "*r*"; the *nūniyya,* poem rhyming in "*n*"; and the *sīniyya,* poem rhyming in "*s*", for which see *Dīwān,* 56–71, 89–93, and 105–8 respectively; in addition there are some fragments, such as that on page 339. These poems, especially the three mentioned, have the unmistakable stamp of Imru' al-Qays.

4. On this, see my article in "Byzantium and Kinda," *Byzantinische Zeitschrift* 53 (1960): 57–73.

5. For the verses, see *Dīwān,* 75–76.

6. On the many *darbs, durūb,* that led into Bilād al-Rūm in Islamic times see Ṭabarī's account of the campaign of al-Mu'taṣim that ended with the capture of Amorium: Ṭabarī, *Tārīkh,* ed. M. Ibrāhīm, vol. 9 (Cairo: Dār al-Ma'ārif, 1968), 57–58.

7. There are three passes that led from Bilād al-Shām into Anatolia, namely the Syrian Gates, the Amanican Gates and the Cilician Gates, for all of which see the map in F. Dvornik, *Origins of Intelligence Services* (New Brunswick, N.J.: Rutgers University Press, 1974), 141. The tantalizingly homophonous toponym Derbe, a city in the province of Lycaonia, not the Cilician Gates, should be completely ruled out as identifiable with the term al-Darb in the verse. For Derbe, see K. Belke, *Galatien und Lykaonien, Tabula Imperii Byzantini,* vol. 4 (Vienna: Verlag der Österreicheschen Akademie der Wissenschaften, 1984), 157.

8. For a description of the Cilician Gates, see F. Hild, H. Hellenkemper, *Kilikien und Isaurien, Tabula Imperii Byzantini,* vol. 2 (Vienna: Verlag der Österreicheschen Akademie der Wissenschaften, 1990), 387.

9. See Yāqūt, *Mu'jam al-Buldān,* vol. 2 (Beirut: Dār Bayrūt and Dār Ṣādir, 1956), 447.

10. See the present writer in "Byzantium and Kinda," (above note 4), 66–70.

11. Cf. Mutanabbī in Shi'b Bawwān where he felt a stranger: see his *Dīwān,* ed. 'Abd al-Raḥmān al-Barqūqī, vol. 2 (Cairo: al-Maktaba al-Tijāriyya al-Kubrā, 1930), 481, line 3:

Wa-lākinna l-fatā l-'arabiyya fīhā   gharību l-wajhi wa-l-yadi wa-l-lisāni.

12. See Cheikho, 32–35.

13. *Dīwān* 212, where the storytellers outdid themselves when they even inserted a Greek sentence τί θέλεις?, *Ti theleis?* ("What do you wish?"), which appears in Arabic as *Ṭīthālis!*

14. See above, note 10. In addition to the sharp differences between Imru' al-Qays and his cousin Qays, which preclude identifying the one with the other, the account about Qays is an official document which could not have made a mistake in transcribing and transliterating his name from Imru' al-Qays to Qays. When an Imru' al-Qays was involved with Byzantium, his name appears correctly transcribed, as happened in the case of the fifth-century figure of that name.

15. On Amorkesos, see my *Byzantium and the Arabs in the Fifth Century* (Washington, D.C.: Dumbarton Oaks Research Library Collection, 1989), 59–91.

16. Reynold Nicholson apparently accepted the story of the poisoned robe. See his *A Literary History of the Arabs* (Cambridge: Cambridge University Press, 1966), 104.

17. On this, see my *Byzantium and the Arabs in the Sixth Century,* vol. 1 (Washington, D.C.: Dumbarton Oaks Research Library Collection, 1995), 532.

18. This may be related to the possibility that in the early 540s, when the poet journeyed to Constantinople, Justinian may have been interested in acquiring allies in Arabia against the Persians and their clients, the Lakhmids of Ḥīra. The emperor possibly thought that the poet's connections in Arabia might be of some assistance in the war effort against Persia, hence his interest in having the poet come to Constantinople for talks.

19. On the Byzantine imperial state post, the *cursus publicus,* with its *veredi/barīd* horses, etc., see Dvornik, 122–29.

20. The term *furāniq,* denoting the official in charge of the *veredi,* is a Persian loanword.

21. On the two verses, see *Dīwān,* 252, lines 3–4.

22. For the verses of Al-Aswad ibn Ya'fur, see Yāqūt, *Mu'jam al-Buldān, vol. 1* (Beirut: Dār Bayrūt and Dār Ṣādir, 1968), 272.

23. On Ma'mūn, see further in this section.

24. C. Foss, "Late Antique and Byzantine Ankara," *Dumbarton Oaks Papers* 31 (1977): 29, 30; on Ancyra, see K. Belke, *Galatien und Lykaonien, Tabula Imperii Byzantini,* vol. 4, 126–30, *s.v. Ankyra.*

25. On this, see Yāqūt, vol. 1*Mu'jam al-Buldān,* 271–72.

26. Quoted by Foss, "Ankara," 46.

27. *Dīwān,* 349.

28. See Cheikho, *Shu'arā' al-Naṣrāniyya,* 35, who speaks of an ancient manuscript as his source but does not specify. G. Olinder refers the reader to de Slane's work on Imru' al-Qays and says that the latter derived his account of the statue from "ms.ar. 490 de la Bibl. du roi," which does not correspond to either no. 490 or Suppl. 490 of de Slane's *Catalogue des manuscrits arabes* (prepared 1830–1872, published Paris 1883–1895). See Olinder, *The Kings of Kinda of the Family of Ākil al-Murār* (Lund: C. W. K. Gleerup, 1927), 114.

29. Abū 'Ubayd 'Abd Allāh al-Bakrī, *Mu'jam mā Ista'jam,* ed. Muṣṭafā. al-Saqqā, vol. 1 (Cairo: al-Ma'had al-Khalīfī li-al-Abḥāth al-Maghribiyya, Bayt al-Maghrib, 1945), 204.

30. A *nisba* from Tawwaz, a town in Persia. Al-Tawwazī's name, according to Yāqūt, was 'Abd Allāh ibn Muḥammad ibn Hārūn. He was a distinguished *lughawī* (philologist) who died in Hijrī year 238 (A.D. 852/3): see Yāqūt, vol. 2 *Mu'jam al-Buldān,* 58.

31. See Foss, "Ankara," 70.

32. Foss suggests that what was erroneously thought to be the tomb of Imru' al-Qays was the Temple of Rome and Augustus in Ancyra, the Augusteum: Foss, "Ankara," 77.

33. See *Dīwān,* 357, lines 1–2.

34. See Abū al-Ḥasan 'Alī ibn Abī Bakr al-Harawī, *Kitāb al-Ishārāt ilā Ma'rifat al-Ziyārāt,* ed. J. Sourdel-Thomine (Damascus: al-Ma'had al-Faransī, 1953), 59.

35. Both provinces, Galatia and Cappadocia, where Ancyra and Caesarea were located, have been carefully examined by toponymists, but no 'Asīb has been found in either province in the relevant volumes of the *Tabula Imperii Byzantini*.

36. See Yāqūt, *Mu'jam al-Buldān,* vol. 4 (Beirut: Dār Bayrūt and Dār Ṣādir, 1957), 124-25; Bakrī *Mu'jam mā Ista'jam,* vol. 3, 943–44.

37. Later legend identified the column of the emperor Julian (A.D. 361–363), erected for him in Ancyra, as the "Minaret of the Maiden" (Turkish Kiz Minaret), and the princess has been identified in Turkish legend with Bilqīs, the queen of Sheba: see F. W. Hasluck, *Christianity and Islam Under the Sultans,* vol. 2 (Oxford: Clarendon Press, 1929), 713.

A propos of royalty associated with Ancyra, the Byzantine princess and the Kindite prince, it might be mentioned that the king of the Vandals, Gelimer, defeated in A.D. 534, spent his years of retirement in Ancyra, arriving in the city shortly before Imru' al-Qays did in A.D. 542: see Foss, "Ankara," 56.

38. For the verses that describe the symptoms of his disease, see *Dīwān,* 106, 107, and the fragment on page 339.

39. The "Justinianic" plague has been treated in detail in two works: see P. Allen "The 'Justinianic' Plague," *Byzantion* 49 (1977): 5–20; and L. C. Conrad's unpublished Ph.D. dissertation "The Plague in the Early Medieval Near East" (Princeton University, 1981). The sources for the plague, especially Procopius, are critically evaluated in these two works.

40. Procopius, *History,* trans. H. B. Dewing (London-Cambridge: Harvard University Press, 1914), 2.22: 29–31.

41. Foss, "Ankara," 56. For the recurrence of the plague in Ancyra, see Foss, 57.

42. See Allen, "Plague," 13. The earliest of these recurrences of the plague, in the 550s, is dated to the year A.D. 553/4. Conrad argues that the first recurrence after the Justinianic one is to be dated to A.D. 558: Conrad, "Plague," 121.

43. See *Dīwān,* 106, line 1; 107, lines 3 and 4.

44. *Dīwān,* 108, line 1.

45. For the two poems, see *Dīwān,* 89–93, 105–108.

46. This point has been well analyzed by Suzanne Stetkevych in *The Mute Immortals Speak* (Ithaca: Cornell University Press, 1993), 241–85.

47. *Dīwān,* 90, line 3.

48. On Jābir, see Sezgin, vol. 2, *Geschichte des arabischen Schrifttums,* 150.

49. On 'Amr ibn Qamī'a, see Sezgin, vol. 2, *Geschichte des arabischen Schrifttums,* 2:152–3.

50. See Gustave von Grunebaum "Zur Chronologie der früharabischen Dichtung," *Orientalia* 8 (1939): 345.

51. See H. K. Ṣayrafī, *Dīwān 'Amr ibn Qamī'a,* Majallat Ma'had al-Makhṭūṭāt al-'Arabiyya, vol. 11 (Cairo: 1965), 44.

52. See Ṣayrafī, *Dīwān 'Amr,* 18.

53. On 'Abīd, see Sezgin, vol. 2, *Geschichte des arabischen Schrifttums,* 2: 169–71.

Imru' al-Qays Praises the Prophet

Julie Scott Meisami

Qifā nabki min dhikrā ḥabībin wa-manzili . . .

Many years and many stopping-places ago, Mounah Khouri introduced a small class of Berkeley Arabists to Imru' al-Qays's "Mu'allaqa." Its rhythms still echo in memory; and though most of us in that class at Berkeley have since traveled on to other abodes, it is to that "rim of twisting sands between Dakhūl and Ḥawmal"—by a somewhat roundabout route—that I return here.[1]

Imru' al-Qays's "Mu'allaqa" is arguably the most widely quoted—plagiarized, imitated, parodied—poem in Arabic. The poet himself was often credited with having invented nearly everything of note in ancient poetry, with having composed the most outstanding, never-to-be excelled verse, or the most striking comparison on some topic or other. In the *akhbār,* which were perhaps invented, or elaborated, to explain his poems, he was both a heroic and a tragic figure; the Prophet called him "the most poetical of the poets, and their leader into Hell-fire."[2] Ancestral voice of the Arabic poetic tradition, his verses, so to speak, are the "touchstones" of that poetry: he was a prestigious and formidable rival for later poets, a source of inspiration and of influence.

Arabic poets seem always to have borrowed from Imru' al-Qays. Ibn Qutayba[3] notes borrowing (and not only from the "Mu'allaqa") by Ṭarafa, al-Nābigha al-Ja'dī, al-Shammākh, Aws ibn Ḥajar, Ka'b ibn Zuhayr, al-Najāshī, Zuhayr, al-Musayyab and Zayd al-Khayl—pretty much the A to Z of the ancients and the *mukhaḍram* poets—and professed to find the source of a problematic line by Abū Nuwās in Imru' al-Qays's famous verses forswearing wine for vengeance.[4] Andras Hamori has studied the echoes of pre-Islamic poetry in the master of the *khamriyya;*[5] and Abū Nuwās is not alone among the early moderns in this respect. As yet, however, these are only echoes (although sometimes very loud ones) and reflect perhaps both a period of transition in which Arabic poetry becomes increasingly "literary" and a certain "anxiety of influence" on the part of the early moderns. But as we move on—as the ancient poetry becomes, through anthologization and through pedagogy, more textualized—we see increasingly a movement from echo towards appropriation.

This appropriation takes place via the related strategies of *taḍmīn* (or *akhdh*), the insertion into a poem of a line or part of a line (or lines) by another poet, and *mu'āraḍa,* the composition of a "parallel poem" based on the same meter and rhyme as its model.[6] The earliest full-fledged *mu'āraḍa* of the "Mu'allaqa" may be 'Alī ibn al-Jahm's (d. ca. 249/863) celebration of the establishment of one al-Mufaḍḍal, a well-known *muqayyin* in Karkh,[7] which begins,

> We alighted by the gate of Karkh, in the best
> of halting-places, among the beauties of al-Mufaḍḍal's *qiyān*.

Increasingly explicit allusions to the "Mu'allaqa" (especially through the use of selected rhyme-words) reach a climax in lines 19–20:

> Stopping-places whose frequenters do not follow the rain,
> nor are all aspects of pleasure remote from them;
> Stations had Imru' al-Qays visited them he would have
> refrained from mentioning al-Dakhūl and Ḥawmal.

The parody is completed by the final "punch-line":

> Then he would have seen me bestow my love on a fawn the
> train of whose gown was gathered up, not flowing loose,
> Who, when night approached our bed, would not say, "You have
> hocked my camel, Imru' al-Qays! now get off!"

Later poets became more playful with the "Mu'allaqa." Ibn al-Mu'tazz (d. 296/908) quotes these "anonymous" verses as an example of *ḥusn al-taḍmīn:*

He sought to protect—when I spent the night as his guest
—his disks of bread, in avarice, by (invoking) *Yā Sīn,*
[And protected his water with spearpoints, serpents and
vipers];
So I spent the night, with the earth my bed, and sang,
"Stop! let us weep for my stomach!"[8]

Usāma ibn Munqidh, discussing *akhdh,* furnishes further examples from the poetry of the secretaries, who transformed the motif of weeping over the ruined campsites to the suppliant's lamentations outside his patron's door. Thus Ibrāhīm ibn al-'Abbās al-Ṣūlī:

I stood at the vizier's door, as if (saying), "Halt,
friends both! Let us weep, recalling a love and a lodging."
If we ask (their help), out of suffering poverty, they
answer, "Don't perish of sorrow; restrain yourself decently!"
"The tears of my eyes overflowed" at their evil answer,
"upon my throat, till my tears drenched even my sword's
harness;"
My frequentation of their door has lasted long; "and what is
there left to lean on where the trace is obliterated?"[9]

Al-'Abbāsī (d. 963/1556), in his chapter on *taḍmīn,* observes that "[many] poets have played with quoting from this *qaṣīda*" and provides a variety of examples, including a "strange" instance "invented" by the Ṣāḥib Fakhr al-Dīn ibn Miknās, in a jesting poem, which does not bear quotation, to one of his friends who had a large nose.[10] But by far the most interesting of al-'Abbāsī's examples, and the one to which this paper will be devoted, is the first.

Noting that *taḍmīn* "may sometimes be of a *bayt* or more, or of a *miṣrā'* or less," al-'Abbāsī states, "The best of this technique is when the meaning is turned away from its original sense," citing in illustration "Abū al-Ḥasan Ḥāzim's quotation of Imru' al-Qays's *qaṣīda,* in which he turned its meanings towards praise of the Prophet."[11] The poet in question is Ḥāzim al-Qarṭājannī (d. 684/1284), who after the fall of Córdoba in 633/1236 migrated first to Marrakesh and from there (some time before 643/1246) to Tunis, where he spent the remainder of his life. A translation of Ḥāzim's *lāmiyya* follows; I have used Arberry's rendering of the "Mu'allaqa" (emended where necessary, as Ḥāzim's quotations often involve a complete change in meaning) to preserve as much as possible the effect of *taḍmīn.*[12]

1 Say to your eyes twain, should you visit the noblest of prophets,
"Halt, friends both! Let us weep, recalling a love and a lodging." (1a)
2 Descend at Ṭayba; be concerned no more for an abode
by the rim of the twisted sands between Ed-Dakhool and Hawmal. (1b)
3 Make pilgrimage to a garden whose sweet scents have long been
spread wide by *the spinning of the south winds and the northern blasts.* (2)
4 Put off your garments; don pilgrim's garb, confirming the truth
(of the faith), *beside the tent flap, all but a single flimsy slip,* (26)
5 Beside a Ka'ba at whose remoteness my tears streamed down
upon my throat, till my tears drenched even my sword's harness. (9)
6 O camel-driver of hopes, take me with you, and do not say,
"There now, you've hocked my camel, Imru al-Kais. Down with you!" (14)
7 My soul has taken an oath to this, and has sworn to me,
swearing a solemn oath that should never, never be broken. (18)
8 And I said to her, "Let there be no doubt; I shall obey; for
whatever you order my heart to do, it obeys." (20)
9 How long she carried her saddle on the backs of resolve
(and oh, how marvellous was her loaded saddle). (11)
10 She upbraided the weakness that impeded her resolution;
and she cried, "Out on you! Will you make me walk on my feet?" (13)
11 —A Prophet of right guidance whose bright light said to
unbelief, *"Well now, you tedious night, won't you clear yourself off?"* (46a)
12 Who recited holy verses whose speech is not rivalled
when they lift it upwards, neither naked of ornament. (34)
13 The nation guided by him alighted all over the earth,
like a Yemeni merchant unpacking his laden bags. (79)

14 It traveled westwards from the east, and displayed itself,
glittering like the folds of a woman's bejewelled scarf. (25)

15 The lands of the east gained of its adornment
half, and the other half, unaltered, lies with us. (17)

16 God's blessing was upon him as he gleamed like a lightning
bolt, *flashing like two hands now in the heaped-up,*
crowned stormcloud. (70)

17 A prophet who warred against his foes among the mountain
watercourses and the hills, *far-reaching his anxious gaze.*
(72)

18 How many a king paid him his due, clad in Najdī garb,
his horse short-haired, outstripping the wild game, huge-
bodied. (52)

19 How many an illustrious Yemeni came to him, wrapped in a
full cloak, reaching almost to the ground, not unarmed, (60)

20 Or a Meccan of al-Baṭḥā', with sword-belt suspended from him,
hung on the neck of one nobly uncled in the clan. (64)

21 At Badr they cast down the foe from their saddles,
just as a smooth rock casts off the rain cascading, (54)

22 And called to their swords, "Let no youthful warrior escape you,
nay, *nor a great chieftain wrapped in a striped jubba."* (77)

23 He scattered the armed masses who came forth against
us, gathering us against them in *a convenient shallow*
intricately undulant. (29)

24 They made hot war's oven at Ḥunayn, as if, *when its ardor*
boils, it roars like a bubbling cauldron, (55)

25 And called out to the arrow of *nab'*-wood in victory: "Be fruitful;
and oh, don't drive us away from your refreshing fruit. (15)

26 "And he at whom you aim your arrows twain: *strike with your*
two shafts the fragments of a ruined heart."(12)

27 Bodies profited not from the armor in which *their breastbones*
were clad, though it were polished, smooth as a burnished
mirror. (31)

28 And to their ruler and lord the foe began saying,
"Don't perish of sorrow; restrain yourself decently!" (5)

29 But he fled in great haste, as one flees, weeping till the pebbles
are dyed with tears *by the tribe's acacias, like one*
splitting a colocynth. (4)

30 —How often he said, "O night of battle, you have gone on too long; *let dawn shine! Yet dawn, when it comes, is no better than you.* (46)

31 "Would that my swift steed had not brought me to battle, *standing where my eyes could see him, not loose to his will."* (69)

32 How many a mountain-ascending moon of theirs with saddled horse, *the eye looking him eagerly up and down, was abashed.* (68)

33 He bridled him with a ring, like the lamp of one who lights a wick, *lowering the oil over the twisted wick.* (71)

34 His eyes gaze with pleasure at a guide above his guide *with the glance of a wild deer of Wajra, a shy gazelle with its fawn,* (33)

35 And he listens with two palm-spathes laid back over curving shanks, his *thick black mane clustering like bunches of a laden date-tree.* (35)

36 They boast in asserting their kinship to him: the quick running of the gazelle fawn, *the springy trot of the wolf, and the fox's gallop.* (59)

37 But he continues on, as a foaming torrent passes, *turning upon their beards the boles of the tall kanahbals,* (74)

38 And strikes the foe like an arrow, or a shooting star, or *like a smooth stone hurled from on high by the torrent.* (53)

39 —Noble steeds, noble men, who have effaced once more the traces of Rustam: and *what is there left to lean on where the trace is obliterated?* (6)

40 The horsemen of the Caesars were put in fear of death by them; slain all *their stragglers, herded together, not scattering.* (65)

41 They captured the passionate wives of the town-dwelling Arabs *—slim, upstanding, frocked midway between matron and maiden.* (41)

42 How many captives, Persian, Byzantine, did they make sleepless (who were once) *sleeping the forenoon through, not girded and aproned to labour.* (38)

43 They seized full moons, the dark nights of whose hair made *the knots cunningly lost in the plaited and loosened strands.* (36)

44 They left behind them, in the land of Syria, heads that
in its furthest reaches, lay like drawn bulbs of wild onion; (81)

45 But the seeds of their hearts did not grow dry in [Syria's]
bottomlands *and its dry hollows, as if they were*
peppercorns, (3)

46 For the sake of a green land where never crept nor sprouted
sand-worms of Zaby, or tooth-sticks of ishil-wood, (39)

47 Whose birds sang in fruit-laden trees with sound roots and
a smooth shank like reed of a watered, bent papyrus; (37)

48 Bound fast to a Garden which shall never wither thereafter,
tied to the mount of Yadhbul with infinite hempen ropes.
(47 var.)

49 How often they traveled by midday in summer's heat, with coats
of mail, armed men like *Duwár virgins mantled in their*
long-trailing draperies. (63)

50 How often they traveled by night, the rainfall, its thunder
throbbing, flinging *off the burnous of the hard, heavy*
rider, (57)

51 Plunging into floods which deluged the desert, after
they kicked up the dust where their hooves dragged in the
trampled track. (56)

52 How many times did they plant a spear in a sand-dune, like
a spindle's whorl cluttered with all the scum of the
torrent. (78)

53 The enemy built no stronghold, from fear of their siege,
nor a solitary fort, save those buttressed with hard
rocks. (76)

54 They were demolished by a sharp sword fastened after its
polishing *by stout flax cables to hard, smooth slabs of*
granite. (47 var.)

55 How many an army stretched its neck to the ends of the earth,
followed by its hindquarters, and rose with its heavy
breast, (45)

56 Trampling smooth the stony ground; if part of it passed by,
its left was yet dropping upon Es-Sitar and further
Yadhbul. (73)

57 Victory and divine support called out to its banners, "Trail
behind us the skirt of an embroidered gown:" (28)

58 A standard with bright-shining spearhead, hungry and keen, like
the lamp kindled in the night of a monk at his devotions, (40)
59 The blood of the foe, on linen strips wound round its head,
like the expressed tincture of henna reddening combed
white locks. (62)
60 Companions who pared the scalps of the foe: how they tracked
down *the grilled slices, some stirring the hasty stew;* (67)
61 How they multiplied the sweet flesh in the pit,
and the frilly fat with fringes of twisted silk. (12)
62 How often they crossed dry dusty tracts whose plants were ever
unwatered, *no, not a drop of sweat on its body.* (66)
63 The perfume of their memories, the bitterness of their battle,
spoke of *the pounding-slab of a bride's perfumes, or the*
smooth stone a colocynth's broken on. (61)
64 —My heart has become enamored of praise of the best of
creation, *and my passion forswears not the love I bear for*
this. (42)
65 Leave him who was enamored of days that suited him
—*and especially a day at Dára Juljul*—(10)
66 And who was unconsoled for *Umm al-Hawarith, and Umm al-*
Rabáb her neighbor, at Ma'sal; (7)
67 And in praising the Prophet become like one who weaves fine
brocades of broidered silk, *plying it with his nimble hands*
by the knotted thread.
68 Contemplate therein the Hereafter, and abandon your worldly
life; for you *enjoyed sporting with her, and not in a hurry*
either. (23)
69 How many occasions are there for a man to scrutinize his heart's
secrets, *sincere in his reproaches, not negligent,* (43)
70 Who cries, "O God, my sin has assailed
me, thick with multifarious cares, to try me. (4)
71 "Be Thou my Protector from the demons of desire,
hankering after my blood, eager every man-jack to slay
me," (24)
72 And sings to his world when she flirts with him,
"Gently now, Fátima! A little less disdainful. (19a)
73 "If you will make fast my bond with good intent, I will bind it
firm; but *if you intend to break with me, do it kindly.* (19b)

74 "Be kind in cutting your bond with me and in severing it;
just draw off my garments from yours, and they'll slip away." (21)
75 —O you who listen to praise of the Prophet: breathe in the scent
of the *zephyr's breath that bears the fragrance of cloves;* (8)
76 Of a garden of praise for the Prophet Muḥammad,
nurtured on water pure, unsullied by many paddlers. (32)
77 But you who refuse to listen: you are not rightly guided,
nor do I see that folly has left you yet. (27)
78 Were I to sing its words to a female with young, she would turn
from error, *and I'd make her forget her amuleted one-year-old.* (16)
79 Were the goats of the mountain to hear it, it would sweep them
away, *sending the white wild goats hurtling down on all sides.* (75)

In commenting on Ḥāzim's poem we may begin with its structure. Its seventy-nine lines are loosely based on units of five, clearly defined in the exordium (1–15) and peroration (75–79), used more loosely in the body of the poem, where they undergo both abbreviation and amplification, especially before and after the central, pivotal line 39, in which *jiyād* ("noble steeds"/"noble men") links the mount passage (30–38) with the battle passage and the references to army and companions (40–48). The basic arrangement of the poem is into macrosegments of 15, 24, 24 and 15 lines, arranged chiastically around the center. (See diagram.)

	1–5	Address to pilgrim (parallels *aṭlāl*)	
15	6–10	Desire for pilgrimage	A
	11–15	Prophet; spread of the faith	B
	16–20	Prophet overcomes all	[E]
24	21–29	Battle section (1): Badr and Ḥunayn	C
	30–38	Mount section	D
1	39	Pivot: *jiyād*	X

	40–48	Battle section (2): success/martyrdom	D'
24	49–54	Hardships	
	55–59	Army	C'
	60–63	Companions	[E']

	64–68	Dedication to praise	B'
15	69–74	*Maw'iẓa*	
	75–79	Conclusion	A'

We may also compare the poem's structure, roughly, with that of the "Mu'allaqa." The resemblances and differences are, as might be expected, most evident in the opening sections where the ruined abodes are replaced by the pilgrimage sites (IQ 1–6; Ḥ 1–5), and where Imru' al-Qays's "Your habit" et cetera, is contrasted with the pilgrimage as true object of desire (IQ 7–12; Ḥ 6–10). They are also seen in the inverted order of the "mount" (Ḥ 30–38; IQ 51b–69) and "journey" (Ḥ 49–59; IQ 41–51a) passages and in the consistent transformation of specific clusters of motifs. This will become more apparent as we attempt a more detailed (though by no means exhaustive) commentary on the poem which will focus on Ḥāzim's manipulation of the "Mu'allaqa" (including some fairly radical alterations of its sense), by means of which he both rejects the pre-Islamic ethos that poem represents and, by appropriation, redeems both poem and poet.[13]

1. The nasīb (verses 1–10)

Ḥāzim addresses the prospective pilgrim (implicitly himself, but with broader implications as well), exhorting him to bid his eyes (rather than the conventional "two companions") to weep when he makes pilgrimage to the Prophet (the beloved) and his tomb at Medina (the lodging). The pilgrim is to dismount at Ṭayba (another name for Medina; perhaps also suggesting Ṭība, a name for the well of Zamzam), avoiding the "twisting sands between Ed-Dakhool and Hawmal," and to visit a garden (*rawḍa,* "meadow," used also in its sense of a "burial place" of a saint), whose perfumes are not effaced, but spread wide by the winds (Imru' al-Qays's *mimmā nasajathā* becomes *limā nasajathā; ṭāba nashruhā* forms a *tajnīs* with Ṭayba; we may note also the sense of *ṭāba li-. . .* as "to become lawful." This abode—unlike the traces wept over by Imru' al-Qays—is legitimized by Islam).[14]

The process of redemption has begun; it becomes more pronounced in verse 4 as, through a major alteration in sense, the pilgrim is bidden to don the *iḥrām,* the sacred garment, in affirmation of the true faith *(muḥriman muṣaddiqan).* The "flimsy slip" of Imru' al-Qays's beloved *(libsat al-mutafaḍḍili,* a housedress), now identified with pilgrim's garb (cf. Lane *s.v. mutafaḍḍil:* "throwing part of a garment over the left shoulder, pulling it under the right arm, and tying it over the breast"), also becomes the "garment of the virtuous" *(mutafaḍḍil,* "one who claims superiority of excellence over others"). While Imru' al-Qays's lady strips for an afternoon of pleasure, the pilgrim strips to become consecrated. Moreover, *sitr* (IQ: "tent-flap") takes on here the specific sense of the *kiswa,* the covering of the Ka'ba (mentioned in the next line) for which the poet yearns.

The second movement of the *nasīb* provides, as it were, comment on IQ 7–12 (*Ka-da'bika . . .*): where Imru' al-Qays's "habit" was the desire for women, Ḥāzim's desire is for the pilgrimage. He exhorts the camel driver to take him, without complaint, to his goal (a legitimate request, not an illicit importuning), to which purpose his soul has sworn a solemn oath that he must obey, even as Imru' al-Qays obeyed his lady. He praises his camel for her endurance; but while Imru' al-Qays frivolously divided the saddle gear of his slaughtered camel among the virgins at Dára Juljul, Ḥāzim's camel steadfastly bears her burden towards his goal.

2. The Prophet (verses 11–29)

This movement begins with a switch from Imru' al-Qays's *nasīb* to his *raḥīl,* and the description of the long night filled with cares. The Prophet challenges the night of unbelief to "clear off" (*tanjalī,* a verb later associated with the dissipation of folly or error [Ḥ 77, IQ 27]). Verse 12—*Talā suwaran mā qawluhā bi-mu'āraḍin idhā hiya naṣṣathu wa-lā bi-mu'aṭṭali*—does major semantic violence to the *taḍmīn.* Where Imru' al-Qays spoke of a lady who showed "a throat like the throat of an antelope, not ungainly when she lifts it upwards *(naṣṣathu),* neither naked of ornament *(bi-mu'aṭṭali),*" these words suffer an amazing seachange at Ḥāzim's hands. *Mu'āraḍin* can be read as "unrivaled," "incomparable" (suggesting the Qur'ānic *i'jāz*), "unopposed" (that is, incontrovertible truth), and "inimitable" (both in terms of *iʿjāz,* and pointing to the *muʿāraḍa* that the poem itself constitutes). *Naṣṣat* "lifted upwards" also carries the sense of "to make manifest, reveal" (as in the Qur'ān), as well as "to fix" (a text; also in connection with Ḥadīth, to specify on whose authority it is transmitted); while *laysa bi-muʿaṭṭali* "not naked of ornaments" (another reference to *iʿjāz,* and to the model—ever unequaled—of Qur'ānic eloquence) also connotes "not invalidated" (a possible allusion to the heresy of *taʿṭīl,* the denial of attributes to God) and "not neglected," that is, ever heeded.

The ensuing lines are no less fraught with wordplay. The Prophet's rightly guided nation settles everywhere like Imru' al-Qays's "Yemeni merchant unpacking his laden bags" (recalling, as does verse 19, that the Prophet is said to have referred to the Anṣār as *yamānī,* i.e., "auspicious," "because they supported Islam. . . . and faith *[īmān]* was linked to them").[15] *ʿIyāb* (sg. *ʿayba*), "bags," means, metaphorically, "depository of secrets"; in yet another Ḥadīth the Prophet said of his Medinan supporters, *Al-anṣār karishī wa-ʿaybatī,* "The Anṣār are my intimates and the depository of secrets (for this and another example of *ʿayba* used in the sense of "a bond of friendship" see Lane, *s.v.*). This line, moreover, is the first to allude to the "storm" movement of the "Muʿallaqa," which, as we shall see, is associated in Ḥāzim's poem with the onslaught of Islam.

Moving westwards, the Prophet's community "displays itself"—like the Pleiades in the early dawn of one of Imru' al-Qays's romantic assignations—"glittering like the folds of woman's bejewelled scarf." The *wishāḥ* is, according to Lane, two strings of jewels or leather adorned with jewels or a pair of necklaces, worn crossed over the upper body, whose ends are thrown over the shoulders (and is thus linked with the *iḥrām*); the term is used metaphorically for a bow or sword because of how they are worn (cf. Ḥ 19) and here anticipates the references to arms and to battles which will follow shortly. Garments and their transferral from one field of meaning to another form a major motif cluster in Ḥāzim's reworking of the "Muʿallaqa." In verse 15, Imru' al-Qays's "unshifted" *(lam yuḥawwali)*—a pseudo-erotic Arberry-ism for "unmoved, motionless"—is transformed into that "half" of the true faith which has settled "with us" (*ʿindanā,* for IQ: *taḥtī*) in the western lands of Islam, and remains there "unaltered."

The next 14 lines extol the Prophet and his early victories. Ḥāzim returns to the storm movement of the "Muʿallaqa" to depict the Prophet, blessed by God, as a flash of lightning in a stormcloud; the torrent he unleashes will obliterate the enemies of Islam. (We may recall both the metaphorical sense of *bāriqa* as "sword," and the Ḥadīth *al-janna taḥta al-bāriqa,* "Paradise lies beneath the lightning bolt/sword," i.e., holy warfare [Lane, *s.v.*].) *Talā'i'*, "watercourses" (verse 17), evokes another Ḥadīth: *fa-yajī'u maṭarun lā yamtani'u minhu dhanbu til'atin,* "And a rain will come in consequence of which the end of a watercourse will not be impeded," denoting abundance; here the apocalyptic overtones are also clear.[16] Ḥāzim replaces Imru' al-Qays's mountain, al-'Udhayb, with the more general *ākām,* "high hills"; and while Imru' al-Qays and his companions anxiously watched the approach of the deluge, the Prophet spies out the enemies of Islam.

In verses 18–20 Ḥāzim describes those who came to declare allegiance and fight for the Prophet, taking up the "garment" motif once more as he incorporates lines from the "Mu'allaqa"'s "mount" passage (IQ 52, 60, 64) in a manner that both transforms them and anticipates the subsequent identification of horses and men. *Fī ziyyi munjidin* (verse 18), "in Najdī garb," is linked also with *minjad,* an ornament adorned with jewels (cf. *wishāḥ*); as a participle of *anjada,* with "one who supports/answers a call"; and with *munājid,* "a fighter, combatant." It is, moreover, linked by a *tajnīs zā'id* with *munjarid,* both "short-haired" and "(a horse) that outstrips other horses in a race." *Wāḍiḥ* (verse 19) means "fair-skinned, beautiful; smiling; noble, illustrious; conspicuous with respect to lineage." Here, too, horses and men are linked, as Imru' al-Qays's horse with a "full tail" *(bi-ḍāfin),* used metaphorically, becomes a chieftain garbed in an enveloping cloak, as *ḍāfin* is restored to the "garment" field in its sense, with respect to *thawb,* of "ample, full, complete, without deficiency"; and *laysa bi-a'zali* takes on the sense, not of "not askew" (i.e., the horse's tail), but of "not unarmed"/"not unlucky, deficient" (i.e., the man). In verse 20, the "Meccan of al-Baṭḥā'" *(abṭaḥī)* must refer to the Prophet's supporters among Quraysh (cf. *Lisān, s.v.*); as "valley-dweller," it contrasts with the "highlander" *(munjid)* of verse 18 (we may note also the *tajnīs, najdī/nijād,* which frames the three lines and seems to emphasize the notion of armed support) and replaces the "beads of Yemen spaced with cowries" which the fleeing herd resembles (IQ 64).

This section concludes (21–29) with mention of the Prophet's early victories at Badr and Ḥunayn. At Badr, the Muslims are compared (21) to the smooth rock (*ṣafwā';* not, *pace* Arberry, a "pebble") that repels cascading rain (*mutanazzili;* also, as the gloss on IQ 54 suggests, someone who seeks to alight), to which Imru' al-Qays compared the broad, smooth back of his horse. Verse 22 returns to the "storm" movement (IQ 77) to transform the "great chieftain wrapped in a striped jubba" (the cloud-wrapped Mount Thabeer) to the enemy chief who will not be spared by the Muslims' swords. In view of the association, in Jāhilī poetry, of mountains with (kin-group based) strength, this suggests that even the most powerful of enemies will not be able to withstand the deluge unleashed by the Prophet.

Verse 23 moves from storm back to *nasīb,* as Imru' al-Qays's "convenient shallow" (IQ 29), the site of a clandestine rendezvous, becomes the gathering place of the Muslim warriors (Badr, south-west of Medina, is surrounded by steep hills and sand dunes); assignation becomes ambush, love becomes death. At Ḥunayn, the boiling of the "hot oven" of war (*waṭīs;* the Prophet himself is said to have coined the phrase, *ḥamiya l-waṭīsu,* "the war/battle became hot"; *Awṭās* [pl. of *waṭīs*] is the name of a place in the territory of Hawāzin to which the fleeing Bedouins were pursued; cf. Yāqūt 1:405)[17] is linked to the vehement neighing of Imru' al-Qays's "fiery" horse—"Fiery he is, for all his leanness, and when his ardour/boils in him, how he roars—a bubbling cauldron isn't in it!"; *jāsha* further suggests *jaysh,* the Muslim troops who boil with the ardor of war. The harvest reaped by the *nab'*-wood arrows (Ḥ 25) is compared to the "refreshing fruit" *(janā)* of sexual pleasure; but what was for Imru' al-Qays the "fragments of a ruined heart" *(a'shāri qalbin muqattali),* struck by the arrows of the lady's eyes, is now a military target: the humbled *(muqattali)* center *(qalb)* of the foe's army in flight (verse 26).

In verse 27 there is another "garment" transformation, as the beloved's "polished breast bones" *(tarā'ibu)* become the breast-bones of the slain foes, whose polished armor (*dira'un,* to which *maṣqūla* is made to refer) could not protect them. The link with eroticism and death which marks this passage culminates in the enemy chief's supporters telling him (*wa-aḍḥat . . . yaqūlūna,* "they began . . . to say to him," also carrying overtones both of the Aḍḥā sacrifice—they are the sacrificial victims of Islam—and of performing the *ḍuḥā* prayer—they submit, willy-nilly, to the power of the faith) to "restrain himself decently" *(tajammali),* and not behave like a lover on the day of separation, as he flees (29) in haste (*munṣā'un,* used of men, or herds, who disperse quickly), "like one who weeps till the pebbles are dyed with tears (*khāḍibun;* cf. the Ḥadīth *bakā ḥattā khaḍḍaba dam'uhu l-ḥaṣā,* the "staining" attributed either to bloody tears or to the color of the wet pebbles; cf. Lane, *s.v.*), just as one weeps at splitting the bitter bulb of the colocynth (*nāqifu ḥanẓali;* cf. the *Dīwān's*[18] gloss to IQ 4: "He means: I stood, bewildered, after their departure, like a colocynth gatherer *[jānī]* who splits it with his nails to extract its pith"). "By the tribe's acacias" *(ladā samurāti l-ḥayyi)* recalls another Ḥadīth which begins *yā aṣḥāb al-samura,* "O people of the acacia," said to have been addressed to persons mentioned in Qur'ān 48:19 (Lane: these are the believers who "swore allegiance to [the Prophet] under the Tree") and thus refers metaphorically to the victorious Muslims. (The verb *samura* also relates to the color *sumra,* "tawny, dusky," used of lances, e.g., by Abū Tammām in his Amorium *qaṣīda.*)[19]

3. Prophet and Mount (verses 30–38)

This passage, in which horses and men seem almost inextricably linked, begins by describing the Prophet's loneliness on the "night of battle"—paralleling Imru' al-Qays's "night of cares" whose "dawn is no better" (we may, however, suspect a pun on *amthali,* meaning, for Ḥāzim, "not alike": the dawn of Islam dispels the night of unbelief)—as he wishes his "noble steed" *(jawādī)* had not brought him there. The "mountain-ascending moons" (the Muslim warriors)[20] on their saddled mounts *(bi-musrajin)* are abashed by the beauty of the Prophet's mount (there is a *tajnīs* between *murtaqin* "ascending" and *taraqqā* "to rise by degrees"), as they raise their eyes towards it. He bridles his mount with a ring "bright as a lamp" *(ka-miṣbāḥi musrijin; musrij,* "one who lights a lamp," is in *tajnīs* with *musraj,* "saddled"; the "moons" are the guiding lights of Islam). The mount himself gazes yearningly at "a guide beyond his own," and is described in terms Imru' al-Qays used of his lady's beauties (Ḥ 34–35; IQ 33, 35). All other beasts boast of deriving (verse 36: *taraffa'a an yu'zā lahu*), through kinship, their speed from him; thus Ḥāzim reverses Imru' al-Qays's conceit (IQ 59) that his horse possesses the speed of the wolf and the fox.

The Prophet's mount passes like a foaming torrent; with respect to the *taḍmīn* (IQ 74, from the storm movement), *yakubbu 'alā l-adhqāni dawḥa l-kanahbali,* "turning upon their beards the boles of the tall kanahbals," we may note that *yakubbu 'alā l-adhqāni* ("overturned; bent; threw down") also carries the sense of prostration (cf. Qur'ān 17:110), while *dawḥ* (sg. *dawḥa*), "a great tree with spreading branches," also connotes "one of generous stock" *(min dawḥat al-karam).*

In the central, pivotal line (39), noble mounts and noble men are linked by *jiyādun,* which can apply to both; together, they have "effaced once more the traces of Rustam" *(a'ādat rasma Rustama dārisan).* This reference to the Muslim victory over the Persians (led by Rustam Farrukhzād) at Qādisiyya suggests a possible allusion (and, as a result, an approximate date for Ḥāzim's poem) to the Mamlūk defeat of the Mongols at the battle of 'Ayn Jālūt in 658/1260, which effectively halted the Mongol advance westwards and was widely celebrated throughout the Islamic world; if this is the case, it lends added significance to the later references to Syria (verses 44–45). This victory links past with present, to the eternal glory of Islam.

4. The Muslims (verses 39–63)

The battle section which follows (40–48) blends past with more recent triumphs over the foes of Islam to culminate in the ultimate reward of the Muslim martyrs on the field of battle: the instant attainment of Paradise. Filled with dread at the Muslim onslaught, the Byzantine cavalry are slain/ vanish from the earth *(ikhtafat),* down to their last stragglers (*jawāḥiruhā;* used by Imru' al-Qays [65] of the herd of wild cows fleeing before his horse; meaning also, "entering into holes or burrows," i.e., seeking refuge), "herded together, not scattering" (*fī ṣarratin lam tazayyali;* also, "in the midst of clamor/in the vehemence of grief or anxiety"). Imru' al-Qays's pampered ladies (IQ 41, 38,36) become the Byzantine and Persian women captured by the Arabs (Ḥ 41–43), maidens and matrons alike, once wont to lie abed till midday but now made sleepless by the bitterness of captivity. But while the Muslim warriors left behind in Syria (an allusion both to battles against the Byzantines and, perhaps, to 'Ayn Jālūt) the severed heads of their victims, like bulbs of wild onion (the *taḍmīn* is from the concluding line of the storm scene with which the "Mu'allaqa" ends and describes the wild beasts drowned by the torrent), their own hearts have not been left there to desiccate, like the *diman* "scattered like peppercorns" that mark the beloved's abandoned campsite (IQ 3); they have been transported to a "green land" (*khaḍrā';* a possible pun on an epithet for Tunis also suggests the transplantation of the Islamic spirit there; cf. verses 14–15), a land not like the deserts of Arabia—for in it "never crept nor sprouted *sandworms of Zaby, or tooth-sticks of ishil-wood*"—but "A Garden which shall never wither thereafter" *(laysa yadhbulu ba'dahā;* perhaps also, "after which there is no Yadhbul," further reinforcing the contrast).

Verses 49–54 describe the Muslims' migrations through heat and rain. Clad in mail (*dawāri'*, "possessing mail"), they are likened to (in Arberry's translation) "Duwár virgins mantled in their long-trailing draperies" (49). The *tajnīs zā'id* calls attention to the transformations Islam has brought, again conveyed through the garment motif. Duwār was the name of an idol round which, in the Jāhiliyya, the Arabs would circumambulate "in imitation of the circumambulants of the Ka'ba, when they were far from the Ka'ba";[21] in Islamic times it designates the Ka'ba itself, the holiest shrine of Islam and the poet's goal in this poem. The "trailing draperies" (*mulā'a,* a "long-skirted garment" made of two pieces of fabric; cf. also *durrā'a,* "tunic"), to which the Muslims' mail-coats are likened, suggest also the *libsat al-mutafaḍḍili,* the *iḥrām,* of verse 4, underlining the holiness of the Muslim enterprise.

The force of the Muslim onslaught is conveyed by a return to Imru' al-Qays's storm passage (Ḥ 52-53; IQ 78,76): the Muslims' spears are, like the mountain peak, "a spindle's whorl cluttered with all the scum of the torrent." Fearing the Muslims' siege, the enemy built no fort that was not "buttressed with hard rocks," but despite this the foe were demolished *(fa-huddat)* by sharp polished swords bound to the firm rock of the faith. Verses 55–59 praise the Muslim armies, who have reached the ends of the earth, described in the image of the camel by which Imru' al-Qays evoked the oppressive tediousness of night (IQ 45). This army is so vast it extends from Arabia—"Es-Sitár and further Yadhbul" (in view of verse 48, "further Yadhbul" may also connote Paradise) over the rest of the world. Verses 57-58 feature another transformation of erotic motifs: where Imru' al-Qays's lady dragged her skirts over the sands to efface the lovers' traces, the Muslim banners trail robes of glory (recalling the *wishāḥ* of verse 14); it is this standard, rather than the beloved (or, should we say, representing the true beloved), that lights the dark night.

The standard, with its sharp spearhead, is lean, bright, and hungry (*ṭāwin;* cf. also *ṭawā l-bilāda* "to traverse the lands"; *ṭawāhu* "he destroyed it"). On the strips of linen *('adhabāt)* which bind the spearhead, the enemies' blood is "like expressed tincture of henna reddening combed white locks." In Imru' al-Qays this referred to the dried blood of the slaughtered prey, spattered on his horse's neck in the hunt; the Muslims' prey is the infidel, whose blood spatters the "white locks" of the linen bands. For the foe it is death; for the Muslims it is consummation, expressed by the association of henna with dyed hair (the Companions, following the Prophetic *sunna,* preferred to dye their hair red rather than black) and with the adornment of the bride on her wedding day, and by the marriage feast (verses 60–61) which rejuvenates them. This feast—described through allusions both to Imru' al-Qays's communal feast after the hunt (IQ 67) and his slaughtered camel provided for the virgins at Dāra Juljul (IQ 12)—constitutes the Muslims' "feast" of victory (alluding back also to the "oven of war" in verse 24; *jafra,* "pit," also means a young lamb, kid, or boy; and we may think of the enemy as sacrificial victim, evoking also the sacrifice of the pilgrimage alluded to by the *aḍḥa* of verse 28).[22]

Verse 63 recapitulates the motif of the Muslims' migrations, transferring the image of Imru' al-Qays's horse, effortlessly attacking the prey with "not a drop of sweat on his body," to the unwatered waste (*fa-yughsali* also has connotations of the *ghusl,* the ritual ablution, which the Muslim warriors would have been unable to perform in these conditions). Verse 63 sums up the themes of the body of the poem, again in terms of the horse description (IQ 16, describing his horse's broad, smooth back):

> 63 The perfume of their memories, the bitterness of their battle,
> spoke of *the pounding-slab of a bride's perfumes, or the*
> *smooth stone a colocynth's broken on.* (61)

Both sadness (for the Muslim dead) and celebration (of the triumph of Islam) are suggested here.

5. Admonition and Peroration (verses 64–79).

Verses 64–68 contrast praise of the Prophet, to which the poet rededicates himself, with Imru' al-Qays's dedication to carnal passion, explicitly rejecting the latter in praise of the former. That carnal passion is identified with love of this world, which the listener is urged to renounce—"for you enjoyed sporting with her, and not in a hurry either" (68); the hearer is enjoined to become, "in praising the Prophet, like one who weaves fine brocades of broidered silk, *plying it with his nimble hands by the knotted thread"* (67). This image, used by Imru' al-Qays to describe the swiftness of his horse, is transformed in the homiletic context: *yuqallibu kaffayhi* means, figuratively, "he turned over his hands, (i.e.) became repentant, grieved for what he had done" (Lane).

Verses 69–74 produce further radical transformations of topics from

Imru' al-Qays's *nasīb*. The harsh, if sincere, enemy who upbraided that poet for refusing to renounce his passion (IQ 43) becomes that part of man's soul which is inimical to evil, as he searches his heart to find its inmost secrets (*nabatha* means literally to dig out dirt from a well or canal, figuratively to "dig up the dirt" about someone, i.e. to discover his faults; *manābith* [69] signifies "occasions for scrutiny of conduct," and cf. also *nabītha,* "elicited secret" [Lane]). The soul-searcher cries out to God (as Imru' al-Qays did to a long night filled with cares): sin has assailed him, "thick with multifarious cares, to try me" (70); he seeks divine protection from the "demons of desire" *(shayāṭini shahwatin)* who are "hankering after my blood, eager every man-jack to slay me," like the vengeful kinsmen of Imru' al-Qays's lady. The death threatened here is, however, a moral one. *Mujīr,* "protector" (71), substitutes for the pre-Islamic notion of *jiwār,* the covenant of protection, the Islamic concept of God as the only Protector (cf. Qur'ān 23:89; God is He "Who grants asylum, but against Whom no asylum is available," *huwa yujīru wa-lā yujāru 'alayhi*), Who alone can grant refuge from this world and her kinsmen, the "demons of desire."

The soul-searcher vacillates; he is still attached to his world, not yet ready to sever his bond with her, and bargains with her in the erotic language of Imru' al-Qays's *nasīb* (IQ 19, 21). In verses 72–73 the world becomes personified, in the form of Imru' al-Qays's "Fāṭima" (the feminine personification of *dunyā* can be traced back at least as far as the *zuhdiyyāt* of Abū al-'Atāhiya). The explicit identification of *dunyā* with Fāṭima, moreover, takes us back to the root meaning of *faṭama,* "to cut, sever" (a bond), "to wean," and to the metaphorical sense of *al-fāṭima,* death (cf. the Ḥadīth *ni'mati l-murḍi'a wa-bi'sati l-fāṭima,* literally "how sweet is the wet-nurse, how bitter the weaner," whose figurative meaning Lane glosses as "Excellent [is] the office of commander, or governor, and the profit, or advantage, which it brings to its possessor; and very evil is death, which destroys his delights, or pleasures, and stops the profits, or advantages, of that office"). Weak man attempts to cajole his beloved *dunyā* into fair treatment or, if not, gentle detachment (74); but it is he who must sever the bond.

The final peroration (verses 75–79) exhorts the listeners (*sāmi'ay;* an allusion to the "two companions" convention of the *nasīb*) to be inspired by the poet's praise of the Prophet: its fragrance is sweeter than that of the beloved or of this world; it is a garden (returning to the *rawḍa* of verse 3), fed by pure streams. The poet transfers attributes of the beloved—redolent of sweet perfumes, white as the ostrich egg "nurtured on water pure, unsullied by many paddlers" (Ḥ 76; IQ 32)—to the true object of desire, the Prophet of Islam. He who will not heed the Prophet's praise is, like the pagan poet, doomed to remain blind to the right course (Ḥāzim, verse 77, substitutes *'amāya,* "blindness," for Imru' al-Qays's *ghawāya,* "folly, error," verse 27; where Imru' al-Qays was rebuked by his lady, the heedless man is rebuked by the poet). The final lines link Imru' al-Qays's *nasīb* with the storm passage which, as we have seen, is used by Ḥāzim to depict the irresistible force of Islam. Were the most superstitious woman to hear his praise, it would make her sure of divine protection, and she would abandon the worthless amulets with which her child is guarded (a final twist in the transformation of the erotic to the pious); its power is comparable to that of the storm which, at the end of the "Mu'allaqa," sent everything hurtling down in its path and thus to the conquering and transforming powers of Islam itself.

What has Ḥāzim accomplished in this poem? Is it merely a rhetorical *tour de force* which takes the use of *taḍmīn* to its utmost limit? Al-'Abbāsī considered it as providing the finest example of that allusive strategy; he does not tell us why, but we may perhaps conjecture. First, the seriousness of its subject contrasts markedly with the playful, not to say trivializing, allusions to the "Mu'allaqa" by, for example, the secretaries. Second, the extent of the effort, through which the poet constructs what is, in effect, a double poem, is unparalleled. (A major aspect of that effort is Ḥāzim's predilection for archaic language in his own verses—not merely a display of erudition, but an attempt to meet, and defeat, the Jāhilī poet on his own linguistic grounds.) Third, and perhaps most important, the transformation which the "Mu'allaqa" undergoes at Ḥāzim's hands is altogether remarkable.

The two sections of the "Mu'allaqa" which receive the most consistent attention and undergo the most systematic reworking are the *nasīb* and the concluding storm passage. Imru' al-Qays's eroticism, which for Ḥāzim figures both pre-Islamic *jahl* and an unacceptable attachment to the deceptive attractions of this world, is on the one hand rejected and on the other transformed into the imagery of devotion to the best of all beloveds, the Prophet. The imagery of the storm movement is consistently used to depict the overwhelming onslaught of Islam, as its torrent, at once destructive and nourishing, dispels the darkness of unbelief. Other motifs are similarly transformed: the commensal pot in which the meat is cooked after the hunt becomes the bubbling cauldron of Ḥunayn (24), the hunted herd the defeated enemy, the feast itself the flesh of the foe. The deserts of Arabia are rejected for the Paradise, which shall never wither, gained by the Muslim warriors who have died for the faith. The Prophet himself is a warlike figure whose determination and courage contrast with the dalliance of the pre-Islamic poet.

In choosing perhaps the most famous of all pre-Islamic poems for his *mu'āraḍa,* Ḥāzim at once opposes and redeems the pagan poet condemned by the Prophet, making him voice the Prophet's praise. This he does by rehabilitating some motifs (especially erotic ones) and by rejecting others, either outright or through what amounts to an explanatory gloss which demonstrates their "true"—that is, false—meaning (e.g., "Fāṭima" as this world). Through Ḥāzim's poem Imru' al-Qays, in effect, changes his allegiance,[23] as his voice—sometimes in unison, sometimes in counterpoint with Ḥāzim's—proclaims his devotion to the "best of messengers," to an abode that the weaving winds will never efface, to a garden that will never fade.

Notes

1. I must express my gratitude to Nadia Jamil, currently completing an Oxford D. Phil. thesis on "Ethical Values and Poetic expression in Early Arabic Poetry," for her invaluable assistance in preparing this paper.

2. A[rthur].J. Arberry, trans., *The Seven Odes* (Cambridge: Cambridge University Press, 1957), 40.

3. Ibn Qutayba, *Al-Shi'r wa-al-Shu'arā',* ed. M. Qumayḥa (Beirut: Dār al-Kutub al-'Ilmiyya, 1981), 47–48.

4. Ibn Qutayba, *Al-Shi'r wa-al-Shu'arā',* 426; Andras Hamori, *On the Art of Medieval Arabic Literature* (Princeton: Princeton University Press, 1974), 48.

5. Hamori, *Medieval Arabic Literature,* 47–50, 67–77.

6. A thorough and informative study of the various types of *imitatio* is found in Paul Losensky's "'The Allusive Field of Drunkenness': Three Safavid-Mughal Responses to a Lyric by Bābā Fighānī," in *Reorientations/Arabic and Persian Poetry,* ed. Suzanne P. Stetkevych (Bloomington: Indiana University Press, 1994), 227–62.

7. See 'Alī ibn al-Jahm, *Dīwān,* ed. by Khalīl Mardam (Beirut: Lajnat al-Turāth al-'Arabī, n.d.), 51-56; see also Julie Scott Meisami, "Abū Nuwās and the Rhetoric of Parody," in *Festschrift Ewald Wagner,* ed. Wolfhart Heinrichs and Gregor Schoeler, vol. 2 (Beirut: In Kommission bei Franz Steiner Verlag, Stuttgart, 1994),246–57; and Julie Scott Meisami, "Arabic Mujūn Poetry: The Literary Dimension," in *Verse and the Fair Sex: Studies in Arabic Poetry and in the Representation of Women in Arabic Literature,* ed. F. De Jong (Utrecht: M.Th. Houtsma Stichtung, 1993), 8–30.

8. Ibn al-Mu'tazz, *Kitāb al-Badī',* ed. by Ignatius Kratchkovsky (London: Luzac, 1935), 64. The bracketed line is from 'Abd al-Raḥīm ibn Aḥmad al-'Abbāsī, *Ma'āhid al-Tanṣīṣ 'alā Shawāhid al-Talkhīṣ,* ed. M. M. 'Abd al-Ḥamīd, vol. 4 (Cairo: Maṭba'at al-Sa'āda, 1947), 157, which identifies the poet as Ibn al-Mu'tazz; see also Usāma Ibn Munqidh, *al-Badī' fī Naqd al-Shi'r,* ed. by A. A. Badawī and Ḥ. 'Abd al-Mājid (Cairo: al-Idāra al-'Āmma li-al-Thaqāfa, 1960), 212.

9. Ibn Munqidh, *Al-Shi'r wa-al-Shu'arā',* 250; for other examples see 249–59, *passim.*

10. Al-'Abbāsī, *Ma'āhid al-Tanṣīṣ,* 4, 158–60.

11. Al-'Abbāsī, *Ma'āhid al-Tanṣīṣ,* 4: 157.

12. Al-Qarṭājannī, *Dīwān* (Beirut: n.p., 1964), 89–96; Arberry, *Seven Odes,* 61–66; line numbers of the "Mu'allaqa" from Imru' al-Qays, *Dīwān* (Beirut: Dār Bayrūt and Dār Ṣādir, 1958), 29–63, follow in brackets.

13. Lexicographical references are to E. W. Lane's *Arabic-English Lexicon* and Ibn Manẓūr's *Lisān al-'Arab;* further geographical information is from Yāqūt's *Geographische Wörterbuch.*

14. Cf. also the Ḥadīth, "Say: this garden *[rawḍa]* is the garden of Islam."

15. Cf. also the Ḥadīth *al-īmānu yamānin wa-l-ḥikmatu yamāniyyatun,* "Faith is Yemeni (m.) and wisdom is Yemeni (f.)."

16. We may note also the topos of ruler-as-raincloud common in panegyric, where it can connote both his life-giving and death-dealing powers.

17. *Waṭasa* means "to break up"; the battlefield is called *waṭīs* because it is broken up by horses' feet *(Lisān). Waṭīs* is, further, the stone over the fire pit on which the cooking-pot is placed (cf. commentary on verses 61–62 below).

18. For particulars of the edition of the *Dīwān Imru' al-Qays* being referred to here, see note 12, above.

19. There may also be an allusion to the colors of the colocynth bulb, the rind dark, the edible pith (of the female colocynth) white.

20. Taking *awṭās* to be a metathesis of *aṭwās,* plural of *ṭaws* "moon"; cf. Lane.

21. Imru' al-Qays, *Dīwān,* 57 n. 1. See also Stefan Sperl, *Mannerism in Arabic Poetry: A Structural Analysis of Selected Texts* (Cambridge: Cambridge University Press, 1989), 129–30, and Lane, *s.v. duwār.*

22. I have not attempted to explore the possible ritual connotations of this imagery, which is typical of war poetry and echoes both Jāhilī conventions and those of the Islamic *qaṣīda* (explored in Suzanne Stetkevych, *Abū Tammām and the Poetics of the 'Abbāsid Age* [Leiden: E.J. Brill, 1991]).

23. Much as did Ka'b ibn Zuhayr in his famous "Burda" *qaṣīda;* cf. Suzanne Stetkevych, "Pre-Islamic Panegyric and the Poetics of Redemption," in *Reorientations/Arabic and Persian Poetry,* ed. by Suzanne P. Stetkevych (Bloomington: Indiana University Press, 1994), 1–57.

Allegory of the Soul: A Reading of Rūmī's Arabic Poetry

Omaima Abou-Bakr

The monumental writings of the great Persian Ṣūfī Jalāl al-Dīn Rūmī (1207–1273) have given rise to numerous translations and studies that expound on his mystical doctrines and teachings. Thanks to the efforts of such scholars and translators as Whinfield, Arberry, Nicholson and Schimmel, Rūmī has been acknowledged as "the greatest mystical poet of Islam"[1] and even "the greatest mystical poet of any age."[2] Despite these studies and surveys of his themes and ideas, however, there has as yet been no focused critical examination of specific poetic techniques used in his work. Few studies directly present aspects of his literary approach with the purpose of yielding analytical insights. If this is generally true of Rūmī's Persian poetry, it is even more true and quite clear in the case of his Arabic poems, which are buried within his mostly Persian *Dīwān-i Shams-i Tabrīz* and so have not attracted much scholarly attention. It has been the fate of these "unassuming"[3] Arabic *ghazals* to be even more overlooked from the literary and critical point of view despite consensus that the digressive, didactic nature of the *Mathnawī* in general contrasts with the unity and tighter composition of the individual lyrics.

The present essay, therefore, is an attempt to fill this gap by focusing on the literary dimensions of this Arabic verse. It will provide a reading that illustrates the use of allegorical technique: creating a certain structure of images which dominate the poem's progress and unfolding. The Soul *(rūḥ)* occupies the center of this allegorical construct, with Ardent Love (*hawā* or *'ishq*) and the Sweet Beloved/Ṣūfī Master (*malīḥ, mawlā, sayyid,* or Shams al-Dīn) as the other two beings. It is the convergence of these three entities that constitutes the spiritual world of poem 275[4] in particular—an immaterial invisible world that is seen by Rūmī as the only real world.

Before the analysis, a word has to be said about how the general principle of allegory came to be manifested in Rūmī's writing and formed a constituent element in his thought. This will lead us to an examination of the actual poetic devices used in the verse. In fact, some basic remarks about the place of allegory in Sufism are also in order.

Peter Heath identifies three thematic trends in the history of what he has termed "Islamic allegory." The first trend marks works of philosophy and theology, for example the works of Ibn Ṭufayl, al-Suhrawardī, and Ibn Nafīs. The second concentrates on morality and the ethical concerns of romance, such as the writings of Niẓāmī and Amīr Khusraw. The third trend is mystical in intent, for example, Sanā'ī, 'Aṭṭār, and Rūmī who represent the beginning of such a rich literary current.[5] It is this last category that concerns us, for in the later centuries of classical Islamic civilization, Islamic culture and its artistic and literary forms of expression tilted in the direction of mysticism and its patterns of thought, particularly the adoption of the hermeneutical principle of dividing levels of perception into esoteric and exoteric *(bāṭin* and *ẓāhir)*.[6] This exegetical schematization of human understanding—the dichotomy of *bāṭin* and *ẓāhir* corresponding to two types of Qur'ānic exegesis, *ta'wīl* and *tafsīr*—was also behind the Ṣūfī notion of cosmic correspondence.[7]

In Sufism the phenomena of nature, as well as man and the Qur'ānic verses themselves, are all called *āyāt,* that is, portents or signs. They may all be diverse forms or existences externally, but actually they are only embodiments, or form representations, of the same internal spiritual essences. Qur'ān 41:53 provides the source from which the Ṣūfīs derived this concept: "We shall show them our portents *(āyāt)* on the horizons and within themselves until it will be manifested unto them that it is the truth." This verse shows the correspondence between the outer universe and man's being—that there are "signs" within the universe and in man. The two phrases in Sufism, "the large man" and "the small world," convey this interrelationship. Hence, the three sets of signs, or *āyāt,* are three basic sets of multiple external forms or figures representing the ultimate divine truth (the totality of man, the universe, the Qur'ān). This intricate network means that "there is a macrocosmic as well as a microcosmic aspect to Revelation, as there is a 'revealed aspect' to both the macrocosm and the microcosm, to both the Universe and man."[8] In other words, all three varied manifestations possess this dual feature: an outer aspect of existence and an inner level of true meaning and significance.

The above is a simplified exposition of one of the aspects in Ṣūfī thought and world view, which shows the strong hermeneutical basis of the allegorical principle as it gradually developed and flourished in medieval Islam. This double vision came to be a manner of perception with regards both to the revelatory text and to the totality of being or existence: every superficial exterior must have a truer, more real interior. Yet, since the Ṣūfī conception focuses itself firstly and primarily within the realm of unseen, spiritual essences, allegory (also in Ṣūfī writings) emerges as the means most suitable to represent their mystical visions. This paradox of expressing the inexpressible, as well as concealing true meanings and secret significations within a composition for the seeker of truth to explore, is a general feature of the mystical intent. It is allegory's major virtue, therefore, that "it possesses the power to depict certain realms, belief in which is notionally or emotionally overpowering but whose adequate portrayal is inherently beyond the limits of empirical representation."[9] Notions about the Divine Essence, the Divine Names and Qualities, the Holy Spirit, the One Being, the soul's life and mystical love can only be dealt with by a Ṣūfī writer (within a literary or poetic composition) in an allegorical manner. Such aspects of the mystical experience can be translated into representational scenes and embodied entities, and so a writer or a poet is provided with the means "to depict concretely an abstract spiritual cosmos that is invisible to the senses but is known by him or her to be more real than the physical world that surrounds us."[10]

Representing the nonrepresentational is not the only paradox at work that unites mysticism and the use of allegory. As was mentioned earlier, the fact that Ṣūfīs felt that only those who had achieved mystical awareness would best understand and respond to secret, esoteric meanings through removing the surface level points to a double intent. On one hand, Ṣūfī writers wish to *conceal* from common people aspects of mystical vision they would not be capable of understanding, while at the same time they wish to *reveal* to those initiated (lovers and seekers of the Divine) secrets they are ready and willing to perceive. This is in accordance with studies of allegory that maintain that it especially surfaces "in a critical or polemical atmosphere, when for political or metaphysical reasons there is something that cannot be said."[11] By the same token, a similar situation obtains when there is something *mystical* that cannot be easily or straightforwardly stated. Hence, this concealing/revealing mechanism points to the process of interpretation, that is, "allegory's inherent demand for interpretation."[12]

We have established so far that this situation of polysemous or multi-leveled texts, together with the expectation of revelation of meanings, is common both to allegory and mysticism. As Northrop Frye puts it, "allegory is a contrapuntal technique,"[13] in the sense that the explicit, concrete, imagi-native or metaphoric level relates almost point by point to a body of doctrinal connotations, a specific conceptual framework. It is my contention that this is how Ṣūfī *allegoria* works. The intricate mystical world view of Ibn 'Arabī (and his basic twin notions of essence and manifestation, the unicity of being, etc.) and Rūmī's continual preoccupation with form versus spirit (and even the *laysiyya* of Abū al-Ḥasan al-Shushtarī) are all primarily abstract ideal conceptions that need allegorical configurations to be expressed poeti-cally. To typify the immaterial and spiritual realities in external or sensuous forms is, therefore, characteristic of Ṣūfī compositions. In the words of Fletcher:

> in allegory there is always . . . an attempt to categorize logical orders first, and fit them to convenient phenomena second, to set forth ideal systems first, and illustrate them second. This latter Platonic idea-image relationship can exist only when one is conscious of the philosophic status of the ideas one is conceiving. . . . one does not need to have a conscious, highly organized view of the interrelationships that bind the system into a unity.[14]

Hence, the existence of an "insistent doctrinal interest"[15] within a certain literary/poetic structure, which we find in Rūmī or in Ṣūfī poetry in general, defines further the allegorical principle.

It is now fitting to turn to Rūmī's mystical views and their relationship to his allegorical method. What Fletcher calls the disjunction of meanings in *allegoria* whose apprehension requires two attitudes of mind[16] is no more evident than in Rūmī's bilevel conceptual dichotomy of spirit and form, unseen truths or essences and visible manifestations, Divine Reality and material existence. The universe is one insofar as the only ultimate truth of the Divine Being or Essence is concerned, but in terms of creation there is a polarization of microcosm and macrocosm. The macrocosm is the universe with all its multiplicity, that is the created universe reflecting the Divine Names and Qualities[17] through many particularizations and modes—in a more outward and objective manner and in detail *(mufaṣṣal)*. The microcosm points to man who also reflects the Divine Names and Qualities but in an inward and subjective manner and in summary form *(mujmal)*. (Notice that both macrocosm and microcosm are visible external shells important only insofar as they represent inner realities and point to the one true Divine Existence.)

The prototype of macrocosm and microcosm in this sense is the Universal or Perfect Man *(al-insān al-kāmil)*, who has all the Divine Qualities contained and integrated within him in such a way as to make him transcend particular, subjective, and superficial modes of existence and become almost wholly spirit. The Universal Man is the principle of all manifestation, with its double aspect of form and spirit, outer shell and inner reality. He is a created form of man, but for him his specific human ego is an outer, inconsequential entity of being, while all other states of existence belong to him internally. "His inward reality is identified with the inward reality of the whole universe."[18] (We will come back to the concept of the Universal Man when discussing the figure of Shams al-Dīn Tabrīzī in the poem.)

Another relevant aspect of Rūmī's Sufism which clearly conveys his abstracted allegorical disposition is his doctrine of the soul or self. In his Arabic poetry Rūmī uses the terms *nafs* and *rūḥ* to point to two facets of the individual being designating two modes of existence: the ego or carnal self *(nafs)* living the lower soul life and the real "essential" self *(rūḥ)* hidden within, which is capable of receiving divine inspiration that reveals, to the Ṣūfī, God in His Beauty and Love. Schimmel uses the phrase "Rūmī's anthropology" to describe his conception of man's faculties in the form of layers or veils—man's body, carnal soul *(nafs)*, partial intellect—which all must be put aside to reach and uncover the wonderful world of the most genuine organ of all: the heart, synonymous with *rūḥ*.[19] This latent or covered soul—*rūḥ*—is higher than male and female, since it is not bound to outward limitations or a specific individualized ego. Nevertheless, one finds that *rūḥ* in these poems is still referred to by either "he" or "she," which paradoxically can better identify the real mystic self than "I" or "we." In fact, we will see that this device is the initial step in the allegorization of the *rūḥ*, and so the whole poem becomes an attempt to represent this real soul in its coming forth after the uncovering and in its attainment of the Divine Spirit. In other words, once that soul is eventually fathomed, it will be found originally invested with the "Truth" (*al-ḥaqq,* the divine noumenon):

> The Truth is yourself, but not your mere bodily self,
> Your real self is higher than "you" and "me."
> This visible "you" which you fancy to be yourself
> Is limited in place, the real "you" is not limited.
> . . . .
> This outward "you" is foreign to your real "you";
> Cling to your real self, quit this dual self.
> . . . .
> Your real self lies hid beneath your outward self.[20]

In this system, love, of course, plays a basic role. It is originally an attribute of God and the means by which the attributes of that illusory individual self are destroyed. In fact, love indicates the realized or actualized aspect of knowledge of the Divine. It signifies the basic attachment of man to God. In Rūmī's mysticism, to truly *know* Spiritual Reality, man's soul must *become* it through love; to "make oneself capable of God"[21] is the only way—rather, the Ṣūfī way. It is this process of actualization or realization of the Divine Spirit within man that is poetically expressed in terms of allegorizing these entities, Soul—Divine Spirit—Love, and showing their interplay. The allegorical method is used to indicate the way of realizing the possibilities of the Divine Essence or Existence inherent in the mystic soul.

From the above doctrinal outline, one can see how for Rūmī every exterior has an interior, every abstraction or esoteric truth has a concrete expressed form, and how his pattern of thought is more focused on the inner essences. His initial concern begins with an abstract esoteric system of belief and then, in the moment of composition, moves to finding concrete images to represent it. This is what Frye meant by the "abstract" approach to symbols (actually indicating the allegorical method) as opposed to the "concrete" approach, which begins with images of actual things and works outward to ideas and propositions.[22] In this regard, critics have also observed that "allegory . . . envisions human life as a continual interchange between temporal event and eternal pattern."[23] As a poet, then, Rūmī's task was to select adequate figural representations of these essences, of this set of ideals and their interrelations. His doctrinal system manifests itself by means of this allegorical technique, hence requiring allegorical reading or interpretation. Heath has noted this presence of conceptual doctrines as a driving force within a certain composition and as an essential feature of allegory. Moreover, the expectation of systematic hermeneutical decoding becomes a fundamental aspect of the reader's experience of the text.[24] I might add that this expectation also occurs on the part of the Ṣūfī allegorist himself.

In more than one instance throughout Rūmī's *Mathnawī* or *Dīwān-i Shams-i Tabrīz,* he has given us clues suggesting we be aware of this allegorical method of writing and reading. One of these key passages in the *Mathnawī* deserves to be quoted in full:

> I said, "'Tis best to veil the secrets of 'the Friend.'
> So give good heed to the morals of these stories.
> That is better than that the secrets of 'the Friend'
> Should be noised abroad in the talk of strangers."
> He said, "Without veil or covering or deception,
> Speak out, and vex me not, O man of many words!
> Strip off the veil and speak out, for do not I
> Enter under the same coverlet as the Beloved?"
> I said, "If the Beloved were exposed to outward view,
> Neither wouldst thou endure, nor embrace, nor form.[25]

This is an introductory conversation between Shams al-Dīn, Rūmī's spiritual master or *murshid,* and Rūmī, in which Shams (identified as "the Friend") importunes Rūmī to compose the *Mathnawī.* Several significant points can be observed here: firstly, the concept of the multilayered text; secondly, the notion of concealing secrets from the ignorant masses who are not yet initiated; thirdly, the major allegorical paradox of "veiling" secrets that require "giving heed" to uncover and interpret them; fourthly, the concept of a fine *balance* between such contraries (as the intent of hiding versus the interpretive, revealing activity—the state of the Universal Man versus the fallen "forgetful" man—perfect union versus the separation from God); fifthly, identifying Shams al-Dīn with the figure of the Beloved, thus implicitly with the Universal Man and the Divine Spirit itself, that is, outlining the primary function of Shams as a major allegorical compound.

Another passage occurs in book 2:

> What is it that hinders me from expounding my doctrines
> But this, that my hearers' hearts incline elsewhere.
> Their thoughts are intent on that Sufi guest;

They are immersed in his affairs neck deep.
So I am compelled to turn from my discourse
To that story, and to set forth his condition.
But, O friend, think not this Sufi a mere outward form,
As children see in a vine nothing but raisins.
O son, our bodies are as dried grapes and raisins;
If you are a man, cast away these things.
If you are, pass on to the pure mysteries of God,
You will be exalted above the nine heavenly spheres.
Now hear the outward form of my story,
But yet separate the grain from the chaff.[26]

Once more we notice the double-layer composition: the "grain" and the "chaff," the outer form and the inner mysteries, telling a story or reciting a poem that ostensibly pleases with its *badī'* and *ghazal* metaphors but also embeds mystical truths. The principle is applied to the figure of the accompanying Ṣūfī guest (probably Shams) who has an outer form of a man but with a deeper, mysterious significance.

This double vision of Rūmī naturally extends to his conception of language: "Every expression is the sign of a state of mind; that state is a hand, the expression an instrument."[27] In other words, to respond correctly to "expression" or poetic utterance, one has to have the appropriate correct "state of mind," that is, being spiritually inclined to read the text allegorically. Rūmī goes on to say, "The pair [hand and instrument] is needed to generate," and by implication to produce meaning.

In a more direct manner, Rūmī describes in another passage secretive or veiled discourse as "words" that are "only the outward form of the language."[28] He stresses over and over again the two-dimensional aspect of poetic expression and explains by example how the appropriate method of interpretation (resembling Heath's "allegoresis") can be carried out accordingly. He uses the example of Zulaykhā (Potiphar's wife), who has fallen in love with Yūsuf (Joseph)—the story being a favorite among Ṣūfīs and taken by them to symbolize the intensity of Divine Passion and the soul's longing for the heavenly Beloved. Rūmī enumerates several supposed statements that might have been uttered by Zulaykhā, seeming like ordinary discourse, but whose true meaning is something else known only to her confidants. These are statements like "The wax is melted by the fire"; "See, the moon is risen"; "The rose tells her tale to the Bulbul"; and others. He then tells us that in reality such discourse also points to her lover, to passion, and to her inner being, and their interaction together in various ways: "Though she gave vent to thousands of names, / Her meaning and purport was only Yūsuf." This shows Rūmī's acute awareness of a surface level in expression that can take a variety of forms and concrete representations versus a more or less unified level or base of "essential" meaning. In the language of critical poetics: the "vehicle" can be multifaceted while the "tenor" is held in common.

We now turn to the poetry at hand for an application of the foregoing mystico-allegorical technique. The following reading does not deal with allegory as formal structural element of narrative presentation in fictional works, but as dominant persistent tropes that govern the development of meaning in individual poems. Certain devices are employed in the poem—namely, personified abstractions (referring to spiritual realities and entities)—so that the referents of these personifications may be endowed with the power of speech, and a pattern of interplay among these allegorical beings may be implied. One sample poem—poem 275—will be examined in detail: it is a mystical *ghazal* that presents us with just such a controlling personified entity from beginning to end in various consecutive images. That entity is the "Soul," *rūḥ* or *rūḥī*. It is extracted from other faculties of the human character, isolated, animated, and assigned an identity. In this poem, the Soul is either "he" or "she"; it sees, beholds, feels thirsty, drinks, goes through all kinds of troubles and afflictions, gets helped, is saved by the kindness of others, and is able to respond in speech to such happenings. In other words, all throughout the lines of the poem, the Soul assumes a personality and is pictured as engaging in activities and responding to events and experiences. The difficulty of describing the soul in the grips of a mystical experience or mapping its visionary journey is overcome by composing an overall allegorical construct: like layers of building blocks, Rūmī heaps or superimposes one metaphor on top of the other until, by the end of the poem, one gets the impression of a quasi narrative in which the figure of the *rūḥ* is the main character and its afflictions and troubles are the events.

The poem begins with "My Soul beheld a sweet one; she was shaken; / My Soul got thirsty, so I wondered what is the matter with her!" Immediately the figure of the Soul is isolated from the person of the speaker and given a separate identity. The first thing that happens to the Soul is her falling in love and so developing a passionate thirst for love. The second line picks up this "thirst" image and follows up on it with the Soul tasting from the wine of passion a "sip" that made her so light that she shed her loads ("took off her burdens") and flew high above. At this point, the Soul in her seeing, tasting, and moving develops a certain look so visually clear that if "a wandering blind man" met her, he would be able to discern her state of being love stricken. Hence, the first part of the poem stresses the "look" or "appearance" of the Soul in an effort to concretize and personify this elusive aspect of the human character as much as possible.

Fletcher uses the term allegorical "agent" for such personified abstractions: "These agents give a sort of life to intellectual conceptions; they may not actually create a personality before our eyes, but they do create a semblance of personality."[29] The agents usually interact within a closely knit system, in which they all modify each other in some way. In other words, "a typical personified agent can act only in consort with other similar agents." In our case, the activities and responses of the *rūḥ* acquire meaning or significance only within the same interpretive modes in which another agent is present: such as the figure of Love *('ishq* or *hawā)*. Love is always present as this paradoxical figure who provides for the Soul the immediate circumstances of her sweet suffering and also her relief and salvation. We have seen that in the first four lines Love looms large and appears five times. So far he is the cause of the Soul's being "shaken" out of a state of normalcy and entering into a state of intoxication.

In a series of metaphors, Love is the "wine" that satisfies the Soul's thirst, the "sky" *(jaww)* into which the Soul flies away, and the "ocean" in which she is "drowned." Especially interesting is the contrastive movement of the Soul between flying upwards and sinking down into the sea, as a result of Love's "wine." The immediate presence of this wine's intoxicating effect is captured in terms of two opposing spatial and physical movements, also implying two different conditions: flying implies lightness and openness (a reaching out), while drowning in the sea suggests heaviness, hiddenness, and a submerged quality. On one level, since intoxication is generally an undefined, vague state of being and mystical intoxication in particular comprises paradoxical, elusive inclinations, this intoxicated mystic Soul is engaged in both modes: *emerging* (out of the lower carnal self) and also *immersing* (in the Divine Being). Both actions are undertaken within the all-encompassing upper or lower realms of Love. (In fact, this double action will be reflected towards the end of the poem through the two images of "birth" and "dressing up.") Here, Love is both the air and the sea, and the Soul is part of it and moves within it, upwards or downwards. On another level, this double image of flying and sinking implies the mystico-allegorical technique of text composition: the two diametrical points of hermeticism, that is, "conspirational invocations for concealing the 'true' significance of the secrets concealed in the [text]," and the "self-confident openness in regard to the real meaning. . . ."[30]

The figure of Love (*'ishq* or *hawā*) appears in several other poems of this Arabic group, as an agent always addressing the mystic Soul, directing and guiding her, as well as persuading her to come closer and join him. In poem 1738, Love sees the mystic flirting with his *ghafla* (forgetfulness), so He cries out to him: "From Tabriz, an embodied spirit has come to you; / For the sake of his love, throw away your money under his feet." In poem 2123, *al-'ishq* again addresses and persuades the poet to come to Him. The poem is an address, ending with the line: "O confused one, come and prosper in my House, what a blessed House it is!" And in poem 2271, Love himself is endowed with the human characteristic of being *mushtāq* (in yearning and longing) for the lovers in reciprocation to their *ashwāq* (passions). In other words, Love—initially an intangible emotion—is presented in these poems in the form of a personified, speaking and behaving being. It should be remembered, nevertheless, that although allegorical personifications display a particular kind of action, it is still "abstracted behavior—behavior that lacks the full breadth and excitement of human involvement."[31] This is an accepted feature of allegorical agents (even in narratives) since they cannot be full-dimensional, rounded characterizations. In fact, the "daemonic principle" shows them as if obsessed with only one idea, a characteristic of a one-track mind, driven compulsively by a certain hidden and powerful force.[32] This also applies here in the figure of Love who is created and patterned according to the one principle of Divine attraction, the "essential" attachment of man to the Ultimate Beauty of the Divine Beloved.

Our poem (275) then proceeds to follow the Soul in her journey, in Love's company: "the ships of Love carrying Her along. . . ." The next unit of imagery (lines 5–8) draws the scene of the Soul as she embarks on the path of love. Whatever riches she acquires, she casts off for the sake of Love. "The ships of Love" *(sufun al-hawā)* are thus sailing along with the Soul in the "seas of riches." Yet, the "eye of my Soul" (presumably the covetous eye of *ḥasad*), gazing upon all this abundance acquired by Love and his ships, takes notice of the great number of "deeds" and "bounties" aboard. As a result, the ships (though at this point the poem seems to be referring only to *one* ship) are hit and are almost drowned, were it not for "Love's helpers" who rush to the rescue and lessen the loads to prevent sinking. Whether the Soul at this point is still with Love and his fortunes *(amwāl)* on the ship or not, the fact that she is portrayed as covetous or envious of Love's possessions calls for pause. Is this a temporary fall of the human self or a lapse into the material state? Do we detect a hint, a shadow of the carnal, lower soul who still cannot get rid of her personal, material desires and petty individuality?

If that is the case, then this descent calls for the Soul to be truly elevated and purified of any contaminating residues. Indeed, the following lines (9–12, marking the heart of the poem) provide signposts signifying spiritual troubles: the Soul—still undergoing the suffering of love—has tried to sing her beloved's praises, but since he surpasses any possible *madḥ* (praise), her words have been subject to *izdirā'* (disdain) because they have fallen short of their goal. The Soul—actually *nafs* is used here—finally knows despair because of this missed or unobtainable union. Line 11 introduces what will prove to be an important figure in the poem's allegorical framework—the *mawlā* (Spiritual Master)—who appears on the scene as *rawḥ* (refreshment), or in a possible pun, as *rūḥ* (a spirit). The line reads, "How lovely it would be! O for the charity of a *mawlā* who—if my Soul coughs—hands her a drink to purify her condition." A serious transformational process is about to befall this mystic, ever-searching Soul.

It is fitting at this point to take note of the minimal quality of allegorical presentation in these poems. Where the *Mathnawī's* style depends on redundancy, digressiveness, and elaborate expositions of various doctrinal points (with a motley of Qur'ānic exegesis, parables, stories, animal fables, verse, and prose), extreme condensation is the key feature of the *Dīwān's* poems (whether Persian or Arabic). Not only are the allegorical agents themselves submerged, move in and out of each other, and so are somewhat enigmatic, but the very style and sentence structure of individual lines and metaphors are also cryptic. Sometimes a single or only a couple of words suffice to evoke the most complex of images intended. All throughout this poem, for instance, Rūmī creates an aura of representational animation, often in a concentrated manner that may give the impression of fragmentary utterances or units, but which in actuality signify the existence of an intricately coded message needing to be deciphered. In fact, this principle of "compartmentalizing . . . a complex notion,"[33] or a careful separating process, is a distinct feature of images in allegorical writing: images sometimes appear to be isolated from each other for purposes of enhancement and for giving the conceptual abstractions a quasi-visual clarity of outline. For example, we have been following the various experiences of the Soul depicted in the poem, progressing from one unit of meaning to the other in what may appear an abrupt manner without transitions or preparations. However, continuity or coherence is achieved through the implicit overall interpretive framework within which the poem's allegorical images function.

With line 13 begins the most central and compound image concerning the mystical transformation of the Soul in her search for Union and for the Divine Spirit. The Soul, now that the poem is drawing to a close and the Spiritual Master *(mawlā)* has appeared, will undergo the experience of birth. The notion of birth naturally encompasses the ideas of hiddenness and revelation, something concealed and invisible taken out and uncovered. Rūmī paves the way for the birth image through this metaphor: Love disappears down in the deep recesses of the Soul in the form of a heavy pearl. Then in the following hemistich, the line reads: "My Soul is burdened (or weighed down) by a pearl that she is carrying." This begins a four-line analogy in which the Soul, in its state of carrying the heavy pearl within, is likened to a chaste woman who is surprised by labor despite all her protective curtains and canopies. However, in the middle of her obvious troubles and bewilderment, a dear noble lord *(sayyid).* who is gentle and kind, takes pity on her. His state is kingly; he is a sun, and he fulfills all her hopes. "He came across my Soul whilst she was in this perishing (ruinous) condition *(radā)*, . . . [and so] she supplicated him with no humiliation." The lines, which began as an analogy comparing a soul to a pregnant woman in labor, end by making this woman merge with the allegorical figure of *Rūḥ* that has been already created from the very beginning of the poem. The *Rūḥ* coincides now with this personified woman giving birth and being helped by a noble virtuous lord.

The mystical implications of this birth image for Rūmī have to be explained. According to Rūmī, when the Divine word/Essence penetrates the mystic's Soul, that is, what the Divine unfolds to man's consciousness and imparts to his soul, "his nature is such that there is born within him a Spiritual Child *(walad ma'nawī)*."[34] In the *Mathnawī,* for example, we find that Maryam is the prototype of the mystic soul because she is penetrated by the Divine word through the Angel's Breath: "The Father speaks the word into the soul, and when the Son is born, each soul becomes Mary."[35] In other words, each one of us has a Christ within him; the suffering of love (labor pains) gives birth to our Christ. This motif, to which Corbin gives the name of "sophiology," is to be found in the mystic theologians and philosophers of the Avicennan or Suhrawardian tradition of Iran.[36] In our poem it is not the figure of Maryam that is used, though her experience of labor and birth as narrated by the Qur'ān is definitely evoked; rather, it is the figure of Shams al-Dīn who is the supreme allegorical personality. It is through his agency that the Soul undergoes and survives the experience of rebirth.

Shams al-Dīn al-Tabrīzī, a real historical personage and the inspiration of the *Dīwān,* is our third allegorical pillar, in addition to Love and Soul, upon which the poem is built. However, this third emblem belongs to a different category. We have seen how intangible emotion, like mystical love, or an invisible human faculty, like the soul, adopts the semblance of speaking, animated, feeling personalities. "This personifying process has a reverse type, in which the poet treats real people in a formulaic way so that they become walking Ideas."[37] The same distinction is the subject of a useful article by R. W. Frank, who differentiates between personification-allegory and symbol-allegory. The first "uses abstractions as though they were concrete substances—people, places, things." The personifications themselves are literal in the sense that they have no second meaning since their names tell what they are (e.g., *Rūḥ* is just what its name indicates, as is *Hawā*). We must, however, find out "the second meaning for the pattern of relationship and activity in which the personifications are placed."[38] The latter type of symbol-allegory (to which Rūmī's Shams al-Dīn and Dante's Virgil belong) presents characters and significant details in concrete form so that "in addition to their literal value they have a figurative value."[39] That figurative meaning is not often stated, but only implied.

The Ṣūfī master has a significant and important position within the tradition of Sufism. In the simplest terms, he supervises the stages of spiritual apprenticeship. The disciple contemplates God, loves the Divine Being, in the mirror which is the soul of his master. Since he lives in the world of the spirit and has transcended the world of forms, "he can reformulate the doctrine in a manner that suits the particular needs of the collectivity which he is addressing."[40] In this sense, the master in Ṣūfī literature eventually turns into a supreme image or emblem concretizing the very object of the mystic's search. That Divine object is hard to grasp mentally and almost impossible to define and express in accurate and appropriate human terms. Hence, the master acquires an important literary function as well, for he becomes at least a clear-cut and named personage that is an objectification of an esoteric, abstract entity—the Divine Reality. In Sufism, particularly in the school of Ibn 'Arabī and Rūmī, this spiritual master stands for the Universal/ Perfect Man we explained earlier. It follows, therefore, that he is the perfect human model who has attained all the possibilities inherent in the human state. In him, the Names or Essence are actualized so that they become the very states of his being.[41] So when treated poetically, he is considered the most suitable allegorical representation of the reality of the Universal Man in the perceptible universe. In other words, Shams is really a reflection of a reflection, or a representation of a representation: he is a figurative representation of the Universal Man who in turn is the manifested actualization and summation of the Divine Names and Qualities. In fact, in one poem (1783), Rūmī directly calls Shams "an embodied spirit," *rūḥ mujassam.* (In another, 268, it is the mystic himself, following his transformation as a result of a divine vision, who is called "an embodied spirit.")

In Sufism, the mystic aspires to this other person "as a mode of being which he must inwardly exemplify in order to exist in the divine manner."[42] Rūmī's Soul in this poem has been searching for the true site of this divine mode, through the adventurous company of Love, only to find it "in" her: "the pearl," or that newborn spiritual child. The Soul has to give birth to itself anew so to speak, to be reborn inwardly. The Ṣūfī, at first, "tends to look outside of himself for the Image which . . . is the very form of his inner being."[43] Indeed, in the poem, it is only after Shams appears to give the Soul a purifying "drink," that she is able to give birth to the "pearl"—the reborn soul inside her. This is the true inward soul (as opposed to the superficial soul destined to die), which after being purified through love's suffering can now attain the inward reality of the Universe and the Divine. For man to know the true significance of his existence, he should be aware that "the totality of our being is not only the part which we at present call our person, for this totality also includes another person, a transcendent counterpart which remains invisible to us, what Ibn 'Arabī designates as our 'eternal individuality.'"[44]

According to Rūmī, only the mystic is born many times, and his experiences of birth, death, and rebirth are allegorical representations of the cosmic movement of the World-Spirit (the Universe and the Divine), with which he is one. In the third and fourth books of the *Mathnawī* he speaks of the development of the soul in an upward movement, expressed in terms of death and rebirth:

I died as mineral and became a plant,
I died as plant and rose to animal,
I died as animal and I was Man.
Why should I fear? When was I less by dying?
Yet once more I shall die as Man, to soar
With angels blest; but even from angelhood
I must pass on: all except God doth perish.
When I have sacrificed my angel-soul,
I shall become what no mind e'er conceived.
Oh, let me not exist! for Non-existence
Proclaims in organ tones. "To him we shall return."[45]

Rūmī, therefore, sees life as a series of rejuvenating deaths; to live means to be transformed: "one should interpret these verses not as pertaining to certain philosophical theories or to metempsychosis but rather as another expression of his conviction that no part of creation can reach a higher level of existence without sacrificing itself in Love."[46]

The last two lines of our poem (275) shift to another scene also involving the Soul: this time taking off her old garment (once more, the old carnal soul) and putting on a special new shirt from Tabrīz (Shams' hometown), whose fabric is "woven with Love." Then she says "proudly": "His bounty has especially chosen me." Then, the poem ends with a final ambiguous hemistich, stating that the Soul got jealous *(ghārat)* after a while, due to something said about her. Images of putting on and taking off clothes in reference to abstractions like Soul or Love or Intellect, et cetera, abound in Rūmī's poetry. This feature enhances the process of personification and stresses the concreteness of the figure created. Another related cluster of images is that of the dwelling place or house (such as *maskan* or *dār,* etc.). In poem 2123, Love addresses the speaker, inviting him to enter into his abode: "Come and prosper inside my house, how excellent a house it is!" Also, in poem 317, the speaker addresses a group of people sitting outside the door of a house; he urges them to enter and take off their clothes amidst the rays of light inside. In doing so, they can be part of the "nation of love" *(ummat al-'ishq)*, whose love is a special "code of manners." Inside, there is no difference between leaders and followers, nobles and slaves. All you see is a "garden of hearts." The precision of the physical details that Rūmī uses in such situations is astonishing. This occurs often in his verse: regardless of the degree of esotericism he is conveying, he still manages to enrich his images with the starkest, most vivid and realistic details (sometimes details taken from daily domestic activity, kitchen, cooking, or animal imagery, etc.). Such a feature would be unexpected in an allegorical, mystical piece; yet, as Rosemond Tuve comments, "great allegories are usually the most concrete of all writings in texture."[47]

This characteristic may also be due to another conception by Rūmī that the two-fold nature of creation, the esoteric and the exoteric, the spiritual essence and physical manifestation, must be kept in balance. The two worlds of the macrocosm and the microcosm are meant to be perceived as continually existing side by side. Paradoxically, the separation from God is a necessary condition for the unfolding of the principal possibilities or archetypes contained in the Divine Essence. If such a separation did not happen, all these possibilities inherent within the Names and Qualities could not be made manifest. The maintenance of the world depends on a balance between the Ṣūfī who continually seeks to realize the state of the Universal Man and the ordinary man who lives in a state of heedlessness *(ghafla)*, completely immersed in the material world of manifestation. Each is necessary for the mystical yearning and quest to be born and played out. In his *Discourses* Rūmī writes:

> Now this world goes on by reason of heedlessness; if it were not for heedlessness, this world would not remain in being. Yearning for God, recollection of the world to come, intoxication, ecstasy—these are the architects of the other world. . . . So He [God] has appointed two sheriffs, one heedfulness and the other heedlessness, that both houses may remain inhabited.[48]

Consequently, each of these short *ghazals,* one after the other, quickly runs the course of the basic mystico-allegorical theme. The poems play out this movement back and forth between the world of physical manifestations and the higher world of pure concepts and Essential Reality. They unfold the mystic's continual yearning to be reintegrated into his primordial center, into the Principle Divine. Heath, in his discussion of Ibn Sīnā's works, hints at this almost compulsive need of such writers to produce self-created allegorical works, since new esoteric texts are continually required as "bases from which the seeker attempts once again to scale the summit of truth."[49] Indeed, once Shams al-Dīn is mentioned towards the end, the poem concludes abruptly, with no sense of real closure or implication that when the Universal Man is realized a final rest will ensue. On the contrary, one always gets the feeling that Shams acts as a tantalizing higher Principle, after which our poet is ready to go through the experiences of yearning, beatific vision, ecstasy, death, rebirth, et cetera, in the garb of another poem.[50]

In this connection, it has been observed that the allegorical image lacks the criterion of surprise present in a regular metaphor. This is quite relevant to Rūmī's case, in which the images of Love and the Soul at the beginning of a poem gradually lose the initial impact of surprise as they begin to fit precisely with the other notions within the poet's overall scheme, notions the poem itself reveals to us by degrees. Fletcher describes this aspect:

> Surprise diminishes as the analogy is extended, because we see more and more clearly the meaning of the hidden tenor. In most cases allegories proceed toward clarity, away from obscurity, even though they maintain a pose of enigma up to the very end.[51]

Rūmī managed to create, out of each of these *ghazals,* wine-songs, or seeming panegyrics, a mystical allegory which projects the stages of the internal mystical life of the human soul. Beneath the traditional *badī'* and courtly metaphors, each poem is a visionary circle within which this soul moves, loves, suffers, dies, transforms itself, and is reborn.[52] In Tuve's view, the overall subject of the pilgrimage man takes through life to death and redemption may be considered "the basic allegorical theme."[53] What we have tried to show is how on more specific grounds Ṣūfī doctrine and aesthetics interact through the allegorical dimensions of the text.

In conclusion, we have seen how the two-fold reality of outer *(ẓāhir)* and inner *(bāṭin)* being functions as the major frame of reference to which several points relate. That umbrella concept operates on four levels. Thematically (in terms of doctrine), we have the Ṣūfī world view of the macrocosm and the microcosm, exoteric and esoteric knowledge, essence and manifestation, spirit and form, which leads to the notion of contemplating Divine Reality in the form of the Universal Man and the notion of the carnal lower soul as opposed to the spiritual true Soul. Secondly, in terms of technique, Rūmī employs the allegorical figures of Soul, Love, Master (Shams or the Perfect Man), and the Holy Spirit to represent his various complex notions and mystical views. Thirdly, from the perspective of readers or recipients of the verse, clear suggestions are provided to determine the appropriate response by interpretation (allegoresis). Attesting to the validity of this textual point are all of Rūmī's comments on the inner core and outer shell of words and on how a reader is to respond by means of his inner spiritual faculties. Hence, beneath the surface of these lyrics lies a deeper intent marked by the distinctive Persian tendency towards mystical allegorical writing.[54] As Frye puts it in simpler terms, "A writer is being allegorical whenever it is clear that he is saying 'by this I *also (allos)* mean that.'"[55]

Fourthly, and in the final analysis, Rūmī's poetry is an attempt to express the inexpressible: to concretize and give shape in the form of a poem to what is ultimately shapeless and noumenal. It is the kind of literary output that illustrates a typical "mythopoetic" vision of existence, as described by Frye, a world of "total metaphor, in which everything is potentially identical with everything else, as though it were all inside a single body."[56] Rūmī himself had already summed up this critical comment, in describing the mystic's ultimate spiritual disposition as the ability "to witness the Ocean gathered in a drop."

Poem 275

1— My Soul beheld a sweet one, and she was shaken;
My Soul got thirsty, so I wondered what is the matter with her!
2— She tasted from the ray of passion's wine—a sip;
She flew away into the sky of Love and took off her burdens.
3— My Soul became drowned in his Love, so much so that
If a wandering blind man met her, he would know her condition;
4— With Love, there is no moon in the two universes like him,
And my Soul—with this Love—has no one like her;
5— Never had my Soul tilted to money, until she loved;
Hence seeking fortunes to spread unto him all her money.
6— Still, the ships of Love are carrying her along, ever since,
In the seas of riches and prosperity.
7— The eye of my Soul struck them, however,
When it counted all their bounties and abundant deeds.
8— Yet the ships were saved after almost perishing; Love's helpers
Took good care of them and lessened their loads.
9— O my Soul, the Love of a heart that is so great and surpassing,
To all praises sung of him, that he despises them.
10— The Self is desperate for a union that seems to have gone,
When she recites from the Book of the Unseen her deeds.
11— How lovely it would be! O for the charity of a *mawlā,* a refreshing spirit,
Who—if my Soul coughs—hands her a drink to purify her condition;
12— Verily, my Soul uncovers encounters from the past,
Then she sees them not, but focuses on things to come.
13— The heavy Passion has disappeared in my deepest conscience—a pearl,
And my Soul is weighed down by the pearl she is carrying;
14— Like a chaste woman going into labor,
Exposed to ruin, unbenefitted by her curtained canopies.
15— Except for a Lord who took pity on her;
Verily my Soul is a hill who took down her ruins.
16— A noble Master, a Lord, perfect in all his affairs,
Sun of religion (Shams Din), a ruler, fulfilled her hopes.

17— That *mawlā* came across my Soul whilst she was in this ruinous condition,
A long time ago; she supplicated him with no humiliation.
18— A shirt—woven with love—has arrived from Tabriz,
In the morning my Soul took off her shirt and put this on;
19— She proudly said: "His bounty has especially chosen me."
Then she was jealous after a while due to some saying about her.

(Translated by Omaima Abou-Bakr)

Notes

1. Arthur J. Arberry, *Discourse of Rumi* (London: John Murray, 1961), ix.

2. Reynold A. Nicholson, preface to *Selected Poems from the Divani Shamsi Tabriz* (Cambridge: Cambridge University Press, 1898).

3. Annemarie Schimmel, *As Through a Veil* (New York: Columbia University Press, 1982), 87.

4. Jalāl al-Dīn Rūmī, *Dīwān-i Kabīr ya Kulliyat-i Shams,* ed. Badī' al-Zamān Furuzanfar, 10 vols., (Tehran: Amir Kabir Press, 1336/1957). The numbers given to the poems in this edition are the ones cited in this essay. All translations of the Arabic poetry are by the author of this essay. See poem 275 translated at the end of the essay.

5. Peter Heath, *Allegory and Philosophy in Avicenna* (Philadelphia: University of Pennsylvania Press, 1992), 5.

6. J. Christoph Bürgel, *The Feather of Simurgh: The "Licit Magic" of the Arts in Medieval Islam* (New York and London: New York University Press, 1988), 16, 40ff.

7. *Tafsīr* is the external interpretation of the Qur'ān, which seeks to explicate the outer level of the revelation, such as the immediate literal meaning and rhetorical and grammatical questions. *Ta'wīl,* initiated and practiced by Ṣūfī exegetes, is the internal interpretation that seeks the inner level of meaning. In Muḥammad Ḥusayn al-Dhahabī, *Al-Tafsīr wa-al-Mufassirūn,* 2 vols. (Cairo: Dār al-Kutub al-Ḥadītha, 1976), 353, *ẓāhir* is the "basic apparent Arabic meaning" and *bāṭin* is "God's aim and intention lying beneath expressions and terms."

8. Seyyed Hossein Nasr, *Three Muslim Sages* (Cambridge, Mass.: Harvard University Press, 1964), 104.

9. Heath, *Allegory and Philosophy,* 163.

10. Heath, *Allegory and Philosophy,* 163.

11. Joel Fineman, "The Structure of Allegorical Desire," in *Allegory and Representation,* ed. Stephen Greenblatt(Baltimore and London: Johns Hopkins University Press, 1981), 28. Hence, there is an elitist, closed-circle tendency that characterizes these allegories (whether mystical, philosophical, political), making them intentionally and avowedly obscurist, in the sense that their meanings are clear only to those already initiated. See Graham Hough, *A Preface to the Faerie Queen* (New York: W. W. Norton, 1962), 106–11. Also, "authors conceal secrets (the solutions to their enigmas or ambiguities) in their texts because they (ostensibly) deem their disclosure hazardous for intellectual, social, or political reasons" (Heath, *Allegory and Philosophy,* 194).

12. Heath, *Allegory and Philosophy,* 198.

13. Northrop Frye, *Anatomy of Criticism* (New York: Atheneum, 1970), 90.

14. Angus Fletcher, *Allegory: The Theory of a Symbolic Mode* (New York: Cornell University Press, 1964), 18.

15. Frye, *Anatomy of Criticism,* 91.

16. Fletcher, *Allegory,* 18.

17. The "Divine Names" *(asmā')* designate Names of the Supreme Essence, or the subjective reality of Oneness itself, where there is no analogy with the creature or creation. The "Divine Qualities *(ṣifāt)* point to the objective manifestations of God in universal qualities, the attributes included in the Divine Essence as immanent in the world.

18. William C. Chittick, *The Sufi Doctrine of Rumi* (Tehran: Offset Press, 1974), 50.

19. Annemarie Schimmel, *The Triumphal Sun* (London: East-West Publications, 1980), 279.

20. Rūmī, *Mathnawī,* Bk. 6 in *Teachings of Rumi: The Masnavi,* trans. E. H. Whinfield (New York: Dutton, 1975), 317. Referred to hereafter as Whinfield, *Masnavi*.

21. Cited in Henry Corbin, *Creative Imagination in the Sufism of Ibn 'Arabī* (Princeton: Princeton University Press, 1969), 172.

22. Frye, *Anatomy of Criticism,* 89.

23. Carolynn Van Dyke, *The Fiction of Truth: Structures of Meaning in Narrative and Dramatic Allegory* (Ithaca: Cornell University Press, 1985), 63.

24. Heath, *Allegory and Philosophy,* 197. Heath also draws our attention to the complementary aspects of "compositional allegory" and "allegoresis," the latter meaning interpretive allegory that depends specifically on the act of exegesis by a reader according to an explicit belief system, "regardless of whether or not such interpretation was intended by the text's original author," 196, 197.

25. Whinfield, *Masnavi,* bk. 1: 7.

26. Whinfield, *Masnavi,* bk. 2: 63.

27. Whinfield, *Masnavi,* bk. 2: 65.

28. Whinfield, *Masnavi,* bk. 4: 319.

29. Fletcher, *Allegory,* 27 and 29.

30. Heath, *Allegory and Philosophy,* 198.

31. Fletcher, *Allegory,* 29.

32. Fletcher, *Allegory,* 40.

33. Fletcher, *Allegory,* 29.

34. Cited in Corbin, *Creative Imagination,* 172.

35. Corbin, *Creative Imagination,* 347.

36. Corbin, *Creative Imagination,* 172.

37. Fletcher, *Allegory,* 27.

38. R. W. Frank, "The Art of Reading Medieval Personification Allegory," *ELH* 20 (1953): 242.

39. Frank, *Art of Reading,* 240. This distinction also resembles Frye's distinction between the "concrete" and the "abstract" approaches to allegory, mentioned earlier; see note 22.

40. Chittick, *Doctrine of Rumi,* 82.

41. Chittick, *Doctrine of Rumi,* 50.

42. Corbin, *Creative Imagination,* 169.

43. Corbin, *Creative Imagination,* 172.

44. Corbin, *Creative Imagination,* 173.

45. Rumi, *Mathnawī,* vol. 3, of *Rumi: Poet and Mystic,* trans. R[eynold] A. Nicholson (London: George Allen and Unwin Ltd., 1944), 103.

46. Schimmel, *Through a Veil,* 123.

47. Rosemond Tuve, *Allegorical Imagery* (Princeton: Princeton University Press, 1966), 29.

48. Rūmī, *Fīhi mā Fīhi: Discourses of Rumi,* trans. A[rthur] J. Arberry (London: John Murray, 1961), 120.

49. Peter Heath, "Creative Hermeneutics," *Arabica* 36 (1989): 207.

50. In a brilliant seven-line poem (1179), Rūmī presents *"Ṣifa"* (Divine Quality) as the womanly figure of the Queen of Sheba *(saba'),* whose "form is human, and whose created being is of fire." In the last line, Rūmī asks "Rūḥ al-Quds" (the Holy Spirit) about this woman's identity, and the answer is one that he should have known: she is one of Creation's Signs. Here, it is not Shams, but the noumenal Holy Spirit that is personified and presented as another allegorical parallel to the figure of the Perfect or Universal Man.

51. Fletcher, *Allegory,* 81.

52. John MacQueen similarly comments, "It is not then surprising that in the Middle Ages when allegorical ways of writing came to dominate, the emphasis tended to move from the external to the internal world . . . ," in *Allegory* (London: Methuen, 1970), 59.

53. Tuve, *Allegorical Imagery,* 145.

54. A. Reza Arasteh, *Rumi: The Persian, the Sufi* (London: Routledge and Kegan Paul, 1965), 3,4, 11.

55. Frye, *Anatomy of Criticism,* 89. Also, "We can . . . call allegory the particular method of saying one thing *in terms* of another in which the two levels of meaning are sustained and in which the two levels correspond in a pattern of relationship among details," Ellen Douglass Leyburn, *Satiric Allegory* (New Haven: Yale University Press, 1956) cited in Carolynn Van Dyke, *The Fiction of Truth* (Ithaca and London: Cornell University Press, 1985), 26. Notice how the Spiritual Master is described in terms of the earthly, secular beloved or mistress, and the Soul is presented as a typical suffering lover.

56. Frye, *Anatomy of Criticism,* 136.

Contributors

OMAIMA ABOU-BAKR is currently an associate professor in the Department of English Language and Literature at Cairo University, where she teaches courses in English and comparative literature. She has also taught courses in comparative literature and Arabic at the University of California at Berkeley, where she received her Ph.D. in comparative literature (specializing in English and Arabic) in 1987. Professor Abou-Bakr is the author of several articles on literary criticism, medieval literature, and Sufi poetry, including "The Symbolic Function of Metaphor in Medieval Sufi Poetry," in *Alif: Journal of Comparative Poetics* (1992) and "Mystical Elements in John Keats," in *Cairo Studies in English* (1995).

KAMAL ABU-DEEB is the holder of the Chair of Arabic at the University of London. He taught at a number of other universities in the West and in the Arab world, including Columbia University, Oxford, the University of California at Berkeley, and the University of Yarmouk in Jordan. Professor Abu-Deeb is the author of a number of books and articles in the fields of comparative literary and cultural studies; he is also a poet and essayist who contributes regularly to leading Arab periodicals, including the avant-garde journal *Mawāqif* where he served as coeditor with the well-known modernist poet Adūnīs. His most recent work, *Al-Thaqāfa bayna al-tashaẓẓī wa-al-ta'addudiyya* (Beirut 1996) examines contemporary cultural and political realities in light of an emerging "aesthetic of contiguity" that appears to be displacing the aesthetics of unity underlying modernity in western and Arab cultures and societies. A shorter version of this study was previously published in English under the title *In Celebration of Difference* (London 1995). Professor Abu-Deeb was born in Safita, Syria, in 1942 and was educated at

Damascus University and Trinity and St. John's Colleges, Oxford University, where he obtained his D. Phil. in 1971.

ROGER ALLEN (D.Phil. Oxford University, 1968) is the author of *The Modern Arabic Novel: An Historical and Critical Introduction* (second edition, 1995), *Period of Time: al-Muwaylihi's "Hadith 'Isa ibn Hisham"* (second edition, 1992) and *Modern Arabic Literature* (1987). He has also written and translated numerous articles on modern Arabic fiction and drama and on Arabic language pedagogy. He is currently professor of Arabic language and literature at the University of Pennsylvania.

ISSA J. BOULLATA was born in Jerusalem, Palestine, in 1929. He earned a First Class B.A. (Honours) in 1964 and a Ph.D. in Arabic literature in 1969 at the University of London. He taught Arabic and Islamic Studies at Hartford Seminary (1968–1975), where he was also coeditor of the *Muslim World*. Since 1975, he has been professor of Arabic literature and language at the Institute of Islamic Studies of McGill University in Montreal, Canada. His publications in Arabic include *Al-Rūmanṭīqiyya wa-Ma'ālimuhā fī al-Shi'r al-'Arabī al-Ḥadīth* (1960) and *Badr Shakīr al-Sayyāb: Ḥayātuh wa-Shi'ruh* (1971), and in English, as editor, *Critical Perspectives on Modern Arabic Literature* (1980) and as author *Trends and Issues in Contemporary Arab Thought* (1990). He has published over seventy-five articles in scholarly journals and translated into English several works from modern Arabic literature, including Emily Nasrallah's *Flight Against Time* (1987), Jabra Ibrahim Jabra's *The First Well* (1995), and Mohamed Berrada's *The Game of Forgetting* (1996).

TERRI DEYOUNG (Ph.D. University of California at Berkeley, 1988) has studied both modern and classical Arabic literature in the United States and Egypt, where she received an M.A. in Arabic Literature at the American University in Cairo. She is the author of *Placing the Poet: Badr Shākir al-Sayyāb and Postcolonial Iraq* (forthcoming) and her articles have appeared in *Al-'Arabiyya, Edebiyât,* the *Journal of Arabic Literature,* and the *Journal of the American Oriental Society,* as well as other venues. After completing her Ph.D. dissertation on the use of myth in modern Arabic poetry under Mounah Khouri's direction at Berkeley, she taught at Rhodes College and Yale University before coming to the University of Washington, where she is currently assistant professor of Arabic language and literature.

ALLEN DOUGLAS is associate professor of history and semiotics at Indiana University. His most recent works include *From Fascism to Libertarian Communism: Georges Valois against the Third Republic* and *Arab Comic Strips: Politics of an Emerging Mass Culture* (with Fedwa Malti-Douglas).

SABAH GHANDOUR has been a senior lecturer in Arabic at the University of Pennsylvania since 1990. She received her Ph.D. in comparative literature from the University of California at Los Angeles in 1995 and has written a number of articles in Arabic and English on the novel. Her recent publications include two forewords to translations of novels by Elias Khoury, as well as several encyclopedia articles and book reviews.

JABRĀ IBRĀHĪM JABRĀ, who died in 1994, is widely esteemed in the Arab world as one of its foremost novelists and poets. He was also an incisive literary critic, who regularly published essays and articles in leading academic journals. His numerous publications include the novels *Hunters in a Narrow Street* (in English, 1953), *Al-Safīna* (The ship, 1967) and *al-Baḥth 'an Walīd Mas'ūd* (In search of Walīd Mas'ūd, 1975), as well as the collections of poetry *Tammūz fī al- Madīna* (Tammuz in the city, 1958) and *Al-Madār al-Mughlaq* (The closed circuit, 1964). Most of his critical essays are collected in *Al- Ḥurriyya wa-al-Ṭūfān* (Freedom and the deluge, 1960), *Al-Riḥla al-Thāmina* (The eighth voyage, 1967), *Al-Nār wa-al-Jawhar* (Fire and essence, 1975), and *Yanābī' al-Ru'yā* (Springs of vision, 1979). Toward the end of his life, he published two very fine volumes of autobiographical reminiscences, *Al-Bi'r al-Ūlā* (The first well, 1987) and *Shāri' al-Amīrāt* (Princess street, 1994).

Jabrā graduated from the Arab College in Jerusalem in 1937, then earned a B.A. (1943) and an M.A. (1948) at Cambridge University in English literature. He taught English literature in Jerusalem at the Rashīdiyya College (1943–1948) and later at the College of Arts, University of Baghdad (1948–1952). After attending Harvard University on a fellowship from 1952–1954 (with Mounah Khouri), he was appointed Head of Publications at the Iraq Petroleum Company (1954–1977), and then became Cultural Counselor at the Iraqi Ministry of Culture and Information until he retired in 1984.

ANTOINE G. KARAM was born in Jizzīn, Lebanon, in 1921. A graduate of the Sorbonne in Paris in 1959 with a *Doctorat d'état* in literature, he taught Arabic literature and Islamic thought at the American University of Beirut, the

Lebanese University, and Beirut College for about forty years. He was the first dean of the Faculty of Arts at the Lebanese University, 1960–1963; chairman of the Department of Arabic and Near Eastern Languages at the American University of Beirut, 1971–1974; and visiting professor at Columbia University, 1967–1968; and at the University of California at Berkeley, 1974–1975. He died in 1979.

His literary and critical works in Arabic and French include books and articles on symbolism in modern Arabic literature, the life and works of Gibran, and various aspects of modern Arabic poetry and fiction. He also published scholarly studies on Islamic and Western philosophy. Special mention should be made of his outstanding work on his personal philosophy of life, the beautiful *Kitāb 'Abd-Allāh* (1969). His translations into Arabic include André Maurois' *Byron* and Alexis de Tocqueville's *De la Démocratie en Amérique*. His posthumous book, *Malāmiḥ al-Adab al-'Arabī al-Ḥadīth* (1980) is exemplary in its literary-critical scholarship, deep insights, and extraordinary sensibility.

AS'AD E. KHAIRALLAH received his Ph.D. in Arabic, Persian, and East-West comparative literature from Princeton University in 1971. He is currently on the faculty of the University of Freiburg in Germany, doing research and teaching Arabic and Persian literature. He has also taught at a number of other universities in the west and the Arab world, including a visiting professorship at the University of California at Berkeley (1987). In 1971 he became an assistant professor in the Arabic department of the American University in Beirut, but in 1976 the civil war forced him to leave Lebanon with his family.

Professor Khairallah has had a long-standing interest in both modern and classical Islamic literature (in both Arabic and Persian) and comparative literature, and has contributed over twenty publications to these fields. His recent works include *Love, Madness, and Poetry: An Interpretation of the Mağnūn Legend* (1980), an Arabic book on the critic Mārūn 'Abbūd (forthcoming), and a monograph in English on modern Arabic poetry, which he is close to finishing.

FEDWA MALTI-DOUGLAS (Ph.D. University of California at Los Angeles, 1977). Her critical works include *Structures of Avarice: The Bukhalā' in Medieval Arabic Literature* (1981, based on her dissertation project completed under Mounah Khouri's direction), *Blindness and Autobiography: Al-Ayyām of Ṭaha*

Ḥusayn (1988), *Woman's Body, Woman's Word* (1992), and *Arab Comic Strips: Politics of an Emerging Mass Culture* (with Allen Douglas, 1994). Her study of the novels and other writings of the Egyptian feminist Nawāl Sa'adāwī, *Men, Women and God(s),* is due to appear shortly. She has also authored several dozen scholarly articles which have appeared in leading English and Arabic academic journals. After graduating from the University of California at Los Angeles, she taught for a number of years at the University of Texas at Austin, and she is currently Martha C. Kraft Professor of Humanities at Indiana University where she also serves as chair of the Department of Near Eastern Languages and Cultures, and as the director of the Middle East Studies Program.

JULIE MEISAMI received her Ph.D. in comparative literature from the University of California at Berkeley in 1971. From 1971 to 1980 she lived and taught in Tehran, Iran; she has also taught at the University of California at Berkeley and since 1985 has been Lecturer in Persian at the University of Oxford. Professor Meisami has written extensively on both Arabic and Persian literature. Her books include *Medieval Persian Court Poetry* (1987); an annotated translation from the Persian of *The Sea of Precious Virtues (Baḥr al-Favā'id): A Medieval Islamic Mirror for Princes* (1991); and an annotated translation of Nizami Ganjavi's *Haft Paykar* (1995). Her articles on Arabic literature have appeared in the *Journal of Arabic Literature, Arabica*, and *Edebiyât.* She is currently coeditor of *Edebiyât: The Journal of Middle Eastern Literatures,* and of *The Encyclopedia of Arabic Literature* (to be published by Routledge).

CORNELIS NIJLAND began his career with a degree in theology and Semitic languages at the State University at Groningen in The Netherlands. He continued his studies in Arabic, Persian, and modern history at the State University of Utrecht and eventually received his doctoral degree from the State University at Leiden. He has worked in the Arabic Department of the Wereldomroep (the international radio station of The Netherlands) and from 1960 to 1993 was at the Netherlands Institute for the Near East in Leiden. He has been editor in charge of *Bibliotheca Orientalis* and continues to supervise the section which deals with the Middle East after the rise of Islam. His publications include an in-depth study of the Mahjar poet Mīkhā'īl Nu'ayma (1975) and numerous scholarly articles on modern Arabic literature. He was born in 1928.

IRFĀN SHAHĪD received his Ph.D. from Princeton University in 1954 and has been interested in the interaction of the peoples of the Greco-Roman world of late antiquity and the Arabian peninsula before and after the rise of Islam ever since he earned his B.A. in classics and Greco-Roman History at Oxford University. His publications in this field include *The Martyrs of Najran* (1971), *Rome and the Arabs* (1984), *Byzantium and the Arabs in the Fourth Century* (1984), *Byzantium and the Semitic Orient before the Rise of Islam* (1988), *Byzantium and the Arabs in the Fifth Century* (1989) and *Byzantium and the Arabs in the Sixth Century* (1995). He is also the author of a study in Arabic on the Egyptian neoclassical poet Aḥmad Shawqī, *Al-'Awda ilā Shawqī* (1986). He has, in addition, authored many articles on this and the subjects of classical and medieval Arabic poetry, and Islamic studies, particularly the Qur'ān, which have appeared in numerous scholarly journals. He is currently Oman Professor of Arabic and Islamic Studies at Georgetown University, where he has also served as director since 1982 of the Dumbarton Oaks project on "Byzantium and the Arabs."

JOSEPH ZEIDAN received his Ph.D. from the University of California at Berkeley in 1982, where he completed his dissertation under Mounah Khouri' s direction. He is currently associate professor of Near Eastern Studies at The Ohio State University. He is the author of two editions of *Maṣāidir al-Adab al-Nisā'ī fī al-'Ālam al-'Arabī al-Ḥadīth* (Bibliography of women's literature in the modern Arab world) as well as numerous scholarly articles on various aspects of modern Arabic literature. His most recent works are *Arab Women Novelists: the Formative Years and Beyond* (1995) and *Al-A'māl al-Majhūla li-Mayy Ziyāda* (The unknown works of Mayy Ziyāda, 1996).

Index